USING DEVELOPMENTALLY APPROPRIATE PRACTICES TO TEACH THE COMMON CORE

Using Developmentally Appropriate Practices to Teach the Common Core: Grades PreK–3 provides current and prospective primary grade teachers with an understanding of the CCSS-ELA and CCSS-M that highlights their compatibility with developmentally appropriate practices (DAP), the instructional approach generally preferred by teachers of young children.

The book begins by framing the CCSS as a distinct improvement over lengthy lists of academic content standards and as a carefully conceptualized and DAP-friendly set of curriculum guidelines. Next, the CCSS-ELA and CCSS-M for Grades K–3 are unpacked, analyzed, synthesized, and cross-referenced to key features of DAP. Finally, several "hot topic" issues—differentiating instruction to meet the needs of all learners, ensuring equitable access to the curriculum for English Language Learners, addressing assessment and accountability expectations, and educating parents and families about the CCSS and DAP—are prioritized and examined in depth. *Using Developmentally Appropriate Practices to Teach the Common Core: Grades PreK–3* is a highly useful guide for both pre-service and in-service early childhood education teachers.

Dr. Lisa S. Goldstein, a former primary grade teacher, is Professor and Director of Teacher Education at Santa Clara University in Santa Clara, California.

USING DEVELOPMENTALLY APPROPRIATE PRACTICES TO TEACH THE COMMON CORE

Grades PreK–3

Lisa S. Goldstein

Routledge
Taylor & Francis Group

NEW YORK AND LONDON

First published 2016
by Routledge
711 Third Avenue, New York, NY 10017

and by Routledge
2 Park Square, Milton Park, Abingdon, Oxon, OX14 4RN

Routledge is an imprint of the Taylor & Francis Group, an informa business

© 2016 Taylor & Francis

Library of Congress Cataloging-in-Publication Data
Goldstein, Lisa S., 1963-
Using developmentally appropriate practices to teach the Common Core :
 grades preK-3 / Lisa S. Goldstein.
   pages cm
 Includes bibliographical references and index.
 1. Early childhood education—Curricula.   2. Common
Core State Standards (Education)   3. Culturally relevant
pedagogy.   4. Individualized instruction.   5. Early childhood
teachers.   I. Title.
 LB1139.4G66 2015
 372.21—dc23
 2014049093

ISBN: 978-1-138-01577-7 (hbk)
ISBN: 978-1-138-01578-4 (pbk)
ISBN: 978-1-315-79414-3 (ebk)

Typeset in Bembo
by ApexCoVantage, LLC

Printed and bound in the United States of America by Publishers Graphics,
LLC on sustainably sourced paper.

Dedicated to my two very favorite people:

the delightful, brilliant, hilarious, creative,
caring, luscious-wuscious young men
I proudly call my sons.

Sam Goldstein and Noah Goldstein
my cotton candy unicorns,
may they prance, forever together,
through waterfalls of caramel.

CONTENTS

PREFACE

The implementation of the Common Core State Standards for English Language Arts (CCSS-ELA) and the Common Core State Standards for Mathematics (CCSS-M) across most of the United States raises significant concern among many teachers of children in prekindergarten through Grade 3 (preK–3). After more than a decade of struggling to maintain child-centered, developmentally appropriate classrooms for their young learners within the constraints of No Child Left Behind's standards-based educational expectations, these teachers are understandably wary about the implementation of new standards.

Prekindergarten, kindergarten, and primary grade teachers' concerns about the negative impact these new standards might have on their students' learning—especially the potential for academic expectations to continue their downward creep through the grade levels—have been amplified by reports of the CCSS' academic rigor, strong emphasis on reading and writing non-fiction, and heightened expectations for student performance.

Although public perceptions of the CCSS have been mixed, commentators agree the cognitive demand posed by the CCSS is much higher than that posed by the lists of disconnected academic skills and knowledge that comprised the state academic content standards implemented in response to the demands of NCLB. For many preK–3 teachers, talk of greater cognitive demand and more rigorous academic expectations suggests that "curriculum shovedown"—the process in which academic expectations typically associated with a given grade level are pushed down into an earlier grade—will be an inevitable side effect of the CCSS.

This book offers a more optimistic perspective on the Common Core. In fact, I argue that consideration of the CCSS in relation to the specific values, priorities, and practices central to early childhood education reveals a surprising alignment between the CCSS and the principles of developmentally appropriate practices (DAP). This fundamental compatibility between the CCSS and DAP creates unexpected educational possibilities for teachers and their young learners. Today, all learning environments that serve children in Grades preK–3 have an opportunity to place developmentally appropriate practices firmly at the center of their Common Core implementation plans. This practical book is designed to help guide that process.

Intended as a resource for preservice and practicing teachers, administrators, and community stakeholders, *Using Developmentally Appropriate Practices to Teach the Common Core, Grades PreK–3* begins by describing the connection points between the CCSS and DAP and presenting a rationale that supports the use of developmentally appropriate practices to teach the CCSS to children from the ages of three to eight years old. The book clarifies relevant CCSS terminology, identifies and describes key pedagogical practices teachers will need in order to implement the CCSS effectively, and offers detailed and specific guidelines for teaching the Common Core using developmentally appropriate practices in different early childhood settings, including:

Prekindergarten
Transitional kindergarten/junior kindergarten
Kindergarten
First grade
Second grade
Third grade

The information, strategies, and ideas provided here will support teachers in interpreting and engaging with the Common Core in ways that facilitate the creation of developmentally appropriate, rigorous, intellectually engaging learning experiences for all young children. The book aims to contribute to the ongoing effort to ensure all students in Grades preK–3 have opportunities to learn the content prescribed by their states in ways that will facilitate and enhance their growth across all developmental domains.

The book is divided into four parts. Part I, FOUNDATIONS, presents the core ideas that frame the book:

1. The Common Core State Standards (CCSS) and developmentally appropriate practices (DAP) form a natural partnership: the CCSS indicate what content should be taught, and DAP indicates how to teach that content to children in prekindergarten through Grade 3.
2. Rigor, when applied to learning environments for young children, has a different definition than when it is applied in Grades 4–12. In early childhood education, an experience is rigorous if it is (1) challenging, (2) achievable, and (3) interesting to the specific learners for whom it was planned.
3. Effective early childhood education requires teachers to know their students as learners and to provide them with custom-tailored learning opportunities aimed at supporting their ongoing growth and development.

4. Early childhood teachers must be intentional in their decision-making, flexible in their instructional practices, attentive to their students' needs and interests, and committed to continual reflection on their work with the children and families they serve.

Part II, SPOTLIGHT SKILLS FOR TEACHING THE COMMON CORE STATE STANDARDS USING DEVELOPMENTALLY APPROPRIATE PRACTICES, foregrounds four key professional practices that are central to successful implementation of the CCSS and DAP: (a) observing, documenting, and assessing students' development and learning; (b) differentiating instruction to maximize learning for every student; (c) planning "integrated-content" lessons that enable teachers to deliver twice as much content as in the past; and (d) educating families about the CCSS.

Part III, UNDERSTANDING THE COMMON CORE STATE STANDARDS DOCUMENTS, provides some introductory, context-setting information, followed by two short chapters: one on understanding and using the CCSS-Mathematics and the other on understanding and using the CCSS-English Language Arts.

Part IV, USING DAP TO TEACH THE COMMON CORE IN EARLY CHILDHOOD SETTINGS, GRADE BY GRADE, provides important information for teachers, student teachers, parents, administrators and community stakeholders. The chapter for each grade level includes

*   information about the age range and typical developmental characteristics one would expect to see in the students of that age;
*   a central metaphor that captures the essence of children in that grade;
*   discussion of a focus topic directly related and relevant to that grade;
*   the complete text of the CCSS-Math and the CCSS-ELA content standards for that grade;
*   annotated complete text of the Math CCSS and ELA CCSS for the grade level, with each standard fully unpacked;
*   top three tips for teachers of students in that grade.

Savvy teachers of young children will embrace the implementation of the CCSS. Committing fully to the Common Core gives preK–3 teachers the opportunity to establish developmentally appropriate practice as the primary means of teaching English language arts and mathematics to children in prekindergarten through Grade 3. The Common Core—with its emphasis on rigor, reasoning, and reflective, metacognitive conversations—will put an end to the low-level skill development activities that have persisted in young children's classrooms in the wake of NCLB. This temporary vacuum will allow early childhood teachers to re-introduce developmentally appropriate practice as the preferred set of instructional strategies for teaching academic content to young children.

ACKNOWLEDGEMENTS

First and foremost, thanks are due to Dr. Kyle Snow of the National Association for the Education of Young Children. He contacted me out of the blue and asked if I would give a keynote presentation about the Common Core State Standards and early childhood education at NAEYC's Professional Development Institute in June 2013. I had no idea what I was getting myself into, but I loved every minute of it. Second, I must thank Alex Masulis of Taylor & Francis/Routledge who asked if I'd considered turning that keynote presentation into a book.

With the widespread adoption of the Common Core, young children's teachers have made enormous changes in their professional lives: they have altered the way they think about the work they do with children; adjusted their beliefs about the types of content and experiences that are most valuable for young learners; explored and mastered unfamiliar instructional practices; engaged with new technologies; and explained all the changes, new demands, and heightened expectations to parents, administrators, and community stakeholders.

Young children's teachers possess many remarkable abilities that are rarely acknowledged and even more rarely celebrated. It gives me great pleasure to have the opportunity to recognize some of my very favorite early childhood educators, each of whom has played a significant role in shaping this book:

Mahalo nui loa to my Hawaiian teammates:
Angela Thomas
Gail Judd
Sue Entz
Lori Carlson
Hilda Gonzales
Marcie McClelland

And big thanks to:
Lisa Suyemoto
Marlee-Jo Burns

I'm very grateful for the generous support of my colleagues at Santa Clara University: Kris Melloy, Pedro Hernandez Ramos and Chris Bachen, Marco Bravo, Angelo Collins, Sara Garcia, Margaret Lucero, Priscilla Myers, Steve Johnson, Harold Hoyle, Cheryl McElvain, Bob Michels, Rick Alves, Bob Lowry, Mike Schadeck, Lynne West, Patrick Adams, Sandy Thang, and Dean Nick Ladany and the staff in the School of Education and Counseling Psychology Dean's Office. My gratitude also goes out to the prospective teachers enrolled in Santa Clara's preliminary teaching credential programs, who make me proud, ask great questions, and always keep me laughing.

My favorite friends and family always deserve my thanks, along with apologies for unreturned phone calls and forgotten text messages. Here they are, in no particular order: Mary Champagne, Michael Champagne, Brian Cunningham, Matt Rebong, Richard and Kellie Goldstein, Simon and Joanne Jones, Daniel Grunfeld, George and Myuh-Myuh; Sadee-Jo, Sunnee-Joe, and Sallee-Jo (my secretary). My newest favorite person is Kevin—a calm, unflappable Genius at the Apple Store in Los Gatos, California—whose thoughtful assistance in a time of complete crisis was truly an invaluable gift.

I'd like to thank my sons, Noah and Sam, for permitting me to include photographs in Chapter 4 of their younger selves learning new skills. Likewise, I'm extremely grateful to Clara Gainer and her father, Jesse Gainer, for allowing me to include Clara's original artwork in Chapter 4.

Finally, thanks are due to Daniel Schwartz and—especially—to "Magical" Trevor Gori at Taylor & Francis for guiding me through the manuscript preparation and pre-production processes. I suspect I required a lot more handholding than other authors they've worked with, and I am extremely grateful for their patience and support.

PART I
Foundations

INTRODUCTION TO PART I

Although teaching is a career with a cyclical rhythm that repeats year after year in a regular, predictable pattern, education—as a state and national enterprise—is continually changing. Observers of preK–12 education in the United States frequently liken the changes in education to the swing of a pendulum, claiming that priorities and values shift from one extreme to the other. For example, "back to basics" may be the emphasis in education today, but fast-forward a few years and you can be sure that "child-centered education" will be on the rise and back to basics will be fading into the background.

The CCSS Determine the Content to Be Mastered

Currently, the Common Core State Standards (CCSS) are the new emphasis in American education. Rigorous and complex, the CCSS emphasize critical thinking, language development, deep conceptual understanding, and reliance on evidence pulled from textual sources, even for the youngest learners. Teachers of young children often gasp in surprise when they look at the CCSS' academic expectations for children aged 5 to 8 years old. For example, Reading Standards: Foundational Skill #2 for kindergarten states (CCSS-ELA, p. 15):

Phonological Awareness

2. Demonstrate understanding of spoken words, syllables, and sounds (phonemes).
   a. Recognize and produce rhyming words.
   b. Count, pronounce, blend, and segment syllables in spoken words.
   c. Blend and segment onsets and rimes of single-syllable spoken words.
   d. Isolate and pronounce the initial, medial vowel, and final sounds (phonemes) in three-phoneme (consonant-vowel-consonant, or CVC) words.* (This does not include CVCs ending with /l/, /r/, or /x/.)
   e. Add or substitute individual sounds (phonemes) in simple, one-syllable words to make new words.

FIGURE PART 1.1 Kindergarten Reading Standards: Foundational Skill #2

Mastery of these skills is the expectation for the end of kindergarten. Nevertheless, these skills may seem to be beyond the reach of many typically developing five-year-olds.

Teachers Determine the Most Effective Instructional Methods

The authors of both the CCSS-ELA and the CCSS-M make it clear that the standards specify only the knowledge and skills to be mastered at a given grade level. Decisions regarding the ways in which the content should be taught are left entirely in the hands of teachers. I find this acknowledgement of teachers' professional capacity and responsibility to make instructional decision very refreshing. Although it sounds almost ridiculous, teachers' well-developed expertise in instructional decision-making is rarely recognized: encouraging teachers to use the instructional methods they believe will be most effective with the specific students in their classes seems like the most obvious solution imaginable.

When early childhood educators are permitted to choose the most effective instructional methods for their students—in preschool, perhaps, or in transitional kindergarten programs—they often return to the tried-and-true activities and experiences that support their knowledge and beliefs about how young children learn. Their students can be found playing freely outdoors and indoors, working with magnets, building with blocks, sculpting play-dough, digging in deep containers of sand, rice, or corn meal and engaging in other hands-on/minds-on experiences. I contend that these developmentally appropriate experiences can and should be used to engage young students in mastering the content in the CCSS.

The three chapters in this part present the key issues and elements that form the foundation of my argument: the relationship between the CCSS and developmentally appropriate practice (DAP), the notion of "rigor" in early learning environments, and the importance of teachers making sustained efforts to know and understand their young students.

A Final Note

In accordance with the laws related to public license, the NGA Center for Best Practices (NGA Center) and the Council of Chief State School Officers (CCSSO) have granted "a limited, non-exclusive, royalty-free license to copy, publish, distribute, and display the Common Core State Standards for purposes that support the Common Core State Standards Initiative. These uses may involve the Common Core State Standards as a whole or selected excerpts or portions" (NGA Center & CCSSO, n.d.). I am grateful that the NGA Center and the CCSSO permit educators and other CCSS advocates to access and use their various materials without charge.

The CCSS documents will be referenced continuously throughout this book. To keep the text reader-friendly, I have chosen to modify the format for in-text citations of the CCSS documents. References to the CCSS-English Language Arts will be formatted like this: (CCSS-ELA, p. X). References to the CCSS-Mathematics will be formatted like this: (CCSS-M, p. X). This format will make it easier for interested readers to go back into the documents to find specific information. The full citation for the Common Core State Standards documents is:

National Governors Association Center for Best Practices, Council of Chief State School Officers. (2010). *Common Core State Standards.* Washington, D.C.: National Governors Association Center for Best Practices, Council of Chief State School Officers.

Reference

National Governors Association Center for Best Practices, Council of Chief State School Officers. (n.d.). *License grant.* Retrieved from http://www.corestandards.org/public-license/

1

TEACHING THE COMMON CORE IN DEVELOPMENTALLY APPROPRIATE WAYS

Young Children: Born to Learn

Young children—from birth through age 8—are focused on a single, unwavering goal: to understand their world. Their curiosity about everything around them seems insatiable, and they are always ready to learn something new. Young children spend most of their waking hours each day thinking, exploring, asking questions, and learning as much as they possibly can.

Young children strive continually to develop new skills, explore different possibilities, challenge themselves (and others), and figure things out. They wonder out loud about how things work, what words mean, why grass is green, and why they have to take a nap when they are definitely not tired. They learn new information eagerly, and create wonderful, unexpected connections between the newly learned information and their existing knowledge base. The opportunity to feed young children's hunger for knowledge and to support them in their tireless pursuit of new skills is what drew many of us into the teaching profession and what keeps us there still.

Policy Impacts PreK–3 Teaching Practices

Young children, their developmental patterns, and their learning trajectories have not changed. However, the policies, expectations, and preferred practices that shape teaching and learning in Grades preK–3 change continually.

The implementation of No Child Left Behind (2001) brought significant changes to the preK–3 world. This federal legislation led states to establish rigid accountability policies that placed a high premium on academic success for all students and imposed penalties on schools that did not meet their government-determined growth targets.

In an effort to address NCLB's accountability pressures, most school districts in most states chose to push academic expectations down into the earlier grades. Presently, many children are expected to begin kindergarten with mastery of skills that were previously associated with the start of first grade. And, in many parts of the U.S., it has become difficult for preK and kindergarten teachers to justify teaching young children using developmentally appropriate practice.

Arrival of the Common Core State Standards

Coming right on the heels of NCLB, the Common Core State Standards (CCSS) have been viewed with some suspicion and concern by teachers of children in Grades preK–3. These early childhood educators fear the full implementation of the Common Core State Standards (National Governors Association Center for Best Practices, Council of Chief State School Officers, 2010) will have a negative impact on young children. Because of the CCSS' emphasis on rigor, academic language, and critical thinking, some early childhood teachers worry the CCSS will further constrain their ability to provide their students with the engaging, developmentally appropriate learning experiences that form the strongest foundation for academic learning in the upper grades.

Preschool and primary grade teachers must accommodate the decisions and demands of their school administrators, yet they also must provide rich and engaging learning experiences for their young students. This tension between ensuring student mastery of the mandated academic standards and providing opportunities for meaningful learning across the cognitive, social, emotional, and physical developmental domains has become a defining feature of teaching in Grades preK–3.

New Opportunities and Possibilities

The implementation of the Common Core State Standards is in its early stages, and has just begun to impact the education of young learners. At this point in the process, teachers in Grades preK–3 still have opportunities to impact the ways in which the CCSS will be implemented in preK–3. There is a very real possibility of *establishing developmentally appropriate practice as the principal instructional method for teaching the content specified in the CCSS to young learners.*

In this chapter, you will find background information on the foundational elements necessary for implementing the CCSS using developmentally appropriate practices in early learning environments. First I provide a brief, general overview of the CCSS. This is followed by a discussion of key features of developmentally appropriate practice. The chapter concludes with consideration of the ways in which the CCSS and DAP are complementary—the CCSS specify what to teach and DAP provides evidence-based guidance on how to teach—and can be brought together to have a powerful impact on young students' learning.

The Common Core State Standards

The Common Core State Standards include two separate documents, each containing K–12 academic content standards: "Common Core State Standards for English Language Arts and Literacy in History/Social Science, Science and Technical Subjects" (which I will refer to as the CCSS-ELA) and "Common Core State Standards for Mathematics" (which I will refer to as the CCSS-M). The decision to adopt the CCSS was voluntary and was made on a state-by-state basis. Forty-four states are implementing the CCSS, as are the District of Columbia, Guam, American Samoa, Northern Mariana Islands, U.S. Virgin Islands, and the U.S. Department of Defense schools. (Alaska, Indiana, Nebraska, Oklahoma, Texas, and Virginia did not adopt the CCSS. Minnesota adopted the CCSS-ELA, but not the CCSS-M. For more information, see http://www.corestandards.org/standards-in-your-state/.)

The CCSS were expressly designed to develop the knowledge and skills that young adults will need for successful entry into college and/or careers at the end of Grade 12. Further, the CCSS were benchmarked internationally to be commensurate with the content, rigor, and organization of the academic content standards used in the highest-performing nations. This will ensure that graduates of U.S. schools will be prepared to succeed in a global economy and society (Common Core State Standards Initiative Standards-Setting Considerations, n.d.).

Like the standards that were adopted before, or in response to, No Child Left Behind, the CCSS are academic content standards: They provide a detailed description of the knowledge and skills students are expected to learn at each grade level—from kindergarten through 12—in English Language Arts and Mathematics. However, the CCSS are *unlike* the previous state content standards in a variety of significant ways. **These departures from the old, NCLB-style**

TABLE 1.1 Shifts That Accompany the Implementation of the Common Core State Standards

The CCSS-English Language Arts require teachers to…	The CCSS-Mathematics require teachers to…
• Provide students with regular practice reading and writing complex text and using academic language.	• Emphasize the key knowledge, skills, and practices specified for their grade level.
• Expect students to support their ideas and assertions using evidence drawn from literary and informational text.	• Create coherence by linking major topics within a grade level and by recognizing the progression of mathematical knowledge that builds across the grade levels.
• Use the reading and writing of content-rich nonfiction to build students' academic knowledge base.	• Attend to students' conceptual understanding, procedural skill and fluency, and application with equal intensity.

standards are what open the CCSS to alignment with developmentally appropriate practice.

The authors of the CCSS identified three significant shifts in both ELA and in Math that distinguish the Common Core from the previous sets of state standards. These shifts were identified and foregrounded by the authors of each Common Core standards document to help teachers and the public understand the classroom-level changes that will accompany the implementation of the Common Core.

In both ELA and Math, these shifts were specifically intended to redress significant shortcomings common to most states' existing academic content standards, to the curricular and instructional materials aligned with those standards, and to the instructional practices employed to teach the content in those standards.

The CCSS bring other important departures from the approach to standards-based education that was enacted in response to the demands of NCLB. Once again, the new priorities and emphases that frame the Common Core enhance their compatibility with developmentally appropriate practices.

"Fewer, clearer, higher" standards. NCLB-style academic content standards were frequently described as "a mile wide and an inch deep" (CCSS-M, p. 3). Every content area had its own academic content standards, and each of those standards documents included more content than could possibly be taught within the 180 days of a typical academic year. Since it was impossible to teach all the required standards, teachers simply did their best to cover as much of the content as possible. Unfortunately, the frenzied pace at which the standards were covered made it impossible for students to engage deeply with the concepts or to master the skills fully.

The CCSS, on the other hand, were deliberately designed to be easy for teachers to use. In addition, the CCSS include only the content most critical for student success (Common Core State Standards Initiative Standards-Setting Considerations, n.d.). The number of standards at each grade level is limited to ensure that students learn the academic content that is most important.

Integration across academic content areas. The Common Core requires age-appropriate reading and writing activities to be integrated into all facets of the classroom curriculum. The CCSS are explicit in the expectation that instruction in English Language Arts will include significant, sustained attention to reading, discussing, and writing non-fiction rooted in the academic content covered in the grade level's social studies, science, and mathematics standards. Likewise, instruction in social studies, science, and mathematics is expected to include explicit attention to developing all students' English reading and writing skills. So, rather than fracturing the curriculum into small pieces that are addressed in isolation—as was often the case during the NCLB era—the CCSS require teachers to develop lessons that are richer and more challenging than the lessons they have written in the past. For example, when implementing the CCSS, reading skills, writing skills, and the development of academic language are expected not only to be integrated into lessons in all the content areas but also to be taught explicitly in those lessons.

Teaching for student understanding, application, and transfer. The Common Core State Standards in ELA and Math share an emphasis on developing children's deep understanding of the academic content they are learning. Further, the CCSS aim to develop students' ability to apply their knowledge and skills to solving real world problems and their capacity to transfer knowledge and skills learned in one context to a new challenge in a different setting or discipline. Since engagement in academic conversations with teachers and peers develops students' intellectual acuity and flexibility, even the youngest students are expected to provide a rationale to support their opinions, to explain their reasoning, to justify their position by referring back to the text or to another source of concrete evidence, and to respond to critical questions or challenges from classmates.

Acknowledgement of teachers' specialized professional expertise. The CCSS specify what students must learn at each grade level in English Language Arts and Mathematics. The CCSS do not offer any prescriptions regarding how that knowledge and those skills should be taught. The CCSS deliberately give teachers the discretion to make independent, principled, intentional instructional decisions that reflect their knowledge of their students, their understanding of the context and the community in which they teach, and the resources available at their school or in their district.

Further, the CCSS are designed to constitute only 85% of the curriculum in any given grade (Gewertz, 2010). This leaves space in which teachers may strengthen and enhance the existing curriculum by including their most effective and time-tested learning experiences, their most powerful excursions and field trips, and the culturally and linguistically relevant activities that most strongly reflect the interests and home lives of the children in their classes.

In addition, the CCSS are nothing like the teacher-proof curricular "cookbooks" and instructional planning guides implemented in the wake of NCLB. In fact, they are quite the opposite. For example, the authors of the CCSS-ELA write:

> "The use of play with young children is not specified by the standards, but it is *welcome as a valuable activity in its own right and as a way to help students meet the expectations in this document.*"
>
> *(italics mine, CCSS-ELA, pg. 9)*

This quote delivers two positive messages for early childhood education. First, the authors of the CCSS-ELA make it clear that teacher discretion is both expected and desired when teaching the Common Core. Second, the authors foreground—and specifically single out—play as both a valuable activity AND as a legitimate means of instruction when teaching young children. This perspective points to an open doorway through which developmentally appropriate practice can re-enter young children's classrooms.

Developmentally Appropriate Practice

Developmentally appropriate practice—often abbreviated as DAP (Bredekamp, 1987)—is a term used by many early childhood educators to describe a shared

Developmentally appropriate practices must be

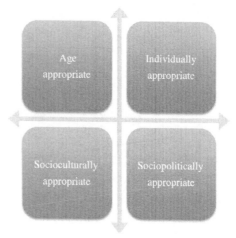

FIGURE 1.1

vision of best practice. DAP is an approach to teaching young children in which learning activities are intentionally selected to be age appropriate, individually appropriate, socioculturally appropriate, and sociopolitically appropriate for the specific children who will be engaging in the activities.

Age-Appropriate Practices

Broad, consistent patterns in the pediatric and psychological research data document the developmental milestones, accomplishments, and challenges common to all typically developing children of a given chronological age. Although each individual child's development is unique and idiosyncratic, children—in general—reach particular developmental landmarks according to a predictable timetable.

Many books and websites describe developmental norms and characteristic traits of typically developing children of a given age (Wood, 2007). Knowing the age of the children in the class enables a teacher to develop a general understanding of the kinds of physical, cognitive, social, emotional, and academic capabilities the students will possess. This body of knowledge, frequently referred to as developmental "ages and stages," creates a solid foundation for effective teaching.

Because child development follows predictable patterns, children of the same chronological age generally exhibit similar behaviors, skills, interests, and needs. Schools in the United States organize children into grade levels based on age because this arrangement has the greatest likelihood of producing groupings characterized by the strongest similarities. When students are grouped with others of the same chronological age, teachers can choose learning activities and experiences that reflect and respond to the typical needs and interests common to children of that chronological age. High quality, commercially prepared curricular and instructional materials that are pre-labeled as suitable for a specific grade level (e.g., a mathematics workbook labeled Grade 3, a storybook for Grades preK–2) are designed to be age-appropriate for children at that grade level.

However, children of the same chronological age mature and develop at different rates. As a result, preK–3 teachers expect to have some students in their classes whose skill levels and/or behavior patterns are less developed than those of their classmates and other students whose skill levels and/or behavior patterns are more advanced than those of their classmates. Thus, learning activities that are generally considered age-appropriate for students at the grade level might prove to be too difficult for some and too easy for others.

Individually Appropriate Practices

Although a group of same-aged children typically share many general characteristics, the developmental profile of each individual child in the group can vary widely. Some children begin losing their baby teeth early in their kindergarten year; others may not start until late in first grade. Children vary in temperament, in approaches to learning, in academic abilities, in self-regulation skills, and so on. Therefore, due to the natural variation in development that characterizes young children, a teacher who chooses an age-appropriate non-fiction book to read to her third graders should expect the book to be individually appropriate for many of her students but individually inappropriate—either too difficult to understand or too basic to be interesting—for some of her students.

Further, each individual child is likely to demonstrate different rates of development in different domains: a kindergartner with an advanced vocabulary and highly developed verbal communication skills (cognitive domain) might have difficulty interacting with age peers (social domain) or with gross motor activities such as throwing, catching, hopping, or balancing (physical domain); a second grader with exceptionally advanced reading skills (cognitive domain) might have weak fine motor skills and poor handwriting (physical domain) or difficulty controlling his temper when he is frustrated (emotional domain).

Although children's development follows established patterns grounded in large data sets gathered over long periods of time, age appropriateness is a broad notion that provides limited assistance for teachers when making day-to-day decisions about curriculum and instruction for their actual, specific students. Because children of the same chronological age can vary widely in their capabilities and interests, the age-appropriate curricular and instructional materials available to teachers at every grade level will never be a perfect fit for the learning needs of every student in a given class. As a result, teachers must be prepared to ensure that all students receive instructional opportunities that are individually appropriate for them.

To know what learning experiences could be individually appropriate for a young child requires the teacher to have a rich understanding of that child. Sources of information include

- observation, documentation, and reflection on all developmental domains
- attention to typical social behavior in the classroom and on the playground
- conversations with the child
- conversations with co-teachers, paraprofessionals, support personnel, aides
- communication with the child's former teacher(s)
- discussions with the child's family

Most young children enjoy attention from adults and are open to answering teachers' questions about themselves and their interests, hobbies, and favorite books, toys, and games. Take notes on a child's responses (i.e., have a documented conversation) and make time to reflect on the ways in which the information you gathered could be used to sharpen and focus your instructional plans for that student. Since young children sometimes develop quickly, a teacher must always be alert to changes in the child's capabilities and interests and continue to adapt instruction to suit the child. Much more detail about the process of observing and documenting student learning is provided in Chapter 4.

Teachers who use developmentally appropriate practice build flexibility into all their lessons. This flexibility is evident when a teacher groups students by ability for leveled guided reading instruction, then regroups them into heterogeneous teams for a hands-on science activity, and then offers a range of centers that feature open-ended activities that can be completed successfully at varying levels of complexity or detail. Teachers can make a lesson more individually appropriate for their first graders who have the capability and desire to go more deeply into a topic or to venture beyond the boundaries of the topic's typical first grade coverage by offering them "challenge problems" and enrichment opportunities. Similarly, these teachers could make the lesson more individually appropriate for their students who may need additional exposure and practice with the material by allowing those students more time to complete a give task or by shortening and focusing the assignment to target the specific area in which any given student needs additional practice.

Culturally Appropriate Practices

The 1997 revision to the DAP guidelines (Bredekamp & Copple, 1997) added a new element to developmentally appropriate practices. The guidelines specified that preK–3 teachers should not only take into consideration the developmental norms associated with the grade level they teach and the specific strengths, interests, and needs of the children in their class when planning instruction. Bredekamp and Copple prompted teachers to integrate acknowledgement and affirmation of the values, beliefs, priorities, and practices that shaping the social and cultural contexts of their students' lives into their curricular and instructional decisions. Cultural appropriateness can be split into two related but distinct categories: sociocultural appropriateness and sociopolitical appropriateness.

Socioculturally Appropriate Practices

In the earliest years of their schooling, young children remain very deeply connected to their families, homes, and communities. The daily challenge of transitioning back and forth between their familiar home and cultural practices and the myriad demands, challenges, and unknowns presented at school can be jarring, even for children whose family, home, and community experiences are very congruent with the culture of schooling.

Teachers serve as a bridge between home and school when they intentionally seek partnerships with parents or guardians and incorporate aspects of their students' home cultures, languages, and practices into the classroom and the curriculum. Some culturally appropriate practices include deliberate efforts to

1. Acknowledge and communicate the value of the cultural, linguistic, and family identities of all the children in the class;
2. Form meaningful and mutually-beneficial partnerships with students' parents and family members by creating as many types of opportunities to participate in classroom life and experiences as possible; actively seek to access the funds of knowledge in the families and their communities and to leverage that knowledge to increase students' learning; ask directly for assistance, suggestions, and recommendations about how to better serve and support their children;
3. Incorporate culturally specific realia into learning centers—enhance the socio-dramatic play area by adding a tortilla press, a wok and chopsticks, and cans and packages from types of food that are familiar to children from the different cultural groups represented in your class; place magazines, books, and other reading materials that reflect the students' cultures and home languages in the library center—and into the classroom environment, such as mounting and hanging photographs of the students and their families, collecting, displaying, and using common household objects that reflect the cultural practices in the students' homes (such as special types of writing tools or paper).

Sociopolitically Appropriate Practices

In the years following the implementation of No Child Left Behind (2001), many early childhood educators had to broaden their understanding of "culturally appropriate practices" in ways that would allow them to attend and respond more closely to pressing sociopolitical demands (Goldstein, 2008a). The standards-based education systems developed in most states in response to the federal requirements associated with NCLB frequently established English Language Arts and Mathematics academic content standards for prekindergarten, kindergarten, and the primary grades that were beyond the capabilities of typically developing children in those grade levels (Hatch, 2002).

Administrators' and teachers' reactions to these NCLB-driven requirements resulted in significant curricular and instructional change in Grades preK–3. The changes, such as heightened academic expectations, intensified emphasis on developing young learners' reading and mathematics skills, and establishing the exclusive importance of assessment data drawn from standardized tests and other formal measures of academic achievement, appeared to be developmentally inappropriate for young learners. These shifts made it difficult for teachers to create child-centered, responsive, engaging, and effective classroom learning environments.

Nevertheless, preK–3 teachers in public elementary schools recognized that the demands of NCLB were a feature of the sociopolitical dimension of culturally appropriate practice (Goldstein, 2008b). The DAP guidelines explicitly acknowledge "the powerful influence of context on all development and learning" (Bredekamp 1997, p. 41) and note that children's "contexts are influenced by many factors—among them are parents' preferences, community values, societal expectations, demands of institutions at the next level of education, and broadly defined values of American culture" (Bredekamp 1997, p. 43). NCLB was a prominent feature of the social and cultural context in which U.S. children were living; thus, attending and responding to the demands of NCLB was an important aspect of culturally appropriate practices.

In order to be developmentally appropriate, then, teachers' practical decisions had to be informed by thoughtful consideration of the demands and expectations associated with NCLB in conjunction with the more familiar, well-established, and widely-accepted dimensions of DAP.

NCLB prompted early childhood educators to think more deeply about vertical alignment of curriculum. Meeting accountability expectations required attention to the big picture and to the long view: Early childhood learning activities and experiences had to be informed by clear, detailed knowledge of the academic and behavioral expectations children would be expected to meet in their future classrooms (Goldstein, 2008b). In order to engage in sociopolitically appropriate practices, prekindergarten and transitional kindergarten teachers had to be aware of the current expectations in the local kindergartens their children would attend and dedicate time and effort to prepare their young students for success in those settings.

For example, when prekindergarten and transitional kindergarten teachers know the kindergarten teachers in the schools in their community expect kinders to sit on their bottoms, remain silent, and pay attention to the teacher for 10 minutes at a time *from the first day of school*, the preK and TK teachers will work to build their students' self-control, focus, and stamina over a period of several months, to help all the students master this skill set, and to rehearse that skill set as often as necessary to keep it strong.

Contradictions and Dilemmas

Teachers in Grades preK–3 encounter contradictions within DAP—mastery of certain academic skills may be sociopolitically appropriate but not age appropriate, for example—but resolving contradictions is already an established feature of developmentally appropriate teaching (Bredekamp 1997, p. 45). Engaging in developmentally appropriate practice is often complicated by tension between what early childhood teachers believe to be best for young children and what is actually required or expected in schools. As the "sitting silently on the rug for 10 minutes" example illustrates, engaging in sociopolitically appropriate practice may require the use of teaching strategies or expectations that could be considered developmentally inappropriate.

Teachers' familiarity with the complexities of working within the DAP framework and their facility as professional decision makers can help determine how to resolve those tensions effectively in relation to the demands of their specific professional contexts. Generally, early childhood educators try to resolve these tensions by avoiding either/or dichotomies and striving for both/and compromises (Bredekamp, 1997). For example, early childhood educators often try to create learning experiences in which content from the CCSS is embedded within meaningful, child-directed, play-based activities.

CCSS and DAP: Natural Partners in PreK, K, and the Primary Grades

The Common Core State Standards are academic content standards: the documents specify the knowledge and skills students are expected to master in each grade level from K–12 in English Language Arts and in Mathematics. Neither of these documents—the CCSS-ELA or the CCSS-M—is a curriculum. The CCSS documents do not provide any guidance about how the knowledge and skills specified for each grade level should be organized or taught. Nor do they recommend specific books, activities, or instructional materials that should be used to deliver the content most effectively. The content in the CCSS could be taught effectively in a wide range of different ways, including the use of developmentally appropriate practices.

Developmentally appropriate practice, by contrast, is a coherent body of research-based guidelines and recommendations regarding the most effective ways to teach any type of knowledge or skills to children from birth to age 8. DAP

TABLE 1.2 Looking at the Common Core State Standards

Body of knowledge	What type of information is this?	What does this information specify?	What does this information NOT specify?
CCSS-ELA CCSS-Math	Academic content standards	The knowledge and skills to be learned by all students in English-Language Arts and Mathematics in a given grade level, K–3	The most effective instructional materials and/or practices to use to teach the specified the knowledge and skills to students

TABLE 1.3 Looking at Developmentally Appropriate Practice

Body of knowledge	What type of information is this?	What does this information specify?	What does this information NOT specify?
Developmentally Appropriate Practice	Coherent body of research-based guidelines and recommendations for instructional practices for young children	The most effective ways to teach any knowledge and skills to children from birth to age 8 in all developmental domains	The knowledge and skills that should be taught using these practices

does not specify the content that young children should learn, nor how selected content should be organized to achieve maximum effectiveness, nor the materials that should be used to teach the content.

The Common Core State Standards and developmentally appropriate practice complement each other: the CCSS specify the ELA and Math knowledge and skills students should learn at each grade level and DAP provides guidance about the most effective way to teach that knowledge and those skills to children in Grades preK–3.

Excellent early childhood education involves numerous and complex judgments "constructed each day by teachers in relation to a specific group of children and within a specific social and cultural context" (Bredekamp, 1997, p. 41). Implicit in Bredekamp's image of teachers' decision making is the notion of multiplicity: There is never a single correct way to teach a concept or skill. The content in the CCSS can be taught using an endless variety of strategies. A teacher might make some small adjustments to a lesson from the district-adopted math series to take advantage of the one-to-one tablet initiative at her school. Another teacher might decide to add depth and complexity to a lesson that was not adequately challenging for some of his students. Teachers frequently change their plans to take advantage of unexpected opportunities—seeing a rainbow, receiving a basket of oranges picked from the tree in a student's

TABLE 1.4 Looking at the Complementary Relationship Between the CCSS and DAP

Body of knowledge	Specifies the content to be taught?	Specifies how to teach the content most effectively?
Common Core State Standards for ELA and Mathematics	YES	NO
Developmentally appropriate practice	NO	YES

backyard, responding to a request from the custodian to help set up the chairs for an assembly—and find ways to weave content from the CCSS-ELA and the CCSS-M into these experiences.

Making curricular and pedagogical decisions that reflect both the needs of their students and the demands of their context is teachers' central responsibility. Teachers in Grades preK–3 can embrace the CCSS, teach the required standards using DAP (to whatever degree is appropriate in their school and community context), and support the healthy development of all their students.

Summary of Key Points

- The expectations that shape the work of teachers in Grades preK–3 are always changing.
- As accountability pressures have increased and academic expectations have been pushed downward into lower grades, many teachers in Grades preK–3 have experienced difficulty maintaining developmentally appropriate learning environments in their classrooms.
- The Common Core State Standards are different from previous content standards in many significant ways. These differences make the CCSS compatible with developmentally appropriate practices.
- During the NCLB era, teachers of children between 3 and 8 years of age developed significant expertise in making curricular and instructional decisions that successfully negotiate the tensions between academic content standards and young children's learning needs. These skills enhance their ability to use DAP to teach the CCSS.

References

Bredekamp, S. (Ed.). (1987). *Developmentally appropriate practice in early childhood programs serving children from birth through age 8*. Washington, DC: National Association for the Education of Young Children.

Bredekamp, S. (1997). Developmentally appropriate practice: The early childhood teacher as decisionmaker. In S. Bredekamp & C. Copple (Eds.), *Developmentally appropriate practice in early childhood programs. Revised edition* (pp. 33–52). Washington, DC: National Association for the Education of Young Children.

Bredekamp, S., & Copple, S. (Eds.). (1997). *Developmentally appropriate practices in early childhood programs. Revised edition*. Washington, DC: National Association for the Education of Young Children.

Common Core State Standards Initiative. (n.d.) *Standards-setting considerations*. Retrieved from http://www.corestandards.org/assets/Considerations.pdf

Gewertz, C. (2010, February 2). States can't pick and choose among Common Standards. *Education Week*. Retrieved from http://blogs.edweek.org/edweek/curriculum/2010/02/states_cant_pick_and_choose_am.html

Goldstein, L. S. (2008a). Teaching the standards is developmentally appropriate practice: Strategies for incorporating the sociopolitical dimension of DAP in early childhood teaching. *Early Childhood Education Journal, 36* (3), 253–60.

Hatch, J. A. (2002). Accountability shovedown: Resisting the standards movement in early childhood education. *Phi Delta Kappan, 83* (6), 457–463.

National Governors Association Center for Best Practices, Council of Chief State School Officers. (2010). *Common Core State Standards.* Washington, DC: National Governors Association Center for Best Practices, Council of Chief State School Officers.

No Child Left Behind Act of 2001, 20 U.S. C. 6301 *et seq.* Retrieved from http://www.ed.gov/policy/elsec/leg/esea02/index.html

Wood, C. (2007). *Yardsticks: Children in the classroom ages 4–14.* Greenfield, MA: Northeast Foundation for Children.

2

PROVIDING RIGOROUS LEARNING EXPERIENCES FOR ALL STUDENTS

The Common Core State Standards specify the knowledge and skills young students must master in Grades K–3 but provide no guidance on how to teach young children the academic content presented in the standards. The National Association for the Education of Young Children (NAEYC) has clearly delineated guidelines for best practices in classrooms serving children from birth through age eight (Bredekamp, 1987); these developmentally appropriate practices can be used to teach any type of content. Teaching the CCSS to young learners using DAP seems like an easy and elegant solution. However, before we can implement this solution, we must address a critical issue raised by the Common Core: the focus on providing learning experiences characterized by "rigor."

Rigor? In Early Childhood Education?

When the Common Core State Standards were first introduced to the American public, we were told these standards were (1) research and evidence based, (2) aligned with college and workplace expectations, (3) rigorous, and (4) internationally benchmarked (CCSS-ELA, p. 3).

Rigor can be a discomfiting term for early childhood educators, especially after our difficult experiences with the intensification of academic expectations and the disregard for young children's learning needs that followed in the wake of NCLB. Rigor evokes images of young children sitting in classrooms endlessly engaged in developmentally inappropriate academic activities. This is image is particularly troubling because students in preK–3 classrooms work harder and learn less when their learning activities are not aligned with the realities of their developmental needs.

Although Barbara Blackburn, a noted authority on the CCSS, states plainly "the foundation of the Common Core State Standards is a focus on rigor"

(2013, n.p.), rigor is barely mentioned in the CCSS documents: The term appears twice in the ELA standards and not at all in the Math standards. Further, neither the CCSS for ELA nor the CCSS for Math provide an operational definition of rigor. So, although we have been told the CCSS are "rigorous," the exact meaning of this word in this specific context is not clearly stated.

The absence of a working definition of rigor suggests the CCSS' authors might not have considered the possibility that their implicit understanding of rigor—which is not identified in the CCSS documents—might be developmentally inappropriate for students in Grades K–3. Further, the authors did not provide any guidelines for adjusting or reframing "rigor" when it is applied to standards or practices in Grades K–3. So, although the Common Core is explicitly intended for use in kindergarten through third grade classrooms, the authors of the CCSS neither explicitly addressed the needs of young learners nor acknowledged that "rigor" in Grades K–3 ought to look and feel very different from the rigor experienced by students in Grades 4–12.

Defining Rigor in Grades PreK–3

The unique needs and priorities of young learners and their teachers are often overlooked in public conversations about preK–12 education. Typically, early childhood professionals find this neglect frustrating. However, in this particular case, early childhood education's relative insignificance actually works in our favor. The Common Core's authors' lack of attention to the primary grades allows early childhood educators to establish our own developmentally appropriate definition of "rigor" specifically for use in preschool and the primary grades.

What would "rigor" look like in an early childhood learning environment? Drawing on recent research literature and on my own observations in preK–3 classrooms, I have framed a working definition of rigor that is specifically tailored to the realities of working with young learners. This definition is grounded in and builds upon the National Association for the Education of Young Children's

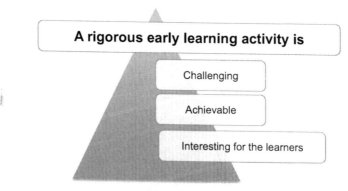

A rigorous early learning activity is

Challenging

Achievable

Interesting for the learners

FIGURE 2.1 Defining "rigor" in the context of early childhood education

ongoing efforts to clarify and exemplify the key traits of high quality learning environments serving children from birth through age 8 (Phillips & Scrinzi, 2014):

> **A rigorous learning activity for young children is challenging, achievable, and interesting for the learners for whom it was planned.**

Let's look at each of those elements in turn.

A Rigorous Early Childhood Learning Experience Should Be Challenging

When my son Noah was in middle school, he made a distinction that has really stuck with me. In an effort to explain his frustration with his never-ending pile of homework, he said, "I like homework that's challenging, but I hate homework that's difficult."

According to Noah, challenging homework involved assignments like solving complex, multi-step math problems; learning new Latin declensions; doing research about historical topics on the Internet; and reading books, plays, and poetry for English class. Challenging homework, Noah said, engaged his brain. Difficult homework, by contrast, involved things like coloring, cutting, and pasting; doing repetitive worksheets; and copying out spelling words. Difficult homework, Noah said, didn't lead to learning.

Challenging homework felt engaging, purposeful, and educative (Dewey, 1938). Difficult homework, by contrast, was endlessly repetitive, took a long time to complete, and didn't teach Noah anything. When I refer to a rigorous learning activity for young children as "challenging, achievable, and interesting to the learners for whom it was planned," I am using Noah's definition of challenging work—interesting tasks that engage learners' brains—rather than the more common definition that links challenge with difficulty, complexity, or complication.

Typically, young children enjoy challenging themselves. Challenges are opportunities for youngsters to test their limits, to exceed their expectations, and to surprise themselves with their capabilities. Mastering a challenging activity bolsters children's self-confidence and can strengthen their willingness to embrace new challenges. Even failure to master a challenge has its benefits. An unsuccessful attempt at a challenging task provides children with concrete feedback about knowledge and skills they need to develop to be more successful and with ideas about how to approach the challenging task in the future.

A Rigorous Early Childhood Learning Experience Should Be Achievable

A child learns by engaging in challenging tasks. However, the level of challenge presented by a task must be reasonable and appropriate for the specific child. In essence, a child trying to learn something new resembles Goldilocks in the story of The Three Bears: She needs challenges with a level of difficulty that is "just right" for her.

A "just right" task falls just beyond the upper edge of a child's current level of capability. For example, a first grade math learner who knows his addition facts to ten and the "counting on" strategy could probably solve $7 + 4 + 2 =$ ___. This equation would allow him to leverage what he already knows and can do in order to complete a task that is slightly more complex and demanding than math problems he has solved before. The novelty in this problem—dealing with three addends and arriving at a solution that is larger than ten—makes it challenging, but the student's existing skill with mental mathematical calculation makes it achievable. This is a "just right" task: It is challenging but achievable. By contrast, solving an equation like $46 + 27 =$ ___ would not be "just right" for this student. This task is challenging, but it is too far beyond his current abilities to be achievable.

Completing new and challenging tasks successfully requires children to exert intellectual effort: Learning new skills or content may require persistence, problem solving skills, self-regulation, knowledge transfer across different contexts, and strategic application of that knowledge in a new domain.

The work of psychologist Lev Vygotsky (1978) is particularly useful when discussing the notion of challenging but achievable tasks. Further, his ideas and theories can help teachers identify the sweet spot where challenge and achievability intersect for any given student. In his examination of the relationship of learning and development, Vygotsky conceptualized three distinct levels: the level of independent performance, the zone of proximal development, and the level of assisted performance.

Level of independent performance: This level of performance, characterized by the swift and successful completion of a task, uses mental functions that are already well developed. When working at this level, children are employing skills and knowledge they have already mastered.

When a task falls within a student's level of independent performance, he can complete the task successfully without any assistance or support. The task is easy for him, and he does not learn anything new by completing the task. This task is *achievable, but not challenging,* for the student.

Zone of proximal development: This level of performance includes mental functions that are in the process of maturation. Working in their personal zone of proximal development creates opportunities for children to think, solve problems, and figure things out, and thereby to master new skills and knowledge.

When a task falls within a student's zone of proximal development (ZPD), the solution to the task lies just beyond her current level of independent performance. The student has the potential to complete the task successfully, but doing so will require her to invest extra intellectual effort. This mental exertion acts as the spark that enables learning to occur. Tasks that fall into a student's ZPD are *both challenging and achievable.* The ZPD is where learning happens.

Level of assisted performance: This level of performance, identified by the successful performance of a task with support from an adult or more capable

TABLE 2.1 Vygotsky's View of Learning

Levels of performance	Student's ability to complete this task	Task's relationship to student learning	Task difficulty
Level of independent performance	Student can complete this task without assistance.	No learning takes place because the task is too easy.	Achievable, but not challenging.
Zone of proximal development (ZPD)	Student can complete this task by exerting intellectual effort (plus receiving appropriate scaffolding, if needed).	Student learns new skills, knowledge, or content by completing this task.	Both challenging and achievable.
Level of assisted performance	Student can complete this task only with the assistance of more capable others.	No learning takes place because the task is too difficult.	Challenging, but not achievable.

peer, reflects mental functions that have not yet developed (but will develop in the future). Children working at this level must rely on assistance from others to bridge the gaps in their cognitive capacity and to assist them in completing the task.

When a task falls within a student's level of assisted performance, she can only hope to complete the task with continuous support from someone who has already mastered it. The task is so difficult for the student that she must rely on the guidance of her support provider to make any progress. This task is *challenging, but not achievable*, for the student, and she learns very little from her attempt to complete the task.

How to Find a Child's ZPD

Targeting learning experiences and activities to fall into your students' zones of proximal development can be difficult. Even within an age-graded preschool classroom of children between 36 and 42 months old, a teacher is likely to find

TABLE 2.2 Using Play to Identify Students' ZPDs

Open-ended activity centers	Flexible learning materials
Sand or water table	Pattern blocks
Socio-dramatic play	Building materials of all kinds
Puppet theater	"Treasure" boxes (buttons, tiles, coins, etc.)
Reading/looking at/listening to books	Colorful scarves
Outdoor play	Clay
Easel painting	

a great deal of variation in physical, socio-emotional, and cognitive capabilities and needs. Offering a range of open-ended activities and providing materials that can be used in a variety of ways enables students to create learning activities and experiences that are responsive to their interests. Children often find their own route into their ZPDs when given interesting materials and time to explore and engage with them.

Scaffolding

Often, the extra effort exerted by a student working in her ZPD is sufficiently powerful to enable her to complete a challenging task without any additional support. At other times, the student tries to complete a task repeatedly and runs out of ideas. When this occurs, a teacher, an aide, or a more experienced peer might assist her by providing a hint, asking a leading question, or offering a recommendation intended to help the student get back on track. The key to supporting a student who gets stuck while working on task you believe to be challenging but achievable for her is to provide the smallest amount of support necessary to get her moving forward again.

Supports of this type are often referred to as "scaffolding"—like the wooden and metal framework you might see on the outside of a building that is undergoing renovations—because they

- Reinforce the student's existing capabilities
- Provide additional stability while the student is building new knowledge or skills
- Are easily removed when they are no longer necessary

With the support provided by supplemental, temporary scaffolding, the student can learn new information and skills more easily and continue making progress toward completing the task. Like a stepstool in front of a sink, a scaffold boosts a child up beyond her current level of ability and thereby puts success more easily within her reach.

There are many different types of scaffolding. For example, a third grade teacher might provide all the students with a graphic organizer that will help them structure a strong summary of the story they just read, or give a student a triangular pencil grip to make the physical act of writing easier and more comfortable. During an instructional unit on farms, a kindergarten teacher could offer all students access to custom-made picture dictionaries with photographs of farm animals labeled in English, Mandarin, and Spanish. If some second grade students are struggling with double-digit addition and subtraction because they have difficulty lining up the numbers in straight columns, their teacher could make one-inch graph paper available to help them organize their equations more neatly.

Teachers are continually inventing new ways to scaffold the learning of students who have a need for temporary support. The very best scaffolds are custom-designed by an attentive teacher who knows the student and the classroom context well. For example, last year a student with cerebral palsy was enrolled in the classroom of an experienced kindergarten teacher who works in a nearby district. This teacher's main concern about teaching this young student was finding a stool or chair that would both provide the student with an appropriate amount of physical support and also would be lightweight and easy enough for the student to carry from place to place without assistance. The teacher wanted the student's everyday experience of sitting and moving around in the classroom—from table to carpet and back to table, from indoor play to outdoor play, from the restroom to the classroom garden—to be safe, effective, easy, and accomplished independently by the student. When she was unable to find any satisfactory options, the teacher decided to design and construct a small support cushion with Velcro straps that the student could attach and remove from almost any chair with ease. Covered in colorful, machine-washable fabric, this cushion was an ideal scaffold for this particular kindergartner: It provided her with the right amount of physical stability while also nudging her to develop greater autonomy and self-help skills.

A Rigorous Early Childhood Learning Experience Should Be Interesting to the Learner

The notion that young children should be provided with educational experiences that are challenging and achievable is well established in the early childhood education literature (Copple, Bredekamp, Koralek, & Charner, 2014). However, I've planned many activities and designed many learning experiences that I knew were challenging and achievable for my students, yet when I implemented them in my classroom they bombed completely.

Honestly, I couldn't believe that no one wanted to take apart my old VCR, even though the activity involved wire cutters, needle-nosed pliers, cool gears, and machinery. Furthermore, the take-apart center was aligned with our science unit on living and non-living things: At that center students were directed to take the machine apart, identify the ways in which it is like a living thing and unlike a living thing, and make a "like-unlike" anchor chart for our class discussion about the activity. How cool is that? Not cool at all, according to my K–1 multiage class. No one visited that center. Obviously, what I'd planned just didn't grab or sustain my students' interest.

Many young children have not yet bought into the expectation that when you're at school you're meant to do what your teacher tells you to do. When they are simply not interested in listening to that book, making trains of 10 with linking cubes, drawing a self-portrait, writing in their journal, playing kickball, or doing any of the activities you've put out in centers that day, young students' behavior communicates their disinterest clearly.

Getting young children interested in school-driven, teacher-selected learning experiences, excited about engaging in the activities you've planned, and enthusiastic about trying new things are among the thorniest problems of practice faced by early childhood educators. It's a mistake to assume that children will engage happily and productively in an activity just because it is challenging and achievable. Activities have to be interesting to the specific, particular students you're teaching in order to entice them into participating.

Here's an example. I once observed a public school prekindergarten teacher who had set out a mathematical puzzle center in her classroom. I was puzzled by the presence of a basket of Beanie Baby toys in the center; I assumed the teacher had placed it there while setting up the centers and forgotten to put it away. But when she introduced the center to her students during morning circle, she described the activity as "helping some Beanie Babies solve fun math puzzles." Even the prekinders who had no desire to solve math puzzles themselves were eager to help Beanie Babies solve math puzzles. By adding the Beanie Babies to the math puzzle center, this teacher inserted a small-but-fun twist—in this case, pretend play—and transformed an activity that students might have considered difficult or dull into the most popular center of the week.

A challenging and achievable activity will support and enhance young children's learning. However, if students are not interested enough in an activity to engage fully with it, they are unlikely to experience the challenge it offers, to achieve success and develop new skills, or to learn anything from the experience. To be rigorous, an early childhood learning activity must be more than challenging and achievable: It also has to capture, respond to, or extend the interests of the students.

Thinking and Talking About Rigor

While it's true that dictionaries define "rigorous" as *rigid, inflexible, or unyielding*, according to EdGlossary.org (2014), "educators frequently apply *rigor* or *rigorous* to assignments that encourage students to think critically, creatively, and more flexibly. Likewise, they may use the term rigorous to describe learning environments that are not intended to be harsh, rigid, or overly prescriptive, but that are stimulating, engaging, and supportive."

A "stimulating, engaging, and supportive" classroom environment in which young learners are encouraged to think "critically, creatively, and more flexibly" sounds like a wonderful place to engage children in learning activities that are challenging, achievable, and interesting to them. Rigor might not be so bad after all.

However, principals, administrators, parents, community stakeholders and legislators—just like the authors of the CCSS-ELA and the CCSS-M—may not have given any consideration to the necessity of an age-appropriate definition of rigor for use with children 3 to 8 years of age. Further, they may not have thought about what rigor might look like in young children's classrooms. Teachers in preK–3 grades must become spokespeople bent on raising awareness that academic rigor looks very different in the classrooms of young children from how it looks in the classrooms of older children.

Summary of Key Points

- Teachers of children in Grades preK–3 can work within a definition of academic rigor that reflects their students' developmental needs: A rigorous learning experience for young children is challenging, achievable, and interesting to the learners for whom it was planned.
- Teachers must reach out to principals, administrators, parents, community stakeholders, and legislators and help them understand that
  - PreK–3 teachers provide a rigorous educational program that is developmentally appropriate for young children
  - Young children think and learn differently from older students
  - Rigor looks different in preK–3 classrooms than it looks in Grades 4–12

References

Blackburn, B. (2013, March 30). *Rigor and the Common Core State Standards: Just the beginning!* Retrieved from http://www.seenmagazine.us/articles/article-detail/articleid/2871/rigor-and-the-common-core-state-standards.aspx

Bredekamp, S. (Ed.). (1987). *Developmentally appropriate practice in early childhood programs serving children from birth through age 8.* Washington, DC: National Association for the Education of Young Children.

Copple, C., Bredekamp, S., Koralek, D., & Charner, K. (Eds.). (2014). *Developmentally appropriate practice: Focus on children in first, second, and third grades.* Washington, DC: National Association for the Education of Young Children.

Dewey, J. (1938). *Experience and education.* New York: Collier.

EdGlossary.org. (2014, August 13). Rigor. Retrieved from http://edglossary.org/rigor/

Phillips, E. C., & Scrinzi, A. (2014). What is developmentally appropriate practice? In C. Copple, S. Bredekamp, D. Koralek, & K. Charner (Eds.), *Developmentally appropriate practice: Focus on children in first, second, and third grades* (pp. 1–3). Washington, DC: National Association for the Education of Young Children.

Vygotsky, L. S. (1978). *Mind in society.* Cambridge, MA: Harvard University Press.

3

KNOWING YOUR STUDENTS AS LEARNERS

The Common Core and DAP should be considered natural partners. Our definition of rigor for preK–3 settings reflects the most current thinking in the field of early childhood education (Copple, Bredekamp, Koralek, & Charner, 2014a, 2014b). Our next step in moving toward a high quality, classroom-friendly synthesis of the CCSS and DAP is to turn our attention to the young children we teach. Knowing our students as learners is a cornerstone of effective early education.

The Role of the Teacher

John Dewey is often admired as the father of child-centered education. Interestingly, Dewey neither thought of education as being centered around the child nor believed young children to be capable of deciding what they should learn or do in school. Rather, John Dewey explained the process by which children become educated like this: "The fundamental factors in the educative process are an immature, undeveloped being; and certain social aims, meanings, values incarnate in the matured experience of the adult. The educative process is due to the interaction of these forces" (Dewey, 1902).

FIGURE 3.1 John Dewey's conception of the process of education

Dewey framed the process of education as an interaction between children and the social aims, meanings, and values embodied in the curriculum. *Interaction* is a key word in Dewey's conception of education, because it specifies that influence and impact flow back and forth between the child and the curriculum. Thus, the child plays an active role in shaping and reshaping the curriculum and, at the same time, the curriculum and its contents are affecting and re-forming the child.

About 35 years after his initial description of education as an interaction between the child and the curriculum, Dewey (1938) acknowledged the crucial contributions of the teacher in facilitating the educative interaction. He asserted that, in order to maximize student learning, the teacher

> must survey the capacities and needs of the particular set of individuals with whom he is dealing and must at the same time arrange the conditions which provide the subject matter or content for experiences that satisfy these needs and develop these capacities. The planning must be flexible enough to permit free play for individuality of experience and yet firm enough to give direction towards continuous development.
>
> *(Dewey, 1938, p. 58)*

In short, Dewey acknowledged that teachers are responsible for facilitating meaningful, intentional interactions between students and the specific content they are expected to learn.

In order to facilitate the interaction between children and the academic knowledge and skills at the heart of the curriculum, teachers must develop deep understanding of (1) their students and (2) the content they are required to teach. This chapter focuses on strategies for deepening your knowledge of your students as learners; future chapters focus on deepening your knowledge of the content you are required to teach: the CCSS-ELA and the CCSS-Math.

Learning About Your Students

In Dewey's vision of the educative process, the teacher is a catalyst. Actions taken, decisions made, and opportunities provided by the teacher spark interaction between the students and the curriculum and increase the speed at which change and growth occur. Because teachers play such a central role in students' learning, we must be sure the instructional and curricular decisions we make each day are informed and intentional.

Informed decisions about teaching and learning are based on careful professional consideration of relevant, meaningful information about students as learners. Your students' parents/adult family members/guardians are an obvious source of insight into their children. Many early childhood teachers develop an information form for parents to complete and return to school; the example provided is called a "parent info snapshot."

Sample Parent Info Snapshot Form

TABLE 3.1 INFO SNAPSHOT FOR _____ **DATE** _____

Child's Date of Birth _____ **This form was completed by** _____

What adults does the child live with?	
Siblings (name, age, grade, school)?	
How does s/he get to school? Where does s/he go after school? How does s/he get there?	
Health issues?	
Other info to share?	

Student's Academic Likes/Interests	Student's Academic Dislikes	Student's Favorite Activities

Parents Comments:

PARENT'S NAMES: _____

BEST DAYTIME PHONE NUMBERS: MOM _____ DAD _____

BEST EVE/WEEKEND PHONE NUMBERS: MOM _____ DAD _____

To continue to learn about our students, teachers gather many different types of evidence and refer to a wide variety of sources (see chart below):

TABLE 3.2 How to Learn About Your Students

Types of relevant, meaningful evidence documenting student learning	Sources of relevant, meaningful evidence documenting student learning
Anecdotal observations	Students' cumulative folders or records
Documented conversations	Results of school/district-mandated screenings
Learning photographs/learning videos	Results of standardized tests
Reflective notes	Scores on benchmark assessments
Work samples showing typical performance	Conversations with colleagues who may know the student(s)
Work samples showing growth over time	Previous teachers
Frequency counts/tallies/time samples	Classroom aides (if any)
Informal formative assessments	Specials teachers (PE, Music, Art, Library)
Checks for understanding (CFUs)	Support teachers (ESL/English Language Development, Speech, Resource Room, etc.)
Teacher-developed assessments	School psychologist/counselor
Behavioral surveys	Special Education staff
	Conversations with students' family members, after-school care providers, nanny/babysitters
	Child development literature/research (including topics such as ages & stages, behavior management, students with exceptionalities)

Informed decision-making requires teachers to gather, synthesize, and interpret a great deal of information and then use that knowledge to make determinations about the most appropriate content, student learning objectives, materials, procedures, adaptations, assessments, extension activities, and so on for the specific children in their classes. Since different tasks challenge different children in different ways, knowing each of your students' strengths, needs, and current capabilities helps you to design the best activities and develop the most effective and appropriate supports for their learning. And, given that young children learn and grow quite quickly, teachers must also attend to the progress each student is making and adjust curricular and instructional decisions accordingly in response to their students' development and growth.

Teachers' knowledge of their students as learners is what enables them to identify and develop learning experiences that are challenging, achievable, and interesting for their students. This knowledge helps teachers to create leveled reading groups and to sort their students into small mixed-ability groups; to create well-paired "study buddies" and to identify any student pairings that should be avoided; and to improve their aim when targeting lessons and activities at the students' zones of proximal development—that powerful sweet spot nestled between activities that are too easy or too hard for a given child—to enable powerful learning to occur.

Learning While Teaching

Although teachers learn about their students by gathering informal assessment data and using other forms of documentation to capture their students' characteristics as learners, teachers truly get to know their students as learners by teaching them daily. Throughout every lesson every day, teachers reflect on their observations and hunches about students' understandings and misunderstandings, take notice of interesting details in students' approaches to learning new content, consider students' reasoning, and wonder about students' questions. The best teachers do this in a continuous instructional loop that continues across the year. The diagram on page 35 illustrates the cyclical nature of the instructional loop.

Let's look at each element in the loop.

1. Observe and Document Student Learning

Meeting students where they are (Epstein, 2007) has long been a central element of developmentally appropriate practice. Teachers' ongoing informal observation and documentation of students' learning are central to the process of identifying where students are—their current capabilities, interests, challenges, life experiences, approaches to learning, and so on—in all developmental domains. Developing broad and deep knowledge about their students' capabilities, needs, and interests enables teachers to plan learning experiences that will be challenging, achievable, and interesting for them. Getting to know students as learners requires teachers to devote time, effort, and thought to observing, documenting, and reflecting on their students' strengths, areas for growth, and progress toward mastery of the academic content standards for the grade level.

This type of ongoing observation and documentation of young students' capabilities and progress across all developmental domains has been a fairly common occurrence in preschool settings, junior/transitional kindergartens, and perhaps even in kindergartens. However, the accountability pressures of the past decade may have prompted primary grade teachers to abandon their customary use of informal, teacher-developed assessments in favor of reliance on the assessment tools adopted and mandated in their school districts. So primary grade elementary teachers might be unfamiliar with these critically important practices. You will have the opportunity to examine a variety of these informal assessments in Chapter 4.

2. Develop Nuanced Understandings of Each Student as a Learner

Checking for understanding during instruction and examining students' completed work are strategies for assessing the degree to which your students mastered the content you taught.

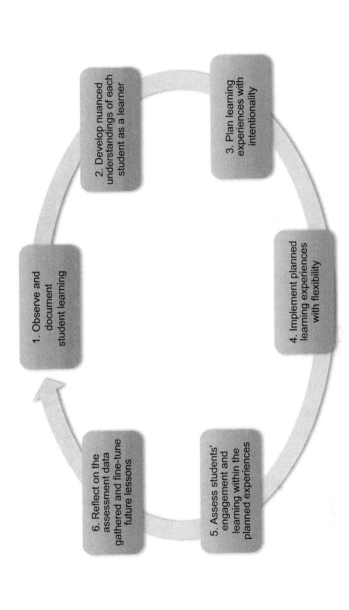

FIGURE 3.2 Developmentally appropriate practices—continuous instructional loop

1. Observe and document student learning

2. Develop nuanced understandings of each student as a learner

3. Plan learning experiences with intentionality

4. Implement planned learning experiences with flexibility

5. Assess students' engagement and learning within the planned experiences

6. Reflect on the assessment data gathered and fine-tune future lessons

Using observation and documentation allows you to capture your insights into your students' lives as learners. Examination and analysis of informal assessment documentation gathered in the classroom (and from other sources), combined with time to consider and reflect, can lead teachers to a deeper and fuller understanding of each student in their class. Unlike more standardized and inflexible approaches to assessing students, informal assessments allow teachers the freedom to observe and document what they believe to be the most important aspects of a particular child's experience in the classroom and, also, to focus not only on the student as a learner, but as a whole child.

3. Plan Learning Experiences With Intentionality

As Dewey pointed out, education is the outcome of teacher-planned interactions between children and curriculum content. Through these interactions, both elements—the children and the curriculum—are changed. Children are changed by the curriculum when their teachers create challenging, achievable, and interesting learning experiences that provide them with opportunities to learn and master the knowledge and skills in the curriculum. The curriculum is changed by the children when their teachers use their knowledge of the students as learners to massage, prod, bend, and sculpt the curriculum into a shape custom-tailored to align with the needs and preferences of their students. Teachers are the change agents that make the interactions between the students and the standards—and the resulting learning—possible.

Because teachers' responsibility for facilitating these critical interactions is of paramount importance to students' learning, teachers must be highly intentional about their practices. Intentional teachers identify specific learning goals and outcomes for their students—both for individuals and for the class as a whole—and strive to make the professional decisions they believe will be most likely to lead the students to attainment of those learning goals (Epstein, 2007). Teachers also demonstrate intentionality by designing learning experiences that are responsive to the current needs, strengths, interests, and developmental levels of the specific children they teach and to the content-specific demands of the curriculum.

This careful consideration of children and content enables teachers to make intentional decisions about teaching and learning—everything from activities and instructional strategies to student grouping and the arrangement of classroom space to the daily schedule and engagement with families.

4. Implement Planned Learning Experiences With Flexibility

Teachers know better than to expect every activity or learning experience to play out exactly as it was written in the lesson plan. However, when conditions change unexpectedly—a sudden rainstorm eliminates the possibility of doing the planned outdoor science lesson, or the light bulb in the projector burns out and makes whole-class editing of the book about last week's field trip impossible—teaching with intentionality makes clear thinking much easier. Rather than scrambling desperately for any activity to fill the now-empty time slot, remind yourself of the student learning objectives of the cancelled lesson—What did you want the students to learn in that outdoor science lesson? Why was whole-class editing of the field trip book so important?—and quickly design a new experience that will give students access to the same learning outcomes by a different route.

A teacher could also use this empty time slot as an opportunity to check on the students' progress toward the long-term goals you set for your class. Whether you set the intention of helping your students use richer and more specific academic language, increase their ability to articulate the reasoning undergirding their solutions to mathematics problems, or converse with each other rather than always directing questions and comments to the teacher, unexpected access to a free block of time offers an opportunity to check in on your students' movement toward attainment of those long-term targeted learning outcomes.

5. Assess Students' Engagement and Learning Within the Planned Experiences

Assessment and documentation of students' learning and engagement should happen continuously throughout every lesson. Teachers check for understanding (CFU) while providing instruction, while students are working on a task, and during the closure of each lesson. As they ask and answer questions, teachers keep track of which students have participated and make quick notes about the level of understanding reflected in these students' responses. Table 3.3 and Photos 3.1 and 3.2 illustrate two different types of record-keeping documents for use while teaching a whole-class lesson.

The first form is called a "class log." Each box contains the name of a student and space for jotting down notes about each student's contributions to the

TABLE 3.3 Simple Class Log

DATE	ACTIVITY
ANYA	MIA
ALEX	MIKA
BIANKA	MYA
BRANDON	ODIN
BRAYDEN	PAULA
CORMAC	PALAK
CLAIRE	SYDNEY
ELLIOT	SORIA
HAILEY	VALEN
JACKSON	WILLIAM

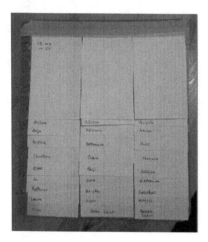

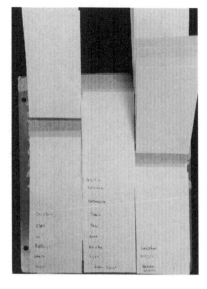

Flippy log, closed   Flippy log, open

lesson and discussion, understanding of the concepts, and so on. Simply write the date and the lesson topic at the top of the page and you have a useful record of your students' knowledge and engagement during a specific lesson.

Another type of class log—something that I call a "flippy log"—is designed to allow teachers to document student learning more easily when circulating among the students during the independent practice segment of a lesson, group work, centers, sustained silent reading, or other independent activities. Flippy logs have more writing space per student than a class log, and are built on a light but rigid piece of cardstock. There is an individual index card for each student, and the cards are taped down in rows—the teacher just flips to the correct card, makes notes, and moves on. The cardstock backing makes it easy to write observations while circulating around the classroom from center to center or from group to group. The relatively large writing surface provided by the index cards enables you to keep track of each individual student's progress over time: For example, a teacher could document each student's reading fluency once per week and note the number of errors made each week. After three weeks, the teacher would have valuable information about her students' literacy development.

While providing instruction, teachers use varied strategies to check for student understanding:

> Individual white boards for responses
> Small discussion and report out (think-pair-share; think-square-share; turn
> and talk)

Have a student use his/her own words to

> Rephrase another student's comment
> Explain how s/he solved the problem
> Explain how another student solved the problem
> Make a connection between two students' contributions

While students are working on the task, teachers circulate and discuss the students' work in progress:

> Talk to students who are successful, students who are getting it, and struggling students
> Crouch down and talk to students face to face. Ask student(s)

>> To explain his/her answer and how s/he arrived at the answer
>> For a different way to get to the same solution
>> What aspects of the task might seem confusing to other kids and why

During closure, teachers ask more CFU questions:

> If you were teaching this process to someone, how would you start?
> Can you summarize the process/task?
> Can you give an example of when you might use this process/task in "real life?"

6. Reflect on the Assessment Data Gathered and Fine-Tune Future Lessons

Structure your daily plans to ensure that at least one of your whole-group lessons will result in a tangible product that documents each student's progress toward mastery of the standards that were linked to the lesson's student learning objectives. After you've collected the students' work, review their papers to recheck for student understanding. Add notes as needed to the class log used during the lesson. Be sure to note which kids mastered the lesson objectives, which kids need more time and exposure to master the lesson objectives, and which kids will need focused attention to master the lesson objectives.

Jot comments and observations about student engagement on your lesson plan, and record potential modifications to the lesson for next year. Use this information to sharpen and strengthen lessons and learning experiences for the remainder of the current school year.

Continue this loop of observation, planning, implementation, assessment, reflection, and adjustment throughout the year. In addition to providing valuable information about student learning, the continuous instructional loop is also a great way to maintain awareness of your students' current interests. You can observe and document what they are talking about, pretending to be, reading, playing with, listening to, or watching at home. Then you can use what you've learned about their interests to make challenging and achievable activities more interesting to your students.

Summary of Key Points

- PreK–3 teachers are instrumental in facilitating the interaction between students and academic content that results in learning.
- Teachers of children in Grades preK–3 are decision makers. Their decisions are informed by evidence-based knowledge of their students' capabilities and are made with a purposeful, deliberate, strategic focus on supporting students' ongoing learning.
- Because young children are continually growing and changing, teachers must observe their students and document the students' progress, strengths, and areas for growth throughout the entire academic year.

References

Copple, C., Bredekamp, S., Koralek, D., & Charner, K. (Eds.) (2014a). *Developmentally appropriate practice: Focus on children in first, second, and third grades.* Washington, DC: National Association for the Education of Young Children.

Copple, C., Bredekamp, S., Koralek, D., & Charner, K. (Eds.) (2014b). *Developmentally appropriate practice: Focus on kindergartners.* Washington, DC: National Association for the Education of Young Children.

Dewey, J. (1902). *The child and the curriculum.* Chicago: University of Chicago Press.

Dewey, J. (1938). *Experience and education.* New York: Collier Books.

Epstein, A.S. 2007. *The intentional teacher: Choosing the best strategies for young children's learning.* Washington, DC: National Association for the Education of Young Children.

PART II

Spotlight Skills for Teaching the Common Core State Standards

Using Developmentally Appropriate Practices

INTRODUCTION TO PART II

As mentioned in Chapter 1, the Common Core State Standards do not include many specific features designed to respond to the unique learning needs of students in Grades preK–3. However, the authors of the CCSS-ELA and the CCSS-M are very clear that these two documents:

1. specify the knowledge and skills that should be taught at each grade level

and

2. leave instructional decisions—HOW to teach the knowledge and skills to students—to the professional judgment of classroom teachers.

In states that have adopted the CCSS, teachers in Grades K–3 are expected to teach the academic content standards specified for their grade level; preK teachers are expected to prepare their young learners for success in CCSS-driven primary grade classrooms. Yes, the content to be taught in Grades K–3 has changed. However, what has NOT changed is this: Developmentally appropriate practice still remains the gold standard of instructional methods for young children. Using developmentally appropriate practices to teach the CCSS is the ideal solution.

Just to clarify, developmentally appropriate practice does not forbid the teaching of academic content to young children. In fact, the most recent DAP documents acknowledge that, particularly in Grades K–3, students *should be* learning academic content (Copple, Bredekamp, Koralek, & Charner, 2013). DAP's only caveat is that the academic knowledge and skills must be presented and learned in ways that are age appropriate, individually appropriate, and culturally appropriate for the students. Potentially effective instructional practices for teaching academic skills to young children include:

Hands-on experiences
Pretend play and dress-up
In-depth conversations with teachers or classmates
Outdoor adventures
Jokes and riddles
Sorting and classifying interesting objects
Building with unit blocks
Open-ended exploration activities
Teacher-guided discussions
Cooking projects
Working in a classroom garden
Dance and movement activities
Painting of all kinds
Modeling with clay
Metacognitive reflection on their own learning

Thanks to the compatibility of DAP and the CCSS, we have been handed an unprecedented opportunity to (re)establish developmentally appropriate practice as the preferred approach to instruction in kindergarten and the primary grades. Let's capitalize on these unique circumstances and use them to our young students' advantage.

Teaching the content specified in the CCSS-ELA and the CCSS-Mathematics to young children in developmentally appropriate ways may require teachers to make adjustments to their instructional methods, develop some new ways of thinking about curriculum, and perhaps refine their implementation of some specific practices. In this part, I present four broad "spotlight skills" that are particularly important in our efforts to keep the learning needs of young children at the center of preK–3 teaching practice and to provide rigorous educational experiences for every student. The spotlight skills are:

1.   Observing, documenting, and assessing student learning
2.   Differentiating instruction to maximize learning for every student
3.   Planning "integrated-content" lessons
4.   Educating families about the Common Core

Each of these skills is discussed, contextualized, and illustrated with examples of real, classroom-tested ideas and practices.

Reference

Copple, C., Bredekamp, S., Koralek, D., & Charner, K. (Eds.) (2013). *Developmentally appropriate practice: Focus on preschoolers.* Washington, DC: National Association for the Education of Young Children.

4

SPOTLIGHT SKILL

Observing, Documenting, and Assessing Students' Learning

Teachers who engage in developmentally appropriate practice typically aim to "meet students where they are" (Phillips & Scrinzi, 2014). In Grades preK–3, teachers strive to plan flexible learning experiences that will support each student's individual growth and progress toward mastery of the content standards for the grade level. Like engaging in developmentally appropriate practice, planning rigorous learning experiences—that is, experiences that are challenging, achievable, and interesting to the learners for whom they were designed—requires teachers to know their students' capabilities and interests. Teachers' knowledge about their students plays a key role in satisfying the CCSS' emphasis on providing children with rigorous academic work.

But how do teachers determine where their students are and what their students need? To do this effectively, teachers must

1. Learn as much as they can about each student in their class and continue learning over the course of the academic year
2. Adapt and adjust instructional plans in accordance with students' learning needs

A useful approach to learning about young students as learners is to engage in continuous informal observation and documentation of their performance and behavior. Unlike standardized behavioral checklists or skills inventories, the informal tools used in observing and documenting student learning are usually developed by a teacher for her own use. These flexible teacher-developed tools can be customized and adjusted as needed to provide access to the specific student learning data needed to inform instructional decisions.

This part introduces six easy-to-use tools for informal, teacher-driven observation and documentation of young students' learning:

- Anecdotal observations
- Documented conversations
- Reflective notes
- Annotated work samples
- Learning photographs
- Learning videos

Observation and documentation of student learning is among the most important features of teaching young children. Because the students grow and change so quickly, preK–3 teachers must always be alert to changes in their needs, capabilities, and interests and ready to respond to those changes by adjusting their instructional plans. In many early childhood classrooms, the teacher engages in informal assessment and documentation of student learning as a daily activity.

This chapter includes samples of each of the assessment tools, explains how each tool is used by early childhood educators, and offers concrete suggestions about integrating informal teacher-driven assessment into your daily classroom practice.

Observation and Documentation Tool #1: Anecdotal Observations

Have you ever told your friend a story about something one of your students said or did—perhaps something funny, or surprising, or revealing, or exciting? If so, I imagine you probably shared some information about the context in which the event took place, described what the student said or did, and explained why you found the student's comment or action so interesting. For your friends, these classroom anecdotes are an enjoyable feature of your conversations. For you, these anecdotes are priceless golden nuggets: Every anecdote provides you with a flash of valuable insight into your student. Each golden nugget reveals something powerful about the student that will help you teach him or her more effectively.

A "golden nugget" anecdote—that is, a short story starring one of your students that describes something you witnessed that provided you with valuable information about a student as a learner—is the start of an anecdotal observation. Let's look at each piece of that definition:

> *A short story*: An anecdote is short and finite. It has a beginning, a middle, and an end.
>
> *Starring one of your students*: Your focus remains solely on the student—this anecdote is a place for him or her to shine brightly.
>
> *Describes something you witnessed*: If you didn't see or hear it yourself, it's not an observation. There are other ways to document the valuable information about a student that is reported to you by someone else (see Observation and Documentation Tool #2: Documented Conversations in the next segment of this chapter).
>
> *Provides valuable information about the student as a learner*: The information you learned—and what the information reveals about the student as a learner—is the heart of the anecdote.

When you experience the "a-ha!" flash of insight that turns an ordinary anecdote into a golden nugget of knowledge, you need to document what you heard and saw, what it revealed about the student as a learner, and why that information is relevant or important. This should be done as soon as possible after the incident occurred.

However, it can be difficult to find time to write up a complete anecdotal observation during the hustle and bustle of a typical school day. If you have a smartphone, you can use the "voice memo" function and just say a few words that will remind you of the anecdote. For example:

FIGURE 4.1 Use your smartphone to record an anecdotal observation

You might carry a small notebook in which to jot down reminders about important anecdotes. Or you might choose a particular color of sticky notes to use exclusively for the bare-bones information that will become an anecdotal observation as soon as you have time to complete the write-up.

> 9/28/14
> Eleanor's "exciting pants!" She's so upbeat and relaxed—she feels right at home in the classroom.

FIGURE 4.2 Handwritten anecdotal observation

Remember, these options are temporary stopgaps to ensure you don't forget key details when you later write up a complete anecdotal observation record.

An anecdotal observation record should be focused and complete. But it should not be a major writing project. See sample record sheet below and a completed anecdotal observation sheet beneath that.

ANECDOTAL OBSERVATION RECORD SHEET

STUDENT'S NAME:

DATE:

WHAT DID YOU OBSERVE?

WHY IS THIS IMPORTANT? WHAT DOES THIS SHOW ABOUT THE
STUDENT AS A LEARNER?

FIGURE 4.3 Anecdotal observation record sheet

Anecdotal Observation Record Sheet

Student's name: Mary

Date: 10/9/95

What did you observe? During Choice Time this afternoon, I found Mary
curled up on the carpet—sound asleep!—under the round table with her thumb in
her mouth. Believe it or not, Misha and Sara were seated at the round table playing
with Legos, and were completely oblivious to Mary's presence.

Why is this important? What does it show about the child as a learner? Wow,
Mary is TIRED! Could this be a factor in her difficulty following directions in
class? I wonder if kindergarten is really overwhelming for her, or if the full day is
too long. What time does she go to bed and when does she wake up? Does she eat
breakfast?

FIGURE 4.4 Completed anecdotal observation document

Always remember to write the student's name and, especially, the date on which
the original event occurred. An anecdotal observation without a name or a date
is destined for the recycle bin.

Observation and Documentation Tool #2: Documented Conversations

Sometimes you want information that you can't observe visually: how a child approached a mathematics problem, how two students resolved their interpersonal conflict, why a kindergartener always curled up into fetal position after a few minutes of sitting on the carpet for Group Time. There's no need to wonder or to guess: The first step in getting the information you're seeking is to ask the student(s) directly. Either during or after your conversation with the student, document what s/he told you in response to your question and what you learned. This tool is called a documented conversation.

Documented conversations are particularly powerful because they allow you to access the child's reasoning, explanations, opinions, and beliefs and then to integrate them into your understanding of the child as a learner. Further, documented conversations can be quick, easy, and even surprising. Here's an example from a kindergarten classroom:

Ms. Rose walks into the block corner where Stacy is playing.

Ms. Rose:	Hi Stacy! What are you working on?
Stacy:	I'm building a pig farm.
Ms. Rose:	Wow! Have you seen a pig farm in real life?
Stacy:	No, but I saw drawings of a pig farm in a book. The boy wanted a pig and his parents bought him one but it had to live on a pig farm far away. The boy and the pig wanted to live together, but they couldn't. So I'm making a kind of pig farm where children and their pigs can live together in peace and happiness.

Ms. Rose sat down on the counter by the block corner and wrote as much as she could recall about her conversation with Stacy:

> Stacy is building a pig farm in the block corner. She told me she'd read a story about a boy who wanted a pig. When he got one, it had to live on a pig farm, not at home with the boy. Even though the boy and the pig wanted to be together, they couldn't. Stacy said she was building a pig farm where kids and their pigs could "live together in peace and happiness." Stacy's compassion and empathy are very strong, as is her desire to make things better for people who are unhappy or suffering. Her goal—"kids and their pigs living together in peace and happiness"— isn't even directly relevant to her life: she doesn't have a pig (as far as I know). But Stacy saw a situation she perceived to be unfair and she wanted to find a solution that would make it right.

A documented conversation can be captured in a number of ways. Writing a summary of the conversation after it occurred is an approach a teacher would use if she had not planned to have a documented conversation. If a teacher learns something unexpected and valuable in the course of a conversation with a student, a summary of the conversation and what it revealed about the student as a learner is an acceptable format.

A documented conversation is meant to be

Substantive: Ask the student things you really want to know, things that are related to their learning, their experience, their thoughts. Make it meaningful.

Casual: You aren't testing the child to determine what he or she knows. It should feel like you're talking with a friend about something that's important to both of you.

Brief: Keep it short and sweet—get in, get your information, and get out.

You can use a documented conversation as a stand-alone tool, as Stacy's teacher did. Or you can use a documented conversation as a ride-along tool—ask each student how s/he solved the number puzzle and write each student's response directly onto the work sample.

You can also use a documented conversation as a follow-up tool, as one of my former student teachers did. She was required to observe and document the learning

---

Student name: Brad Z.

Date of photo: 10/16/06

Description of activity: Group time on the carpet in Mrs. G's kindergarten classroom

What learning is being documented in this photo: This photo shows Brad actively disengaging from the learning experience provided by his teacher. The teacher is reading a story aloud to the class. Brad, curled up into a ball, is face-down on the carpet with his back to the teacher. I consider this a non-learning photo!

What does the photo reveal about the child as a learner? This photo captures Brad's typical behavior during group time: He's quiet and doesn't disrupt the class, but his body language makes it clear that he is bored and restless. The other children were sitting "criss-cross applesauce" and appeared to be enjoying the story; Brad was not engaged at all. This type of behavior during group time is typical for Brad.

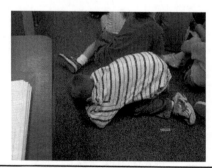

FIGURE 4.5 Learning photograph of Brad

of one child in her field placement classroom. The documentation tool below is a called a learning photograph, which you will encounter later in this chapter.

Concerned and curious, the student teacher decided to have a documented conversation with Brad to get more information about his experiences and behavior during Group Time on the carpet.

Student name: Brad Z.

Date and time of conversation: 10/18/06, 9:35 am

Place conversation occurred? Mrs. G's kindergarten classroom

ME: Brad, I've noticed that you wiggle around a lot during group time. And you often put your head down on the carpet. Why do you do that?

Brad: I'm bored.

ME: Do you dislike the story we're reading? Or do you dislike what Mrs. G talks about?

Brad: No, it's just boring.

ME: Do you like to read at school?

Brad: Not really.

ME: Why not?

Brad: Because I like to choose the books. I like the books I have at home that I picked out. The ones here are boring.

ME: What kind of books do you like?

Brad: Science books. I like to read about animals. My favorite book is called "Amazing Bats." It's really cool.

My thoughts about the child's response/What did I learn about the child as a learner? I had no idea why Brad—someone who is generally a happy, relaxed, easy-going kid—frequently acted up during group time, so I decided to ask him. I'm glad that I did. I had a feeling that the slow pace of the whole-class discussions could be tedious for him and now I know that I was right. I'd like to share what I learned with Mrs. G and see if we can come up with ways to keep Brad engaged when whole-group activities are taking place.

FIGURE 4.6 Documented conversation with Brad

You might find it easier to have documented conversations with your students if you record the conversations on your smartphone (as a video or as an audio file). That method is quick and easy. However, a recorded documented conversation is most useful as an assessment of student learning when it has been transcribed, like the conversation between Ben and his student teacher. Locating a specific quote or comment made by a student in a recorded documented conversation involves listening closely to your recordings: The process is so tedious that you might not even bother to search for the quote or comment, regardless of its value. You can find key information much more quickly by skimming a transcript, but transcribing interviews can be tedious and time consuming too.

Documented conversations are a powerful tool. If you ask honest questions—things you really want to know—young children tend to appreciate your interest and take your request seriously. Your conversation with a student can encompass any topic, run for any length of time, and will deepen your teaching-learning relationship with the students you teach.

Observation and Documentation Tool #3: Reflective Notes

Teachers become very familiar with our students—we know their likes and dislikes; their hopes and fears; their favorite movies, books, games, and activities—but we don't always remember to synthesize the myriad bits, snippets, and scraps of information into a coherent whole. Just as documented conversations allow you to learn what your students think, reflective notes are a tool that allow you to synthesize your own thoughts about a student's performance, behavior, attitudes, approaches to learning, social skills, and so on.

Reflective notes create an opportunity for a teacher to take a step back and think holistically about a student as a whole person. Who was she on the first day of school, and who is she now? What have been her greatest successes and her biggest struggles at school his year? What makes her laugh? What does she find frustrating? How does she deal with change? With failure? With classmates who push her buttons? What does she care about, think about, wonder about? What do you see in her future? Reflective notes strengthen your understanding of your students as learners, deepen your connections to them, and engage your responsibility for supporting your students' continued growth and development.

Reflective notes are also useful when a thought about a student just pops into your head. Here's an example:

Mingus—Reflective Note   10/23/06

I think Mingus is a very bright student. He always understands the assignments and completes them diligently. However, he throws a lot of tantrums. For example, today when he needed help opening the glue bottle, he started screaming instead of asking the teacher nicely. I think that if he had the tools to communicate effectively, his tantrums and outbursts in class might stop!

FIGURE 4.7 Student teacher's reflective note

This seems to be more of an "a-ha!" note than a reflective note: Things suddenly clicked for this teacher and she wrote it down so she wouldn't forget. That works too! However, there are some important differences between these two tools.

TABLE 4.1 Comparing Anecdotal Observations and Reflective Notes

	Anecdotal observations	*Reflective notes*
What is this tool used for?	Describing something you saw/ heard that gave you insight into a student's learning	Expressing your thoughts about a child's learning, developing theories, making plans, raising questions
Why would you choose to use this tool?	Because you just observed an spontaneous incident that shed light on a student's learning	Because you had insights and ideas about this student and the opportunity to jot them down
When would you use this tool?	"In the moment" or as soon as possible afterwards	Once you've had time to think about what you've been seeing

Observation and Documentation Tool #4: Annotated Work Samples

Young students' schoolwork catches adults' eyes for a wide variety of reasons: its quality (high or low), its aesthetic properties (will look great on the refrigerator), its sentimental value (oh, isn't this sweet), and so on. For preK–3 teachers, though, this work provides detailed, specific insight into students' capabilities, including academic skills, self-regulation, ability to understand and follow directions, fine motor skills, perseverance, and other approaches to learning. Students' work provides the most immediate, straightforward, and unadulterated evidence of what students know and are able to do under typical, day-to-day, classroom conditions.

However, a piece of student work—a drawing, a math worksheet, a story, a compare and contrast Venn diagram graphic organizer—is not useful as an assessment of a student's capabilities without a cover sheet that explains what the work reveals about the student as a learner and why that revelation is important. It is this annotation, written by a teacher, a parent volunteer, or a paraprofessional, that transforms the student's work into an assessment of the student's learning.

An annotated work sample always has two parts:

1. A piece of student work that reveals something about the student's skills, habits, or learning

2. A cover sheet that provides specific, detailed information about what the work sample shows about the student as a learner and why what is shown is important

This is a drawing. It is not an annotated work sample.

FIGURE 4.8 Clara's drawing

However, it becomes an annotated work sample when it is accompanied by a teacher's meaningful documentation. See below:

Child's name: Clara G.

Date: 10/12/2002

What was the activity? Free choice

What does this show about the child as a learner?

Clara wanted white clouds, but there weren't any white markers. She came up with an innovative solution: draw the outline of clouds, but leave the inside of each cloud blank so the white paper is visible. Then color the background to make the clouds stand out and appear white (see upper left corner of drawing). This solution shows two of Clara's significant strengths: her creativity and her sophisticated problem-solving skills.

FIGURE 4.9 Clara's drawing becomes an annotated work sample (Image reproduced with permission from Clara and Jesse Gainer.)

A piece of student work without interpretive annotation would still be considered a work sample. However, unless the meaning of the work is clear and the importance of the work is very obvious, an interpretive annotation is necessary to foreground the significance of the work.

The required elements of a work sample cover sheet are shown in Figure 4.10.

Student name:

Date the work was completed:

Activity during which the work was completed:

What does this work show about the student as a learner?

FIGURE 4.10 Work sample cover sheet

Write the cover sheet as soon as possible after the student completes the work. You may feel certain that you'll always remember why you pulled that particular piece of work to serve as a work sample, but it can be very easy to lose track of all the pertinent details.

While it's always preferable to save the original piece of work, it's not absolutely necessary: After all, the work belongs to the student, not to you. Most student work can be copied, scanned, or photographed easily. If you are using a copy or photograph of the original work, you must attach your cover sheet to the document that remains in your possession.

Observation and Documentation Tool #5: Learning Photographs

A learning photograph is an assessment document that shows a student involved in doing something that provides information about him as a learner. Taking a learning photograph is quick and easy—especially if you have a smartphone—and it feels very natural.

However, there's an important distinction between a learning photograph and what I call a "happy snappy" of a student. Learning photographs show one or more students actively engaged in a learning experience; happy snappies show students posing for the camera, perhaps holding up completed work. There's nothing wrong with taking happy snappies of your students (provided that you have parent permission to do so). But teachers must be clear about the distinction between the two types of photographs of students: A learning photograph provides information about the student as a learner and a happy snappy does not.

The photograph below was taken by an orchestra teacher during her students' first concert. Is this a learning photograph or a "happy snappy?" Why or why not?

PHOTO 4.1 Noah (Photo taken by author and reprinted with the permission of Noah Goldstein.)

PHOTO 4.2 Noah plays his bass (Photo taken by author and reprinted with the permission of Noah Goldstein.)

What about this photograph? Could it be a learning photograph? Why or why not?

Like a work sample, a learning photograph requires a cover sheet that provides explanatory information about the student and his learning:

The student's name
The date on which the photo was taken
The activity in which the student was involved
What the photo reveals about the child as a learner

The photo above truly becomes a learning photograph when the cover sheet is completed and attached:

Learning Photo Cover Sheet

Student's name: Noah G.

Photo date: 10/27/05

Activity: Beginning orchestra concert (Halloween costumes required)

What does the photo reveals about the child as a learner: Noah is using appropriate finger placement and holding the bow properly. It is not clear whether he always looks at his fingering or if he is also reading the music.

FIGURE 4.11 Learning photograph, with all necessary documentation (Photo taken by the author and reprinted with the permission of Noah Goldstein.)

A series of sequenced learning photos can be used to document a student in the process of learning a new skill. Photos taken over time—daily or weekly, for example—make a student's progress visible. The learning photo series on pages 60-61 documents my son Sam's first efforts at learning to surf.

Although the captioned photos describe Sam's surfing experience, on their own they don't offer much insight into Sam as a learner. Ideally, each time you document a student's learning, your knowledge of the child as a learner deepens and expands in ways that enable you to become a more effective teacher for that student. So, in addition to providing short captions for each photo, I recommend that teachers also write up a quick cover sheet on which to document the more general, transferable skills and dispositions you noticed (and, of course, any recurring challenges or difficulties you noticed). This enhances the power of a learning photo series tremendously.

Although a learning video (see next part) would have captured every detail of Sam's first attempt at surfing, most of Sam's 75 minutes in the water involved waiting for suitable waves and falling off his surfboard. A series of carefully chosen learning photos that portray the key elements of Sam's learning process capture the most significant elements of the experience and can be viewed quickly and efficiently.

Like a single learning photograph, a series of sequenced learning photographs needs appropriate documentation to become an assessment of student learning: At the minimum, your documentation should include the student name's, date (or dates) on which the photographs were taken, the activity, and what the photos reveal about the child as a learner. There are many different ways to approach this: add captions directly onto the photos (as I did on some of the surfing photos), insert the photos into a PowerPoint presentation and type text into each slide, or create a single cover sheet for the entire series and save the photos and cover sheet in a folder.

Photo Series Cover Sheet

Student name: Sam

Date: 1/3/05

Activity: Learning to surf

What do these photos show about the student as a learner?

Sam was willing to take risks and work outside his comfort zone: Surfing is a physically demanding activity that he'd never tried before, and there was no guarantee of success.

Despite his frustration, Sam was able to maintain high levels of perseverance, focus, effort, and self-control throughout the process.

Sam benefited from the use of a combination of teaching strategies: direct instruction, guided practice, time to reflect and regroup, observation, one-on-one attention, support, and feedback.

FIGURE 4.12 Documenting Sam's learning experience. Documentation of student learning always requires a cover sheet with interpretation and background information provided by the observer. (All photos were taken by the author and are used with the permission of Sam Goldstein and Noah Goldstein.)

HOW TO DOCUMENT
SERIES OF
(All photographs were taken by
the permission of Sam Goldstein

PHOTO 4.3 One-on-one direct instruction;
Sam asks questions and receives answers
from Chris, his instructor

PHOTO 4.4 Guided practice with Chris

PHOTO 4.7 11:52 a.m.

PHOTO 4.8 Sam takes time with Mom to
reflect and regroup

PHOTO 4.11 12:16 p.m.

PHOTO 4.12 Sam keeps trying (12:19 p.m.)

PHOTO 4.5 Chris watches Sam's technique

PHOTO 4.6 11:43 a.m.

PHOTO 4.9 12:02 p.m.

PHOTO 4.10 Sam and Chris watch Noah. Chris points out some strengths of Noah's technique and suggests strategies for Sam to try.

PHOTO 4.13 Sam's hard work pays off (12:22 p.m.)

PHOTO 4.14 Sam achieves more consistent success (12:29 p.m.)

Observation and Documentation Tool #6: Learning Videos

Documenting student learning and behavior with a video can be the very best way to capture—objectively and in real time—how students act and work the classroom on a day-to-day basis. But, unfortunately, video can also be the most difficult tool to use: It's almost impossible to deliver a lesson or to lead morning circle while simultaneously videotaping a single student's behavior or engagement in learning. Further, many young children are accustomed to being videotaped by their parents or other family members, and they may be in the habit of performing for the camera, acting silly, or demonstrating behavior quite different from their typical classroom behavior.

Nevertheless, the benefits of documenting student learning and behavior with video outweigh the limitations. Here are some suggestions that might help support your use of this valuable tool:

1. Videotape frequently to get kids accustomed to your smartphone or camera and your use of video in the classroom. Record video footage as you circulate from table to table while students are working, during the independent practice segment of a lesson, or during choice time. Take video daily until your students stop caring about whether or not you're videotaping them.

2. Do not show any of your assessment videos to your students. You are taking these videos for your own professional purposes, not to entertain the students. Once the students know that you really are not going to share your videos with them, they'll stop asking you if they can watch them.

3. Delete most of what you record. If you are videotaping frequently, much of what you capture each day is not going to be particularly valuable. Do not waste your time re-watching daily video to see if you caught anything interesting. If you don't want to delete your videos—just in case there might be something there that could be helpful in the future—upload each daily video to the cloud before you leave your classroom. You'll be able to find it there if you need it.

4. If you feel the presence of your phone is distracting to your students (or to you), try doing your daily videotaping using the camera in an iPad or another tablet. Holding an iPad looks very different from holding a smartphone, and that might be enough to put the kids at ease. Also, most teachers I know favor the iPad—not their personal phone—as a general classroom tool, so it might be more unobtrusive.

5. Keep your videos short. If you are videotaping student behavior and learning with the intent of sharing the video with your students' parents or with a Student Support Team, you will want a short video—60 seconds or less—that captures the essence of what you want to communicate about the student as a learner. If your video footage is longer than a minute, edit it down using an easy do-it-yourself application like iMovie.

6. Pair up with another teacher at your school site and become "video partners." Each of you agrees to make yourself available to video record in the other's

classroom at a time when she is providing instruction. Because you are not teaching, you have the freedom to move around the room and document anything your partner requests, from an aspect of her own practice to the behavior of a single student to the work being done by the parent volunteers.

Like all the other informal observation and documentation tools presented in this chapter, learning videos require the "info stamp" that communicates the most central information:

Student name
Date:
Activity:
What does this video reveal about the student as a learner?

This information can be provided on a separate cover sheet, embedded into the iMovie, or on an electronic cover sheet placed in the same folder as the video.

Combining Tools for Maximum Impact

Each of the tools presented in this chapter works as a stand-alone documentation of student learning. But the tools can also be used in combination to tell richer, more nuanced stories of students as learners. Here are three examples:

1. Work Sample Plus Documented Conversation

If you spot something in a student's work that strikes you as unusual, interesting, or unexpected, you might take that work and use it as annotated work sample: You would write a cover sheet that indicates the name, date, activity, and what the work reveals about the student as a learner. But the information written on the cover sheet reflects only YOUR interpretation of what the work reveals about the student as a learner. A quick conversation about the work with the student can enrich your understanding of the work and the child. Document that conversation and file it away with the scanned work sample and the work sample cover sheet and you'll have a more nuanced interpretation of the work.

2. Anecdotal Observation Plus Reflective Note

An anecdotal observation is a brief note that captures a moment or incident that provides an "a-ha!" insight into a student. This a-ha could be something delightful, surprising, puzzling, troubling, thought-provoking, funny, unusual, and so on. A teacher writes up the anecdotal note, provides the info stamp, and it's done. But sometimes it's just not done. Sometimes the incident sticks around in the back of the teacher's mind, raising questions and making connections with other observations she's made and incidents she's witnessed.

When this occurs, the teacher can write a reflective note that spells out the questions she's considering and the connections she's making upon reflection on that incident. A reflective note is a tool that enables a teacher to focus her thoughts on a single student and dig more deeply into that student's experiences in life and in the classroom. Although the teacher would not show the anecdotal observation or the reflective note to the parents of this particular student or to anyone else (as FERPA regulations require), she may feel a professional responsibility to go beyond her initial anecdotal observation and to document her thoughts about this student as a learner.

3. Video and Work Sample

A work sample provides clear, concrete evidence of a young child's capabilities as a learner and as a student. A work sample is made even richer when accompanied by a learning video that documents the student while she is working on the task. Did she complete it easily? Was she focused or distracted? Rushed or patient? Did she encounter any challenges? If so, how did she resolve them? Viewing the work sample and the video together provides a fuller picture of the student by showcasing both the process and the product.

Managing and Safeguarding Your Observation Documents

Years ago, teachers' efforts to document their students' learning and development required careful discernment: The tools available to support this work were rudimentary, expensive, intrusive, and difficult to access (for example, the video camera had to be reserved at the district office two weeks in advance). As a result, teachers had to make intentional and deliberate choices about which type of documentation would offer the most "bang for the buck" for any given activity.

Even with their tight focus and deliberate choices regarding which work provided the richest and most revealing information about each student, those teachers still had challenges organizing and storing the artifacts and documentation. For each student in her class, a teacher might have a pile of work samples; a file folder filled with anecdotal observations, reflective notes, and other teacher-developed assessments; an audiotape documenting the child's growth in oral reading fluency; learning photographs (some still in the photo developers' packets, others unlabeled or misplaced, and maybe even some Polaroid instant photographs); and sometimes even bulky VHS videotapes capturing the student at work in the classroom.

Today, technological advances have made both the experience of observing and documenting student learning and the process of organizing informal assessment documents much easier. A teacher with a smartphone can photograph students and/or student work, videotape and audiotape students in action, transfer those files from their phone to "the cloud," and retrieve them whenever necessary.

In many ways, the work of observation and documentation has been transformed by technology. However, the fundamental challenges of observing and documenting student learning—**knowing which observations and documents are the clearest and most compelling, which reveal aspects of a student's performance that could be predictive of future successes or future problems, which are the strongest evidence of significant growth and progress**—remain the same. Teachers' professional judgment is still the most important piece of this practice.

Another feature of this practice that has not changed is the need to ensure that every piece of assessment documentation—learning photograph, work sample, anecdotal observation, learning video, reflective note, and documented conversation—is linked in some permanent manner to the basic information necessary to make sense of the document. This is an "info stamp" that must be present on all informal observational documentation of student learning:

Student name:
Date:
Activity:
What this documentation reveals about the student as a learner:

Without this information—particularly without the last entry on what this documentation reveals about the student as a learner—you do not have a documentation of student learning.

Once you have completed the "info stamp" (and added any other information you feel is necessary), the assessment document is ready to be filed. Digital documentation—video, audio recording, learning photographs (digital or scanned as a jpg file), and all the cover sheets, anecdotal observations, documented conversations, and reflective notes that were typed using a word processing program—should be stored on a computer or external hard drive.

Student work samples are also best stored in digital format: not only because the work will be easier to store as a digital file, but also because any original student work belongs with the students and their families. Some student work samples—writing samples and drawings, work completed in a journal or during a mathematics lesson, a note handwritten by a child and left on your desk—can be digitized easily using a copy machine, scanner, or a digital camera. Generally, one of those tools will allow you to create a clean duplicate of the work in which the elements you intend to highlight are clear and easy to see.

However, depending on the type of work (is it textured or fragile?) and the dimensions (is it on oversized paper?) of the work and what you most want to highlight in the work sample, digitizing the work may require access to some additional equipment such as a

Digital camera with high resolution
High-quality scanner
Color copy machine (so that a high-resolution color copy can be scanned nicely)

Privacy, Confidentiality, and Professionalism

For more than 150 years, teachers in the U.S. have had three legal responsibilities: to instruct, to supervise, and to provide for the safety of their students. Today, in the 21st century, providing for the safety of our students must also include taking steps to protect their privacy and maintain their confidentiality.

Privacy is a term that applies to the students as individuals. Teachers can protect students' privacy by avoiding the use of their names in conversations with colleagues when it is not necessary; safeguarding the phone numbers, addresses, and other personal information of the students and their families; and choosing to access only the information about their families that is relevant to our work with them.

Confidentiality applies to protecting the data that can be linked directly to the student. Teachers can maintain confidentiality by keeping students' paper files (such as student work, records, and other documents) in a locked filing cabinet or closet and returning the folders to their secure location immediately after using them to keep them away from prying eyes. For electronic data, teachers should always use password protected folders and files. Teachers should use password protection on all documents that include any student performance data.

The Family Educational Rights and Privacy Act of 1974 (FERPA) regulations protect the privacy of students' education records and provide parents with certain rights to access those records. FERPA also specifies the types of information that are legally considered part of a student's education record and the types of information that are not considered part of a student's education record.

This distinction—what "counts" as part of a student's education record and what does not—is extremely significant for teachers. Parents have the legal right to access their child's education record; however, parents' right to access a teacher's *personal records about their child* (such as informal assessment data) depends on the way the teacher used and stored those personal records.

Current FERPA regulations state student "records that are kept in the sole possession of the maker, are used only as a personal memory aid, and are not accessible or revealed to any other person except a temporary substitute for the maker of the record" (FERPA, 2012, pg. 6) are not considered part of a student's official education records.

So, a teacher's informal documentation of students' learning and behavior that has been

1. Kept in the teacher's sole possession
2. For use as a personal memory aid, and
3. Not accessible or revealed to anyone other than a substitute teacher

are not considered part of a student's education record and, therefore, would not be available or accessible to parents. In this way, FERPA protects teachers' professional privacy as well as students' privacy.

TABLE 4.2 Protecting Student Privacy and Confidentiality

Type of assessment documentation/information	Privacy protection tips
Assessment data in digital form: videos, documents, photographs, audio recordings, scanned work samples, cover sheets	Make a password-protected folder for each student in your class, and password-protect each document you place in the folder.
Assessment data in paper form: informal reading inventories, large-size work samples, completed student work to be sent home	Store in a locked filing cabinet or closet. Consider digitizing documents that provide numerical information about student performance.
Student work on display: bulletin board of "great work," student writing, art projects, displays related to curriculum units	Write students' names (and their grades/scores) on the back of the work before mounting it.
Charts displaying individual students' names matched with the number of books they have read, their ability to count to 100, etc.	Use students' initials or numbers rather than names.
Teacher files or folders that contain lists of leveled reading or math groups, names of students with IEPs or 504 plans, students who qualify for gifted/talented programs or free/reduced price lunch, etc.	Keep all sensitive information in a locked desk drawer. If you need regular access to this information throughout the day, keep it in your phone or tablet.
Anecdotal observation and/or information about the behavior or performance of a student in your class, informal documentation that supports your concern about the student	Follow your school's procedures for this type of situation: discuss it with the appropriate school administrator, counselor, or school psychologist; consult with the Student Support Team; etc.

Most of the informal assessment data you collect is likely to be completely appropriate to share with parents or colleagues: work samples, learning videos and photos, anecdotal observations, and most (if not all) of your documented conversations. These informal assessments focus exclusively on the child. However, I strongly recommend keeping your reflective notes under the protection of the FERPA regulations: in your sole possession, for use as a personal memory aid, and not accessible or revealed to anyone. Although reflective notes are focused on individual students, the teacher's thoughts and feelings, hunches and questions, comprise the bulk of every reflective note. The notes reflect on or interpret the students' actions, experiences, intentions, or learning and reveal much more about you than students about whom you are writing. These assessments are for your eyes only, and should be safeguarded to avoid unnecessary problems.

You are responsible for ensuring that all confidential information about students that is stored in your classroom is properly protected and remains confidential. This is particularly important if you have many parent volunteers moving in and out of the room doing different types of tasks.

Check with your school administration to find out whether or not parent volunteers are permitted to work directly with students, to know which students are placed in which reading groups, to file student work into take-home envelopes, or to have any other forms of information about students' academic performance or classroom behavior. Giving parents access to this information may be a violation of FERPA regulations.

Because early childhood educators attend to each student as a whole child, it would be impossible to develop and implement a battery of age-appropriate formal assessments to capture and provide all the information a teacher needs to be effective with every child. The informal observation and documentation tools presented in this chapter, when used in combination, have all the ease, flexibility, speed, and power necessary to ensure that every student is learning every day.

References

Family Educational Rights and Privacy Act of 1974, 20 U.S.C. § 1232g (1974).

Family Educational Rights and Privacy Act (FERPA) Regulations. (2012). Retrieved from http://www2.ed.gov/policy/gen/guid/fpco/ferpa/index.html

Phillips, E. C., & Scrinzi, A. (2014). What is developmentally appropriate practice? In C. Copple, S. Bredekamp, D. Koralek, & K. Charner (Eds.), *Developmentally appropriate practice: Focus on children in first, second, and third grades* (pp. 1–3). Washington, DC: National Association for the Education of Young Children.

5

SPOTLIGHT SKILL

Differentiating Instruction to Maximize Learning for Every Student

Students in preK–3 deserve rigorous learning experiences: In other words, their experiences should be challenging, achievable, and interesting to them. However, the inevitable idiosyncrasies of young children's development guarantee the students in any given classroom will vary in their academic and intellectual capabilities, their approaches to learning, their interests, their capacity for self-regulation, and their social skills. How does a teacher plan lessons that will be challenging, achievable, and interesting for every student in a developmentally, culturally, and linguistically diverse class? One way to do this effectively is to provide differentiated instruction.

Differentiated instruction is an approach in which all the students in a class work toward mastery of the same learning objectives, but they do so in a manner and at a level of complexity that aligns more tightly with their current developmental capabilities. As a result of their teacher's intentional planning, certain students may receive small instructional adaptations—which I call "tweaks"—that alter a given activity or task slightly to provide those students with learning experiences that are more individually appropriate for them.

Tweaks can be used to make a lesson more or less academically challenging, longer or shorter, more structured or more open-ended, more accessible to a student who is an English learner: Teachers' ability to "tweak" instruction creates learning experiences that are a better fit for the specific students in the class. Although the accommodations, modifications, or instructional supports provided to students who have Individual Education Plans (IEPs) or Section 504 plans are required by law, these adjustments can also be described as "tweaks" to the students in the class. This type of pedagogical flexibility allows a teacher to ensure all students are completing an activity that (1) allows them to connect with relevant, age-appropriate learning standards; (2) in a manner that is challenging, achievable, and interesting for them; and (3) in ways that generate richer and more accurate evidence of their learning.

Implementing differentiated instruction is a highly effective way to address the varied needs and interests of your students. Many of the approaches commonly used to differentiate instruction are complex: They require the establishment of elaborate classroom infrastructures and the development of routines and procedures that the students must master. Those are not the best approaches for implementation in prekindergarten through Grade 3: when working with young children, a practice should be easy (both for the teacher and the students), flexible, and open to individual interpretation.

Two approaches to differentiation meet these criteria:

1. Differentiating instruction using open-ended materials.
2. Using tweaks to adjust the complexity, procedure, expectations, or outcomes of an assignment or lesson.

Both methods can be used in age-appropriate ways in preK–3 classrooms. Both work well for a single child, a small group, in centers, and for whole group instruction. These differentiation methods can be used with students who are English Language Learners, students identified as gifted and talented, students who receive special education services, and students who struggle to master the grade-level standards due to unspecified learning challenges, emotional difficulties, or behavioral issues. There is no single right way to implement these approaches; I encourage you to experiment and see what works best for you and your students.

Providing Differentiated Instruction Using Open-Ended Materials

As mentioned in Chapter 1, young children typically have the greatest variation in their developmental profiles across the cognitive, social, emotional, and physical domains. Therefore, any teacher of young students is guaranteed to have a class of students whose capabilities vary widely. In addition, a single child's development will vary across the domains. Consider Sammy, a four-year-old girl: Her cognitive development might be in the range that is typical for four-year-olds, her social and emotional development could be ahead of the norms for four-year-olds, and her physical development could be below those norms. Another four-year-old child in Sammy's class will also have uneven development across the domains. However, his developmental profile—the ways in which he is progressing and growing in his cognitive, social, emotional, and physical skills—will be different from that demonstrated by Sammy or by the child who is sitting next to him in morning circle time.

The wide range of developmental capabilities in any same-age group of young children requires preK–3 teachers to be prepared to provide students with learning experiences that are highly flexible. Because young children of the same age may vary widely in their development, they frequently perceive and engage with the same instructional materials in very different ways. Providing students access to open-ended materials and time for exploration, investigation, and play allows students to differentiate their own instruction. Open-ended materials enable children to engage in self-directed play and create learning experiences for themselves that are challenging, achievable, and interesting. A child rolling a strip of clay against the table is thrilled because—finally!—he can make a snake all by himself; he is unconcerned that the child seated next to him is working on coiling her clay snake around and upwards to form a teacup for her stuffed panda.

Clay, like other open-ended materials commonly used in teaching young learners, meets children where they are. Clay's endless possibilities enable children to design challenging, achievable, and interesting learning experiences for themselves. Aware of the benefits of giving young children time to engage freely with interesting materials, most early childhood teachers—especially in prekindergarten, transitional kindergarten, and kindergarten—give their students access to interesting, open-ended materials for building, exploring, and tabletop play on a daily basis.

Because children don't always realize that they're ready to move on to more demanding tasks, attentive teachers are often the first to recognize the need to increase the challenge provided by any given material. For example, after a period of time even the most avid block-builders lose interest in building the same type of block structures over and again. When the materials feel stale and boring, the block area—formerly a place characterized by industrious work, effective conflict resolution, and sustained focus—may become a place for roughhousing, argument, and disruption. These behaviors suggest that some students in the group are ready for a new challenge.

An attentive teacher might offer the group a big tub filled with Kapla blocks and invite the students to integrate the new blocks into their structures. The children who are not interested in adding Kapla blocks don't have to accept the offer: The work they are doing is challenging, achievable, and interesting to them right now. The children who are working together to build a complex vertical structure are focused tightly on their task and don't hear the offer: They, too, are engaged in work that is challenging, achievable, and interesting to them. The students who respond with enthusiasm to the offer are demonstrating their readiness for an additional challenge. They accept the Kapla blocks and get back to their work.

Likewise, some children are hesitant when asked to complete a new type of activity or engage with an unfamiliar process. A three-year-old child may be intrigued by the huge container of buttons on the manipulatives shelf. He knows about buttons, and he remembers crying when he was not able to button the fancy shirt he wore to his uncle's wedding. He wants to stick his hands in the container, but he hesitates: Buttons once made him cry. When his teacher notices his interest in the button jar, she offers to pull it out so he can play with the buttons. He shies away, whispering to her that he's not good at buttons. She offers to sit with him while he gets started. They talk a little about what makes the buttons the same and different from each other; he mentions colors, sizes, and shapes. The teacher leaves and the student follows his own path. The littlest buttons are too hard for him to pick up, so he focuses on picking out the big buttons. He lines them up along the edge of the table and calls the teacher over to share his work. He works with the buttons—intent and fully focused—all week. On Friday he calls the teacher over and says, "Why do the little buttons sometimes have more holes than the big buttons? I think big buttons are bigger so they need more holes and little buttons are smaller so they need less holes. This doesn't make sense."

This young boy didn't engage with the buttons in a manner that would be typical of an older child: He didn't sort the buttons, classify the buttons, or make patterns with the buttons. But, in the course of a single week, he went from being a boy who wasn't good at buttons to a careful observer able to generate an interesting question about buttons that most adults would be unable to answer. This student's attraction to the button jar and his keen eye for detail kept him engaged and interested for a much longer time than would be typical for a three-year-old. The buttons themselves—colorful, varied, and unfamiliar—scaffolded this student long enough to enable him to identify patterns (small buttons have more holes, big buttons have fewer holes), develop a theory (small buttons should have fewer holes than bigger buttons), and frame a novel and intriguing question for further investigation.

Open-ended materials allow teachers (and young students) to ratchet the complexity of a task up or down, to expand or contract the time frame for completing the task, and to customize the expectations in ways that make the task challenging, achievable, and interesting for each child. The two menus on the next page list different open-ended materials that I have used in my work with young students (Column A) and different ways in which students can engage with the materials (Column B). Quick, flexible, open-ended learning centers can be created by choosing a material from Column A and a task (or more than one task) from Column B.

In addition to the benefits already discussed, engaging with young learners as they work with open-ended materials creates exceptionally powerful opportunities for helping students develop academic language. A quick glance at Column B foregrounds some of the specialized vocabulary that is commonly heard in classrooms but rarely heard in family or community contexts. To meet the demands of the CCSS, students will need to be able to communicate their thoughts clearly and with specificity. In order to be prepared for success in kindergarten and beyond, young learners need exposure, instruction, and guided practice in understanding and using the unfamiliar vocabulary typically found in the academic register.

It is just as easy to teach children high-leverage academic words—such as "estimate" or "predict"—and to model and encourage the use of these words in classroom discussions as it is to default into using a blander and more common word, such as "guess" (which could be used in place of both "estimate" and "predict"). Language is powerful: A child who arrives in kindergarten already aware of the differences between estimation and prediction is better prepared for academic success than a child who just knows how to "guess."

Sadly, exploration and engagement with open-ended materials is much less common in the upper primary grades than it is in preK, TK, and kindergarten. Perhaps the emphasis on the rote mastery of academic skills in Grades 1–3 is a carry-over from the days of No Child Left Behind. However, one of the great strengths of the CCSS-Math is the emphasis on "pursuing conceptual understanding, procedural

TABLE 5.1 Materials and Processes That Meet Students Where They Are

Column A Open-ended materials	Column B Tasks that engage students with the materials
Assorted buttons (different colors and sizes)	Counting
Unit blocks (and any other types of blocks)	Sorting
Linking cubes	Classifying
Counting bears	Organizing
Pattern blocks	Building
Geoboards and rubber bands	Creating designs
Sand (provide measuring cups, funnels, sieves, containers of different shapes and sizes, small plastic dinosaurs or insects; substitute birdseed for outdoor play with no cleanup!)	Making patterns
	Pretend play
	Measuring
	Estimating
Water (provide measuring cups, funnels, sieves, and containers of different shapes and sizes; mix with food coloring to make and blend different colored waters; put colored water in spray bottles; use eyedroppers for moving colored water)	3-D construction
	Sculpting
	Comparing
	Discussing
	Wondering
Clay/dough (make from scratch with student assistance; provide rolling pins and cookie cutters, artists' sculpting tools, bakers' tools for working dough, play-dough "fun factory" types of tools)	Writing
	Drawing
	Stringing
	Manipulating
Small shaped tiles	Stacking
Dyed macaroni	Exploring
Shaving cream	Developing and testing theories
Assorted nuts, bolts, washers, screws	Representing their ideas visually
Magnets	Documenting their work visually
Small unbreakable mirrors (pair with pattern blocks)	

skill and fluency, and application with equal intensity" (*Key Shifts in Mathematics*, n.d.). The focus on helping students develop conceptual understanding of mathematics begs to be satisfied by purposeful engagement with base ten blocks, pattern blocks, Linking cubes, and many other hands-on learning materials.

There are mathematics concepts in the CCSS for Grades 2 and 3 that would be best explored and internalized through work with manipulatives. Examples from the standards for mathematical content include reasoning with shapes and their attributes in Grade 2, and developing understanding of fractions as numbers in Grade 3. In addition, the standards for mathematical practice emphasize the need for students to model with mathematics in Grades K–12, another important reason for using manipulatives. Kindergarten and primary grade students are still young children who learn best by doing. Allowing young students to establish their foundational understanding of mathematical modeling using manipulatives—repeatedly, and in a range of ways—is strong preparation for the kinds of reasoning and abstract thought required in the upper grades and beyond.

Using "Tweaks" to Differentiate Instruction

Differentiated instruction does not require writing a personalized instructional plan for every student in each content area each day. In a differentiated lesson, all students engage with the same academic content standards at the same time. However, the students might be engaging with the standards in different ways, at different levels of complexity, by completing slightly different work, or by spending different amounts of time on the given tasks. Teachers determine which students need instructional adjustments—what I refer to as "tweaks"—and which specific adjustments would be appropriate based on their knowledge of their students as learners (see Chapter 3).

Teachers begin this type of differentiation by planning lessons that are keyed both to the CCSS and to the academic capabilities and developmental needs of the majority of their class. Then they add recommendations for a variety of small adjustments—"tweaks"—that alter the lesson procedures, products, or expectations in minor ways that serve to tailor the lesson more closely to the needs of students who (a) have not yet mastered the foundational skills necessary to complete the lesson fully; and/or (b) are clearly struggling to complete the "at grade level" activity; and/or (c) have already mastered the concepts taught and practiced in the lesson and need to engage with the material at a level or in a manner that provides greater challenge.

I call these small instructional adjustments "tweaks" because that word evokes something quick, easy to implement, easy to change, and easy to undo. Tweaks allow teachers to fine-tune their lessons in ways that align them more tightly with their individual students' needs. Sometimes a teacher might build tweaks into a lesson as part of the planning process: allow students to dictate their story into an iPad rather than write it by hand, create an optional graphic organizer for students who need assistance in structuring the mathematics challenge problem of the day, let students choose whether to work alone or with a partner. Tweaks also allow teachers to make small changes to a lesson while it is already in progress—sort of like fixing an airplane while it is flying—that improve the lesson's effectiveness for certain students.

Tweaks are like accommodations (adaptations to instructional practices which are exclusively available to students who receive special education services) in that they are informed by data-based evidence about the students as learners and are designed to enable the students to succeed more easily. Tweaks are unlike accommodations in that they are available to every learner and are implemented only when the teacher or child recognizes that certain adjustments would make the lesson more effective. Tweaks enable all students to work on mastery of the content standards in ways that are challenging, achievable, and interesting/appropriate for them.

Seven Types of Tweaks

Imagine that you are circulating among your students as they work on an activity, and you notice one student struggling to complete the task. You can use your knowledge of the student as a learner to identify the area of difficulty and—if necessary—tweak the lesson using one of the many tweak strategies in your repertoire. Seven types of tweaks are described below, in terms general enough to provide a clear sense of what that type of tweak entails and offer an example or two. There are many different ways to enact each type of tweak: Each time a student presents a new challenge, you have an opportunity to invent a new tweak.

1. Tweak the Quantity of Work Required

When might you use this tweak? Students who struggle with academic content, skills, or processes tend either to work very slowly or to rush through their work, making careless errors and leaving parts of the assignment undone. These students benefit from explicit instructions regarding the number of sentences they must write or the number of problems they must solve. Likewise, students who have already mastered the knowledge or skills taught in a lesson have no reason to complete the entire assignment: They, too, would benefit from a straightforward statement about what they need to accomplish before moving on to more individually appropriate academic challenges.

    How to use the tweak? Determine the amount of evidence you need to see—for example, the number of sentences that must be written or mathematics problems that must be completed—in order to assess whether or not a student has fully mastered the lesson's objectives. Set that number as the minimum for the students who warrant this kind of tweak.

2. Tweak the Time Allowed for Completion

When might you use this tweak? When you believe a student could satisfy the minimum expectations for an assignment by rushing through it and you want her to invest more time and effort in the work, or when you have a student who would not be able to finish the entire assignment even if he were given two hours to complete it, you can adjust the amount of time a student must dedicate to a particular activity. Both the speedy student and the slower student could be told to write in their journals for 7 minutes and then stop, or to work on their story problems until it's time to get ready for lunch. Having a finite amount of time—especially if it's a fairly brief amount—allows a student to see the light at the end of the tunnel from the very beginning.

    How to use the tweak? Approximate how long it would take for a student to complete enough work on the specific assigned task for you to be able to judge the student's mastery of the lesson's objectives and set that as the time limit. This may be difficult at first because students work at different speeds and have different levels of academic stamina. But your knowledge of the students as learners will help you fine-tune this tweak over time.

3. Tweak the Level of Support Provided

When might you use this tweak? Public schools in the United States expect young children to develop independence, self-discipline, and autonomy. However—as teachers in prekindergarten, transitional kindergarten, and kindergarten know well—those character traits develop slowly over time. Further, in many of the diverse cultural contexts that comprise U.S. society today, family practices encourage young children's interdependence with people who are older than they: For example, some young Hispanic children learn to rely on their older siblings or cousins for assistance, while many native Hawaiian children have grandmothers or "Aunties" who prepare and serve their meals and assist them with difficult tasks like opening juice boxes or cutting meat.

How to use the tweak? Just as children have learned these family-based practices from their families, they must also learn school-based practices and expectations in school. As you begin the process of teaching your students the appropriate behavior and expectations for life in school, some of your students might benefit from tweaks that keep them connected to their established and familiar procedures. Allowing students to work in pairs or small groups rather than requiring them to work alone (or vice versa) or establishing a big buddies/little buddies relationship with a class of older students could be effective ways to do this.

Likewise, there may be students in your class who are independent and competent. These children might prefer working independently, or one-on-one with an adult, or by examining a completed example or model of the end product of an assignment. Tweaks in this area must be responsive to what you are observing and experiencing with the particular students you teach.

4. Tweak the Instructional Input Method

When might you use this tweak? In early education classrooms, the teacher's voice is the tool typically used to teach new concepts and skills. This works well much of the time. However, some young children have difficulty listening and learning in a loud, busy classroom. Students who are English language learners may have difficulty understanding the vocabulary used by their teacher, which then prevents them from accessing the academic content they need to be successful. And children whose knowledge already surpasses the CCSS' expectations for their grade level may be ready to move on before the lesson even begins.

How to use the tweak? When adjusting methods of instructional input is the intent of a tweak, technology offers the most powerful options. If, after experiencing your lesson, some students need more opportunity to engage with the content or more time to master the objectives, they can revisit key concepts by watching a video or DVD, looking at pictures online, or watching video clips on YouTube or on discipline-specific websites. These particular students—as well as those students who had already mastered the standards before the lesson began—might be interested in creating slide presentations that can be used to re-teach the content to the class and/or as a resource for future students. English learners can look at age-appropriate picture books on the topic in their home language or look at books in English using a translation app on a tablet. Listening to an age-appropriate audiobook or podcast that connects to the lesson could also be helpful to many of the students. Implementing tweaks that involve the use of technology might require the presence of an aide, a parent volunteer, or upper grade students who can assist your students if they need tech support.

5. Tweak the Difficulty/Depth/Breadth

When might you use this tweak? When planning a lesson, teachers zero in on the grade level standards and the specific needs of the majority of the students in the class: That's the way to get the most "bang for the buck." But what happens to the students who have already mastered this content? And what happens to the students who do not have the foundational skills necessary to engage fully with this content?

How to use the tweak? The children who have already mastered the content you intend to present to the class need the complexity of the lesson to be ratcheted up, perhaps with interesting extension or enrichment activities designed to deepen their engagement with the content presented in the lesson. The best enrichment activities add complexity and ambiguity the topic and push the students to apply their existing knowledge and skills in a new context and make connections within and across disciplines. On the other hand, the students who lack the background knowledge, academic skills, or English ability needed to engage successfully with the content could participate in the lesson and complete a graphic organizer specially designed to push the key take-aways of the lesson into the foreground and make them more accessible and memorable.

6. Tweak the Expectations for Participation

When might you use this tweak? The student's role at school is to be an active participant in a series of carefully planned learning experiences each day. However, there are many different ways in which students can participate in a lesson.

How to use the tweak? Consider the needs of your most educationally vulnerable students—ELLs, students with identified special needs, students with unspecified learning or behavioral challenges, gifted and talented students—when creating your initial plan for the lesson. What participation structures would help to ensure the ELLs with limited English proficiency have the opportunity to engage with the content and meet the learning objectives of the lesson? Working with a partner? Working in a triad with two ELLs and one native English speaker? Viewing a PowerPoint presentation—that includes vocabulary in English and Spanish and related images—created last year by two students who had already mastered the content presented in this particular lesson and needed a more complex and open-ended challenge? Getting in the habit of always considering the most vulnerable students' needs while planning lessons will help you become an expert at inventing tweaks that support your students.

7. Tweak the Product

When might you use this tweak? There are so many different ways young children can show what they learned in a lesson or a unit, and there are so many ways that teachers can capture and document their students' learning. The key with this tweak is to suit the product to the purpose.

How to use the tweak? If your purpose is to document students' mastery of certain specific skills, choose a product that will highlight those skills: If you want to showcase your students' progress with their handwriting (either manuscript or cursive), a handwritten work sample from each student would provide ideal evidence of the class' mastery. However, if the product's purpose is to give students an opportunity to share what they learned in a social studies unit, in their literature circles, or on a field trip to a museum, you would need to develop a product that will allow all students to express—in an authentic and meaningful way—the ideas, facts, and skills that were most powerful for them. You might have decided that every student will make an illustration of something learned in the unit and write three sentences about the illustration. Although this will lead to a lovely, neat, uniform bulletin board display, it might not truly allow all the students to document their personal learning experiences.

Giving the children voice and choice will enhance the quality of their product. For example, you might consider making a menu of options and asking children to choose one focus area, one type of illustration medium, and one style of poem they will use to represent their learning. The example below was developed to document a second grade field trip to a(n unexpectedly and extremely muddy) archeological site. The field trip was part of our social studies unit about the Ohlone Indians, the indigenous population who lived in our California town long ago, and we were halfway through an English Language Arts unit on poetry. The menu I developed looked something like this:

TABLE 5.2 Learning Poem Choice Board

Pick one focus topic Circle your choice	Pick one illustration tool Circle your choice	Pick one type of poem Circle your choice
Something I learned	Colored pencils	Couplet (2 rhyming lines)
Something I saw	Crayons	Free verse (no rhyme)
Something I liked	Markers	Haiku (5/7/5 syllables)
Something surprising	Pastels	Limerick (d'dumble d'dumble d'dum . . .)
Something I want to remember	Chalk	Rap (rhythm, word play, power)

And here are my reconstructions of two poems that were produced by students in this activity:

<table>
<tr><td align="center">Something I learned
A couplet by Jamie</td><td align="center">Something I liked
A haiku by Sasha</td></tr>
<tr><td align="center">Ohlones lived a life so muddy.
Now archeology's what
I want to study.</td><td align="center">Mud, mud, pottery!
A shard?!? No, it's just a rock.
Rocks and shards and mud.</td></tr>
</table>

Tweak Menu

The "tweak menu" below is a tool designed to remind teachers of the many ways that any given lesson may be adjusted in response to students' demonstrated learning needs. These adjustments also strengthen a lesson because, when used judiciously, they ensure every student will experience a challenging, achievable, and interesting learning experience.

TABLE 5.3 Tweak Menu for Differentiating Instruction

Tweak Menu
Adjust the quantity of work required
Expect students to complete more or fewer problems, sentences, examples
Adjust the time allowed for completion
Expect students to work at different paces
Adjust the level of support provided
Allow students to work with a buddy, dictate to an adult, refer to a completed model of the expected product
Adjust the instructional delivery
Use video, books on tape, computers, visual aids, books in students' home languages, translation apps, and other technology
Adjust the difficulty/depth/breadth
Expect students to work at different levels of complexity and ambiguity
Adjust the degree of participation
Allow students to engage in an activity in different ways
Adjust the product
Allow students to demonstrate their mastery in different creative ways

Documenting Your Tweaks

Sometimes a tweak is no big deal. An activity had much more coloring than Jessika could manage in the allotted time, so you told her to stop and move on to the next step ("adjust the quantity of work"). Conor dropped his waffle—syrup side down!—in the car on the way to school, dragged himself into the classroom after the bell had already rung, and promptly sat down on a glue stick; since the paired writing activity was almost over, you allowed Conor to do the activity on his own ("adjust the level of participation").

However, sometimes tweaks can become a problem. Most typically developing children should not need continual tweaks to be successful with academic content appropriate for the grade level. If you find yourself regularly providing the same tweak(s) for the same student(s), it's time to ask yourself some questions: Is that tweak truly necessary for this student *academically*? Or is it just a preference, or a comfortable habit, or a deliberate ruse? Would she struggle to finish the task without the scaffolding provided by that tweak?

Next, start keeping notes about the tweaks you're making each day: Note which students requested and received tweaks, what tweaks you provided, the success of the tweak, and your next steps for supporting the student.

If there are difficulties, keep track of any elements that seem relevant to the circumstances:

☐ What times of day?   ☐ Which days of the week?   ☐ Partner work?
☐ Which tweaks?   ☐ What type of activities?   ☐ Whole group lesson?
☐ Which content areas?   ☐ What came before this?   ☐ Independent work?

Gathering data to document what is currently happening in your room is always a good place to start any investigation. Once you have collected enough

TABLE 5.4 Keeping Track of Tweaks

TWEAK RECORD					
Date	Student	Content area/ activity	Tweak provided	Level of success attained using tweak?	Next steps?
10/09/14	Lily	Math practice	Do every other problem.	High! She Completed 9 out of 10 problems, ranging from the easiest to the toughest.	Contact Lily's mom to discuss this tweak and answer any questions
10/10/14	Sadie	Journal writing	Write for 7 minutes and stop	Unsuccessful—she played with and/or stared at the timer for four minutes before starting to write.	Ask Sadie to come up with a tweak that would support her in completing her writing assignments

evidence, you will find patterns in the data that can guide your efforts to get your class back on track. Ideally, a teacher should strive to maintain a reasonable balance between the needs of the students and the demands of the content.

Moving too far toward the children's needs and desires undermines their learning. Moving too far toward the content's demands also undermines the students' learning. Differentiated instruction is a strategy that must be used thoughtfully and with intentionality.

Supporting the Success of Students With Specific, Identified Learning Needs

Early childhood teachers typically think about each of their students as a unique individual. We aim to meet every child wherever he or she is *right now*—developmentally, personally, culturally, linguistically, and individually—and then move forward, together, from that point.

Labels and classifications affixed to a child by others, such as English Language Learner, identified as gifted and talented, receives special education services, has a 504 plan, or qualifies for free/reduced price lunch provide important and useful information that helps us understand our students' specific needs more thoroughly. For example, students who receive special education services have an Individual Education Plan that indicates the specific accommodations, modifications, and/or supports required for them to be successful in the general education classroom. Likewise, students with a 504 plan have official documentation of the instructional adaptations and adjustments that must be provided for them to learn effectively. English Language Learners are assessed and classified by their English proficiency levels; this information allows teachers to target instruction appropriately.

However, each label reveals only one facet of the child as a learner. Every English Language Learner, every student with a 504 plan, every student identified as gifted and talented is unique. Effective teachers work continuously to blend the information they receive from students' IEPs and case managers, 504 plans, and other official records with their own observations, assessments, and documentation to create a rich and nuanced understanding of each student; this understanding guides teachers' instructional plans for the class.

Supporting the Success of Students with Unidentified Learning Needs

Students with documented learning needs enter classrooms with diagnoses, assessment information, and recommendations for instructional practices. This information gives teachers a place from which to start their work with these individual students. The rest of the students do not come to school with any guidelines to help their teacher provide them effective instruction targeted to their needs. Teachers begin each year using age-appropriate activities and watching closely to see how things progress.

As they get to know their students, teachers begin to provide appropriate tweaks that customize the classroom learning experiences to address their specific needs more directly: Some children might receive a tweak that helps them control their behavior while sitting on the carpet, others might receive a tweak that enables them to participate more successfully in whole-group learning experiences or that supports them in completing age-appropriate academic tasks. Teachers might not identify the perfect tweak for a particular student on the first attempt, but experience, persistence, and trial and error generally lead to success.

Sometimes, despite all the adjustments and adaptations a teacher has attempted, some students continue to demonstrate learning needs or behavior challenges that require more systematic, specialized intervention and support. This is the point at which the teacher would request a Student Success Team meeting to discuss her concerns, share documentation of her unsuccessful interventions, and seek input and assistance from colleagues and administrators.

Differentiating instruction is more than just a buzzword. Differentiation ensures that every student participates in rigorous learning experiences and experiences the satisfaction that comes naturally with success.

Reference

Key shifts in mathematics. (n.d.) Retrieved from http://www.corestandards.org/other-resources/key-shifts-in-mathematics/

6

SPOTLIGHT SKILL

Planning "Integrated-Content" Lessons

For many of us, the Common Core State Standards for ELA and Math still seem new. However, the CCSS may not be the only unfamiliar academic content standards preK–3 teachers are expected to implement in their classrooms. Now (or in the near future), many preschool and primary grade teachers may be expected to integrate content from the *Next Generation Science Standards* (NGSS Elementary Standards, 2013); the *College, Career, and Civic Life Framework for Social Studies State Standards* (C3; National Council for the Social Studies, 2013); and from any other new standards developed or adopted by their state, such as California's recently revised English Language Development standards (California Department of Education, 2012), into their CCSS-driven classroom curriculum. Doing so will require teachers to sharpen and refine the skills required to create effective, developmentally appropriate lessons that provide simultaneous instruction in more than one academic discipline.

Integrating content from more than one academic discipline within a single lesson is the hallmark practice of teaching the Common Core. For example, CCSS-M lessons frequently integrate CCSS-ELA standards, such as requiring students to write a brief description of the process they used to solve a mathematics problem or an explanation of how they know their solution is correct. However, the bold step taken by the authors of the ELA standards document—pushing expectations for language arts instruction deep into the domains of history/social science, science, and technical subjects—is the clearest example of the CCSS' dedication to content integration.

To meet the expectations of the CCSS, teachers of young children will be expected to create "integrated-content" lessons. These lessons integrate content standards, student learning goals, and procedures drawn from more than one content area; provide instruction in both content areas; and assess students' mastery of the learning goals in each content area.

Moving Beyond Interdisciplinary Lessons

An integrated-content lesson is unlike an interdisciplinary lesson. Although an interdisciplinary lesson might draw on knowledge and skills from several different content areas, a single academic discipline generally dominates the lesson. The content standards and student learning outcomes are drawn from the dominant content area; the other academic disciplines involved in the lesson are typically called upon as tools by which students demonstrate their mastery of the lesson's student learning outcomes.

For example, assessment of student mastery of the concepts and skills taught in a social studies or science lesson typically require students to write responses to questions, to draw pictures, or to illustrate text. Teachers collect and examine students' work to determine how thoroughly each student understood the material taught in the lesson. Then teachers use these data about their students' understandings to make appropriate adjustments to the instructional plans for subsequent lessons. However, this raises a problem: Although writing skills and drawing techniques were not taught in the lesson itself, the students' writing and drawing skills play a critical role in communicating their mastery of the student learning goals. Students who understand the social studies or science concepts thoroughly but do not write or draw well may be unable to document their understanding fully or accurately. Therefore, the teacher's evidence of these students' mastery—the written work or drawings—provides an inaccurate picture of their learning and their knowledge of the content covered in the lesson.

The CCSS' focus on reading and writing in the academic content areas is different from this familiar approach. To meet the expectations of the CCSS, that same social studies or science lesson would need to include student learning objectives from two academic disciplines:

- Student learning objectives tied to concepts and skills in the state's adopted content standards for the grade level in science or social studies
- Student learning objectives from the grade-level CCSS-ELA that focus on the development of the specific reading and/or writing skills that are taught or practiced in the lesson

The CCSS-ELA's expectations for students to write informational text and to support an argument by citing textual evidence are best and most easily met within content-area instruction. The academic disciplines of social studies and science provide students with engaging ideas, questions, and situations about which to read and write. And each of these academic disciplines presents unique challenges. In social studies, young students must begin to learn how to read and interpret primary source documents, to distinguish facts from opinions, and to write clear informational text. And in science, preK–3 students will be expected to develop hypotheses, to describe the processes by which they tested their hypotheses, present their findings, and draw evidence-based conclusions.

Reading and writing are the backbone of the CCSS-ELA; however, reading and writing are not confined within the CCSS-ELA. Rather, reading and writing are considered an integral part of teaching and learning in mathematics, social studies, science, and other academic disciplines, such as visual and performing arts, health education, and physical education. Teachers must fully integrate ELA content into other academic disciplines to be successful within the CCSS.

What Is Content Integration?

Content integration describes instruction that intentionally provides students with the opportunity to engage with and master academic content standards from more than one content area within a single lesson. Content integration requires that a lesson include:

- Academic content standards from at least two content areas
- Student learning objectives in both content areas
- Equal focus and emphasis on both content areas during instruction
- A student activity that facilitates engagement with knowledge/skills in both content areas
- Documentation and assessment of student learning in both content areas
- Feedback to students and families on progress toward mastery of standards in both content areas

An integrated-content lesson does double duty. Essentially, a teacher presents two intertwined lessons at the same time. When teaching integrated-content lessons, teachers remain mindful of the intended student learning outcomes in both content areas and remember to pay equal attention to assessing students' mastery of the knowledge or skills in both disciplines.

The key to integrated-content instruction lies in the lesson plan: an integrated-content lesson has student learning goals in more than one content area, explicitly teaches knowledge or skills from both of those content areas, and assesses student learning in both content areas. See Figure 6.1 for a graphic representation of the step-by-step process of planning an integrated-content lesson.

I've used this planning process to frame five integrated-content lessons that draw on the CCSS-ELA and typical social studies content taught in prekindergarten, kindergarten, Grade 1, Grade 2, and Grade 3. Although I have chosen to use social studies in these examples, this approach is equally useful when integrating the CCSS-ELA with mathematics, science, visual and performing arts, physical education, health education, or any other academic content area (for example, Catholic school teachers could use this integrated-content lesson format to integrate the CCSS-ELA and religion instruction).

Creating an integrated-content lesson

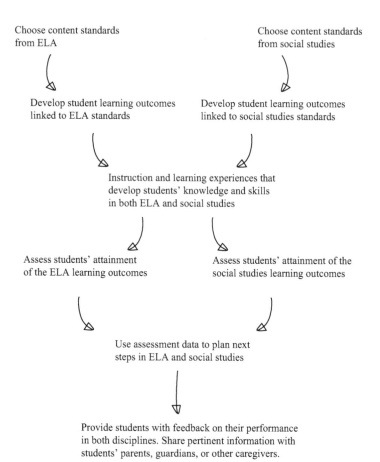

Choose content standards from ELA

Choose content standards from social studies

Develop student learning outcomes linked to ELA standards

Develop student learning outcomes linked to social studies standards

Instruction and learning experiences that develop students' knowledge and skills in both ELA and social studies

Assess students' attainment of the ELA learning outcomes

Assess students' attainment of the social studies learning outcomes

Use assessment data to plan next steps in ELA and social studies

Provide students with feedback on their performance in both disciplines. Share pertinent information with students' parents, guardians, or other caregivers.

FIGURE 6.1 Creating an integrated-content lesson

Integrated-Content Lessons, PreK–3: CCSS-English Language Arts with Any Content Area

An integrated-content lesson is expressly designed to help students master age-appropriate standards from two different academic disciplines. Throughout an integrated-content lesson, the teacher maintains equal, balanced emphasis on the knowledge or skills to be mastered in each content area and on students' progress toward the learning outcomes in both content areas.

The lesson plans below present integrated-content lessons in ELA and social studies for prekindergarten through Grade 3. The prekindergarten content, for both ELA and social studies, is taken from the New York State Prekindergarten

Foundation for the Common Core (New York State Education Department, 2011). The K–3 lessons draw their ELA content from the CCSS-ELA for Grades K–3 and their social studies content from the *History-Social Science Standards for California Public Schools* (California Department of Education, 1998).

Prekindergarten Integrated-Content Lesson: CCSS-ELA and Social Studies

Most U.S. states have adopted early learning standards that describe what typically developing young children could be expected to know and be able to do prior to entering kindergarten at age 5. The states' visions of a child who is "ready for kindergarten" vary, as do the knowledge and skills identified in each of their frameworks.

New York State was an enthusiastic early adopter of the Common Core State Standards. In 2011, the state intentionally reframed their early learning standards to align tightly with the CCSS. The resulting document, entitled *New York State Prekindergarten Foundation for the Common Core* (2011), offers a research-based, developmentally appropriate presentation of the (anticipated) capabilities of young children approaching kindergarten entry. The document's close alignment with the CCSS and its respectful appreciation of young children's individual variations are the reasons I chose to use these specific early learning standards. If your state has adopted its own early learning standards for prekindergarten, those specific skills and knowledge can be plugged into this framework in place of the New York state standards.

Play is how young children learn. Hearing about traditions and looking at photographs of classmates and their families participating in traditional practices is a good place to start. However, pretending to participate in a variety of family traditions in the house corner—especially if the traditions are modeled by the students whose families practice them—will enable prekindergartners to understand and remember those traditions much more clearly.

Kindergarten Integrated-Content Lesson: CCSS-ELA and Social Studies

In kindergarten, ELA lessons often provide students opportunities to practice their listening, speaking, and self-expression skills. Doing this practice in a whole group setting also enables kindergartners to work on exercising self-control, patience, and respect for others. This particular lesson plan provides opportunities for teachers to tap into their students' prior knowledge about national symbols; teachers can extend conversations in response to the students' contributions and areas of interest (e.g., where have they seen these symbols before, what do they know about these symbols/icons, and so on).

The CCSS-ELA standard and the History/Social Science standard chosen for this lesson were not an immediately obvious match. However, the decision to pair these two standards was intentional. This lesson works because it presents *complementary*

TABLE 6.1 Integrated-Content Lesson for Prekindergarten

Prekindergarten/TK-ELA and Social Studies Different Family Traditions	
Content Standards From ELA	**Content Standards From Social Studies**
Writing/Text Types and Purposes 2. With prompting and support, use a combination of drawing, dictating, or writing to compose informative/explanatory texts in which they name what they are writing about and supply some information about the topic.	Geography 2. Demonstrates awareness and appreciation of their own culture and other cultures (a) Talks about and/or shows items related to his/her family and cultural traditions to others; (c) Describes some of the holidays, etc. related to his/her own culture; (d) Demonstrates an understanding of similarities and differences between and among different people and families.
Student Learning Outcomes-ELA	**Student Learning Outcomes-Social Studies**
Students will produce a self-portrait (using scribble-writing, letters, words, pictures) that depicts themselves participating in a family cultural tradition. Students will also describe the activity aloud in a small group of peers and listen to their peers' descriptions of their family tradition.	Students will look at each self-portrait and listen to each of their small group members' comments, and ask questions (optional). When prompted, will students will be able to identify one similarity and one difference among the group members' family traditions.
Instruction and Learning Experience/Activity That Focus on Both ELA and Social Studies	

Part 1: Thinking about family traditions
After reactivating students' prior knowledge and experiences within this unit, teacher does a guided read-aloud of Families (Easterling, 2007) or another book that highlights the differences and similarities of families around the world. During the read-aloud, teacher draws students' attention to cultural traditions and family practices and asks students to share their family traditions.

Before dismissing the group, teacher does a quick prewrite activity—teacher instructs students to imagine they are participating in a special tradition in their family. What are they doing? Are they wearing or holding or using anything special? Why are they doing it—what's important, what's the meaning? Teacher explains that the students will go to their work tables, draw a picture that shows the tradition they just imagined, and write something about the tradition.

Teacher gathers the portraits/writing and creates pairs or trios for Part 2 of the lesson (could be later in the same day or the next—waiting too long will make Part 2 less meaningful and less productive).

Part 2: Sharing family tradition self-portraits
Students are grouped in pairs or trios with a teacher. Each student shows self-portrait and describes the tradition depicted. Teacher and other group members may ask questions for clarification or further information. When all students have shared, teacher reminds students that all families are similar in some ways and different in other ways. With prompting and support, each student should be able to identify one way that their family tradition is similar to another student's family tradition and one way that their family tradition is different from another student's family tradition.

Assessment of Students' Understanding of the Learning Outcomes-ELA	Assessment of Students' Understanding of the Learning Outcomes-Social Studies
Collect student self-portraits and assess each student's progress with fine motor skill development, letter formation, conventions of print, and sound-symbol correspondence. Make notes of your observations. Copy or photograph self-portrait for student file; clip teacher notes/cover sheet to portrait.	Teacher takes brief notes on each student's presentation and participation in small group discussion and ability to identify similarities and differences among families. Copy notes; file originals, clip copies to the self-portraits for later review.
Provide Feedback to Students and Parents Regarding Student Learning-ELA	**Provide Feedback to Students and Parents Regarding Student Learning-Social Studies**
Feedback is given orally to students during Part 2 of the lesson (small group sharing). Family traditions self-portraits are mentioned in the newsletter and sent home; parents should be encouraged to ask their children about what they learned about their classmates' family traditions.	Same as ELA section.
Use Assessment Evidence to Plan Future Instruction-ELA	**Use Assessment Evidence to Plan Future Instruction-Social Studies**
Students who are having difficulty writing letters due to poor fine motor skill development should be given tasks that will strengthen their pincer grip (spray bottles, screwing nuts onto bolts, working with play-dough, playing with small Lego® blocks).	Identify students who were withdrawn or had difficulty articulating their thoughts in the small group part of the lesson. Make time to talk one-on-one with these students to ensure they understand the family traditions content. Also, if appropriate, ask those students how you could help make it easier for them to share their ideas with their classmates and teachers. Document these conversations for future reference.

Extension/Re-teach Activities

Attend to students' engagement in this topic. If they are showing interest in family traditions, invite families to send in age-appropriate materials/realia that could be used by students in the socio-dramatic play area. Photographs of families participating in their tradition (lined up in matching dresses in front of the Christmas tree, lighting candles for a festival or holiday, etc.) could also be hung up in the classroom. When appropriate, teacher should point out similarities and differences in the family traditions represented in the classroom.

TABLE 6.2 Integrated-Content Lesson for Kindergarten

Kindergarten-ELA and Social Studies Important American Symbols and Icons	
Content Standards From CCSS-ELA	**Content Standards From Social Studies**
RI K.1 With prompting and support, ask and answer questions about key details in a text.	K.2 Students recognize national and state symbols and icons such as the national and state flags, the bald eagle, and the Statue of Liberty.
Student Learning Outcomes-ELA	**Student Learning Outcomes-Social Studies**
Students will be able to name one national symbol/icon and pose and/ or answer a question about the meaning of the symbol/icon.	Students will be able to identify at least one national symbol/icon and offer an explanation of what it represents.
Instruction and Learning Experience/Activity That Focus on Both ELA and Social Studies	
Teacher reads *One Nation: America by the Numbers* (Scillian, 2002) or *O, Say Can You See? America's Symbols, Landmarks, and Inspiring Words* (Keenan, 2004) and highlights key details of the most important U.S. symbols and icons. Check for students' prior knowledge and ongoing understanding throughout the read-aloud.	
Teacher projects images of significant national symbols/icons, including the U.S. flag, the Statue of Liberty, the White House, the U.S. Capitol, the Lincoln Memorial, the bald eagle, the Great Seal, the Declaration of Independence, the Liberty Bell, Uncle Sam, etc., one at a time.	
Students work in self-selected pairs/small groups to formulate (1) a description of the symbol/icon; (2) a statement/observation about what the symbol/icon represents; and (3) one question about the symbol/icon.	
Small groups report out; each group member participates in sharing the group's question or observation. Teacher leads whole group summary discussion of that symbol/icon and moves on to the next. This process can continue for as long as the students are willing/able to engage.	
Assessment of Students' Understanding of the Learning Outcomes-ELA	**Assessment of Students' Understanding of the Learning Outcomes-Social Studies**
Teacher listens to each group's description, comment, and question; notes participation quality and level of each student.	Teacher listens to each group's description, comment, and question to assess students' understanding of what the symbol/icon represents.
Provide Feedback to Students and Parents Regarding Student Learning-ELA	**Provide Feedback to Students and Parents Regarding Student Learning-Social Studies**
Document which students are placed into each vocal participation group as evidence of their baseline participation in group conversations. Share this information during parent conferences.	Post images shown during lesson on class website and in class newsletter; suggest that parents ask their children to explain what those symbols/icons mean.

Kindergarten-ELA and Social Studies	
Important American Symbols and Icons	
Use Assessment Evidence to Plan Future Instruction–ELA	**Use Assessment Evidence to Plan Future Instruction–Social Studies**
Note the most and least vocal students. During the next lesson in which engaging in small-group conversation is a student learning outcome, use homogeneous groups—highly vocal, often vocal, rarely vocal—to change up the participation dynamic.	Check for understanding during each small group's mini-presentation to determine the degree to which students' contributions reflect emerging clarity about attributes—freedom, diversity and unity, opportunity, equality, fairness—associated with the United States symbols.
Extension/Re-teach Activities	
• Invite students and families to share photographs of themselves visiting places or holding representations of the symbols/icons associated with the U.S.A. • Invite students and families to share images of important symbols and icons from their heritage countries: flags, crests, images of money, statues or artworks, etc. • Encourage students to think about what's important to them, what they love, etc.—and then to find or develop icons or symbols that represent themselves (or their families).	

content standards from two different disciplines: *it pairs a skill* from ELA—asking and answering questions based on information in a text—*with academic content* from social studies—recognition of and knowledge about United States symbols and icons. The social studies content provides students with something interesting to think about, talk about, and wonder about, and this prompts students to raise and to answer questions related to the topic, which engages them with the ELA standard. Maintaining a balanced focus on two content areas throughout a lesson can be challenging, but it becomes much easier when the content standards and learning objectives in each content area complement each other.

Grade 1 Integrated-Content Lesson: CCSS-ELA and Social Studies

This first grade lesson introduces and/or strengthens students' understanding of critically important academic terminology: compare/contrast. Comparison and contrast are "high-leverage" academic language because the compare/contrast process is used in many different content areas to analyze and interpret information and to draw conclusions. Young students who learn to compare/contrast in a social studies lesson are likely to recognize the process when they are asked to compare/contrast in a lesson in science or visual arts. To develop students' vocabulary further, a teacher could use and highlight the range of words that can be used to engage in the process of compare/contrast, such as like/unlike, same/different, and similarity/difference. This would help prepare students to recognize these paired terms in future lessons and to understand that they are being asked to compare and contrast.

TABLE 6.3 Integrated-Content Lesson for Grade 1

Grade 1-ELA and Social Studies Similarities and Differences Around the World	
Content Standards From CCSS-ELA	**Content Standards From Social Studies**
RI.1.3 Describe the connection between two individuals, events, ideas, or pieces of information in a text.	1.4 Students compare and contrast everyday life in different times and places around the world and recognize that some aspects of people, places, and things change over time while others stay the same.
Student Learning Outcomes-ELA	**Student Learning Outcomes-Social Studies**
Students will learn to use a Venn diagram graphic organizer to compare and contrast life in our community with life in other communities around the world.	Students will be able to understand that some aspects of daily life are common to everyone around the world and other aspects of daily life are different in different parts of the world.
Instruction and Learning Experience/Activity That Focus on Both ELA and Social Studies	
Teacher reads *In A Country Far Away* (Gray, 1991), using a document camera to project the illustrations. Ask students to pair share with their elbow partners and describe what they see in the two settings that is the same and what they see that is different. Give each table group the opportunity to share once during the read-aloud.	
Remind the students about the meanings of the words "compare" and "contrast." Present the Venn diagram as a tool for comparing and contrasting things that are alike in some ways and different in other ways. For Spanish-speaking ELLs, refer to "comparar y constratar" as well as compare and contrast.	
Use two hula hoops on the floor to remind students how Venn diagrams work—bring up groups of students who are similar in some ways and different in other ways and position them in the hula hoops.	
Distribute chart paper pre-drawn with a 2-circle Venn diagram. Have each table label each part of the diagram (only here, both places, only there) and write examples from the book in each section of the diagram with specific details from the book.	
Post completed graphic organizers (with table names) and encourage students to read each other's work and leave comments on each poster using sticky notes.	
Assessment of Students' Understanding of the Learning Outcomes-ELA	**Assessment of Students' Understanding of the Learning Outcomes-Social Studies**
Check for understanding by circulating as students are working to ensure that English learners and students who are struggling readers/writers are (1) engaging in the conversations and (2) using compare/contrast and similarity/difference accurately. Look at completed Venn diagrams to determine if student work demonstrates understanding of similarities/differences, compare/contrast.	Check for understanding by circulating as students are working to ensure that English learners and students who are struggling readers/writers are (1) engaging in the conversations and (2) referring to examples in the text for evidence to support their statements. Look at completed Venn diagrams to determine if students took away key similarities and differences discussed during the read-aloud.

Grade 1-ELA and Social Studies Similarities and Differences Around the World	
Provide Feedback to Students and Parents Regarding Student Learning-ELA	**Provide Feedback to Students and Parents Regarding Student Learning-Social Studies**
Revisit the completed Venn diagram charts at least once after the activity is complete; point out some of the things you noticed in their work that demonstrated their understanding of the content discussed in the lesson. Ask the students if they have found themselves comparing and contrasting other types of things at home, etc.	Photograph each table's Venn diagram and post photos on class website; include in electronic newsletter (and paper newsletter if there are families in the class who do not have easy access to the Internet). Encourage parents to ask the students to explain the activity and describe what they learned.
Use Assessment Evidence to Plan Future Instruction-ELA	**Use Assessment Evidence to Plan Future Instruction-Social Studies**
Discuss how two interchangeable words can have slightly different meanings and encourage students to look for those nuances: Is there a difference between "same" and "similar"? If so, what's the difference? Is there a difference between "different" and "unlike"?	Create a writing center that provides opportunities for repeated engagement with similarities and differences across time and across cultures. Gather books like *Bread, Bread, Bread* (Morris, 1993), *Shoes, Shoes, Shoes* (Morris, 1998), or *Houses and Homes* (Morris, 1995) that show differences and similarities around the world (e.g., we all eat bread, but in many different forms); provide page-sized Venn diagram graphic organizers on which students can document the content in the books.
Extension/Re-teach Activities	
Create a "Venn diagram center" with hula-hoops and groups of large objects that can be sorted (this can also been done as a tabletop activity using embroidery hoops and smaller objects like buttons or sea shells) to provide more opportunities for practice. Provide page-sized Venn diagram graphic organizers on which students can document their sorting decisions to share with the class.	

Based on currently available information about the standardized tests developed to assess student mastery of the CCSS-ELA and the CCSS-M, it appears likely that students will be prompted to compare/contrast in their answer to some of the constructed-response (essay) questions. Introducing this process early, several years before testing begins in Grade 3, will help ensure that students are familiar with this particular structure and have a good sense of how to respond.

Grade 2 Integrated-Content Lesson: CCSS-ELA and Social Studies

The second grade content standards presented in the CCSS-ELA are ambitious and pose relatively high levels of cognitive demand. Try to approach the

CCSS-ELA standards with a flexible outlook: Acknowledge your students' varied capabilities when setting expectations for learning outcomes, use technology as a support for all students (keyboarding on a computer might make it easier for some students to express their thoughts, other students might prefer to record their "opinion piece" as a podcast or a video or to dictate their piece to a class-mate or parent volunteer scribe), or allow students to work in side-by-side pairs (each student writes his/her own opinion piece, but does so in ongoing consulta-tion with the partner).

Getting students engaged in the ELA and social studies content, as fully and deeply as possible, is central to this lesson. But writing a fairly long opinion piece by hand might be difficult for some of the younger second graders. Making small adjustments and adaptations to your instructional plans to hook the students and keep them focused on their work will enhance learning outcomes for all students. This activity could also be the starting point for something larger, like a "hero

TABLE 6.4 Integrated-Content Lesson for Grade 2

Grade 2-ELA and Social Studies *What Makes Someone a Hero?*	
Content Standards From CCSS-ELA	**Content Standards From Social Studies**
W 2.1 Write opinion pieces in which students introduce the topic or book they are writing about, state an opinion, supply reasons that support the opinion, use linking words (e.g., because, and, also) to connect opinion and reasons, and provide a concluding statement or section.	2.5 Students understand the importance of individual action and character and explain how heroes from long ago and the recent past have made a difference in others' lives (e.g., from biographies of Abraham Lincoln, Louis Pasteur, Sitting Bull, George Washington Carver, Marie Curie, Albert Einstein, Golda Meir, Jackie Robinson, Sally Ride).
Student Learning Outcomes-ELA	**Student Learning Outcomes-Social Studies**
After reading a biography of a historical figure who could be considered a hero, students will write an essay in which they introduce the hero, explain how s/he made a difference in the lives of others, and provide three pieces of evidence from the biography they read to support their opinion about the hero.	Students will understand that any person can become a hero and make a difference in the lives of others by acting bravely to create a necessary change in the world.
Instruction and Learning Experience/Activity That Focus on Both ELA and Social Studies	
This assignment, the culminating project of a larger unit on biography that focuses specifically on people making a difference in the lives of others, will be written in class.	

Grade 2-ELA and Social Studies	
What Makes Someone a Hero?	
Assessment of Students' Understanding of the Learning Outcomes-ELA	**Assessment of Students' Understanding of the Learning Outcomes-Social Studies**
Assignment Rubric: Introduction of the hero; opinion about how the hero's actions impacted others; three pieces of evidence drawn from the biography read that support the opinion; conclusion. Accuracy of all factual information; use of evidence and facts to support opinion about the hero; relevance of evidence presented; attention paid to making a difference in the lives of others. Teacher may also include additional comments about progress since a previous essay assignment. Complete a rubric for each student; make copy of essay and rubric for records.	Assignment Rubric: Accuracy of all factual information; use of evidence and facts to support opinion about the hero; relevance of evidence presented; attention paid to making a difference in the lives of others.
Provide Feedback to Students and Parents Regarding Student Learning-ELA	**Provide Feedback to Students and Parents Regarding Student Learning-Social Studies**
Write a complimentary note to student on the rubric that points to two significant strengths in the work (one related to ELA and the other related to social studies); share with student one-on-one before rubric is sent home. Send assignment and rubric home in weekly work folder. Use this essay as an example of student writing during parent-teacher conferences.	Same as ELA section.
Use Assessment Evidence to Plan Future Instruction-ELA	**Use Assessment Evidence to Plan Future Instruction-Social Studies**
Identify students who had difficulty meeting the assignment expectations. Determine whether the difficulties were mainly related to the ELA expectations or the social studies expectations and provide them with targeted support as needed. Take notes on support and interventions used for each student; place notes in files.	Same as ELA section.

Extension/Re-teach Activities
Develop writing/speaking activities/games *linked to students' interests* that involve supporting an opinion with evidence (e.g., "*Star Wars: A New Hope* is the best Star Wars movie because (1) supporting evidence; (2) supporting evidence; (3) supporting evidence.")
Students can write and illustrate mini-biographies of family members, classmates, athletes, and celebrities that focus on the ways in which their chosen individual makes a different in the lives of others. Appropriate evidence must be provided to support the opinions expressed in the biography.

museum" exhibition in which your students dress up as their heroes and visitors to the "museum" can learn about each hero.

Grade 3 Integrated-Content Lesson: CCSS-ELA and Social Studies

Like the kindergarten lesson, this integrated-content lesson has complementary standards and goals: The social studies standards supply the content, and CCSS-ELA specify the process by which students will show what they know. Choosing complementary content standards—skills from the CCSS-ELA and content from social studies, for example—makes lessons efficient and effective.

Making intentional, deliberate decisions when planning integrated-content lessons—such as choosing complementary standards, as seen in the kindergarten lesson and the lesson for Grade 3—blends the two content areas in a seamless, natural way.

TABLE 6.5 Integrated-Content Lesson for Grade 3

Grade 3-ELA and Social Studies Understanding Rules	
Content Standards From CCSS-ELA	**Content Standards From Social Studies**
SL 3.4 Oral report on a topic or text, tell a story, or recount an experience with appropriate facts and relevant, descriptive details, speaking clearly at an understandable pace.	3.4 Students understand the role of rules and laws in our daily lives and the basic structure of the U.S. government.
Student Learning Outcomes-ELA	**Student Learning Outcomes-Social Studies**
Students will include one significant fact and one relevant detail in a brief oral presentation to the class.	Students will be able to explain the purpose and importance of a school or classroom rule.
Instruction and Learning Experience/Activity That Focus on Both ELA and Social Studies	
Post a list of the school rules and the classroom rules for student reference during the activity. Use equity sticks to divide the class into as many groups as there are individual rules on the combined lists. Each group member works independently to write a three-sentence presentation that states their group's rule in their own words, the purpose it serves, and specifies how the rule helps children learn. English learners and students with learning challenges may use a prepared sentence frame and/or other appropriate supports as needed. Determine the best schedule for allowing each group to share their rule (depending on the number of rules, the size of each group, etc.). Share one rule at a time—hearing the purpose and importance of the rule repeated in different words by different classmates will help everyone recall all the rules—over 1 to 3 days.	

Grade 3-ELA and Social Studies Understanding Rules	
Assessment of Students' Understanding of the Learning Outcomes-ELA	**Assessment of Students' Understanding of the Learning Outcomes-Social Studies**
Create a rubric for the presentation: three sentences; rule clearly stated, purpose explained thoroughly, how it helps students learn clarified. Note which students used sentence frames. Complete a rubric for each student. Make copies for records.	See description in ELA section.
Provide Feedback to Students and Parents Regarding Student Learning-ELA	**Provide Feedback to Students and Parents Regarding Student Learning-Social Studies**
In the class newsletter and on the class website, prompt parents to ask their child about the school and classroom rules. Send home completed assignment rubric in the weekly work folder.	See description in ELA section.
Use Assessment Evidence to Plan Future Instruction-ELA	**Use Assessment Evidence to Plan Future Instruction-Social Studies**
Check in with the students who used sentence frames to complete their presentation and ensure they understand their rule and can describe its purpose/importance in their own words.	Same as ELA section.
Extension/Re-teach Activities	
Students can make a big book listing the class rules and school rules illustrated by photographs of classmates modeling adherence to the rules. (Students could also do a "Goofus and Gallant"-style rule book in which there are side-by-side pictures of each rule being upheld and being violated.)	
Students who demonstrated weak oral presentation skills (too quick, too quiet, too many ums and likes) could create a contract with the teacher aimed at increasing their participation in lessons and discussions: a certain number of contributions over a certain number of days might receive a special sticker or lunch with the teacher.	

Planning Integrated-Content Instruction From Scratch

Regardless of whether you are planning to integrate the CCSS-ELA with the CCSS-M or with content from one of your state's current standards documents, the process of planning integrated-content lessons follows the same basic steps.

1. Identify Complementary Content Standards From Two Different Academic Disciplines

Choosing appropriate standards from each discipline is the first step in the process. As the foundation of the lesson, the content standards must be chosen with intentionality and care. Identifying complementary content standards—that is, standards from each discipline that create an effective, aligned, and coordinated partnership when paired together—is an ideal way to begin.

The integrated-content CCSS-ELA and social studies lessons for kindergarten and Grade 3, seen earlier in this chapter, feature complementary content standards. Both lessons include *academic content from the social studies standards* (symbols and icons that represent the United States for kindergarten; reasons for rules and laws for third grade) and *a skill from the CCSS-ELA* (asking and answering questions about a text for kinders; presenting an oral report for third graders). Pairing a skill or process standard from one academic discipline with a knowledge standard from another academic discipline works well because students learn both new knowledge and a new process in which to use the knowledge. Pairing knowledge from two different content areas in a single lesson is unlikely to be effective: Students need something to do with the new knowledge they learned in order to make it their own. Likewise, pairing skills or processes from two different content areas is also likely to be ineffective: Learning new processes without applying them to something specific does not help students internalize what they learned.

Another way to find complementary standards from different content areas is to look for areas of overlap between the content areas; content standards in different disciplines sometimes cover the same knowledge or skill, usually in slightly different ways. Combining those similar standards in a single lesson creates another type of complementary pairing because teaching the similar standards in the same lesson provides students an opportunity to develop a richer and broader understanding of the standard. For example, the CCSS-M indicate students in Grade 1 will "organize, represent, and interpret data" (p. 16) and the *Next Generation Science Standards* (NGSS) specify that first grade students will "demonstrate grade-appropriate proficiency in . . . analyzing and interpreting data" (NGSS Elementary Standards, 2013, n.p.). These two standards are not identical, but pairing them in a single lesson enables students to develop a fuller and more coherent understanding of data analysis and interpretation.

2. Develop a Balanced Instructional Plan for Presenting the Content in the Chosen Standards to Your Students; Be Sure Your Plan Offers Students Equitable Opportunity to Engage With and Learn the Content From Both Academic Disciplines

Although lesson planning is always depicted and taught as a linear process in which Step One is followed by Step Two, my experience suggests lesson planning can often be messy, circular, and shaped by thunderbolts of sudden insight and flashes of inspiration. Once you've settled on the content standards you intend to teach, it's possible that you already have ideas about how you plan to engage the students with the content from both disciplines. Perhaps you even switched out one (or both) of the standards as part of your process of honing your instructional plan. Pulling things together and making adjustments that improve the lesson is part of the planning process.

The most critical issue at this juncture is remaining vigilant: Your lesson plan must give equal time and emphasis to both the standards you're teaching. If it helps, think of those two academic content standards as beloved identical twins who expect to receive the equivalent amount of attention from you, and equal recognition from the outside world. This is your responsibility as a teacher: You must lead your students to mastery of both content standards included in the lesson. Be disciplined and strict with yourself.

3. Determine How You Will Assess Students' Mastery of Both Content Standards

Generally, the instruction and guided practice you provided and the learning experience you developed to engage your students in meaningful work with the specified content requires students create and complete a product that you collect and evaluate to determine the degree to which each student mastered both objectives of the lesson. If you did not yet develop a means by which you can effectively assess student learning prior to this point, you should do it now. Remember: Assess student mastery of both standards.

4. Once You've Finalized the Plan and the Assessment Process, Frame Student Learning Objectives/Learning Outcomes for Each Content Area

You have chosen content standards in two academic disciplines; made plans to engage the students with the content in meaningful, exciting ways; and identified a strategy for assessing student learning that grew organically from the students' experience in the lesson. Now that all these pieces are in place, it becomes very easy to frame two student learning objectives for the lesson: Simply align both learning objectives with (a) the content standards and (b) the assessment activity.

Shoehorning?

The integrated-content lessons presented in this chapter were created from scratch. However, it is not necessary for teachers to re-build all their lessons from the ground up. There are other strategies that can be used to create successful integrated-content lessons. The easiest strategy is something I call "shoehorning."

A shoehorn is an old-school tool—shaped like a small, hand-held garden trowel—that old-time ladies and gentlemen would use to ease their feet into their stiff leather shoes. A shoehorn makes it easy to insert the foot while also preventing damage to the shoe.

One easy way to create integrated-content lessons is to take an existing lesson—one designed to teach content from a single academic discipline—and shoehorn standards from the CCSS-ELA or the CCSS-M into the lesson. Shoehorning is a lesson-modification strategy that most teachers use frequently but are hesitant to discuss in public.

Shoehorning simply refers to interweaving standards from the CCSS-ELA and/or the CCSS-M into already-existing lesson plans. You can shoehorn the CCSS into instructional materials you developed yourself, and into commercially prepared instructional materials, and even into lessons lifted from older basals and textbook series that are not aligned with the CCSS. All the curricular and instructional materials you've saved over the years—the activities and plans you knew to be too effective, too enjoyable, or too meaningful to toss into the recycle bin—can be redeemed and updated by shoehorning the CCSS into the materials.

Do It Yourself

Almost any existing lesson can be reshaped to align with a CCSS-ELA standard; those that can't be reshaped can be augmented by the addition of CCSS-ELA standards via shoehorn. Likewise, ELA standards can be shoehorned into existing lesson plans in social studies, science, and other subjects. Given the CCSS' emphases on complexity and rigor, teachers must commit to the following in order to shoehorn successfully:

1. Attend to Text Complexity and Richness

Ensure that any text associated with a lesson is sufficiently complex. If the text used previously is too basic, replace it with something richer and more intellectually challenging for your students. This includes both the texts you intend to read aloud and the texts you selected for the students to read independently.

2. Use Academic Language When Teaching and Speaking With Students

Model the use of academic language while teaching every lesson and to encourage your students to use academic language as much as possible. As teachers of young children, we play an important role in supporting our students' language development. I have found it just as easy to teach children a "hard," high-leverage word as to teach them an "easy" common word. Why not try things like

The flu is contagious.
The president is charismatic.
I feel disappointed.

Students are especially excited if you promise to teach them a "hard" word. Young children already know that knowledge is power, so each "hard" word they know and use regularly makes them a bit more powerful.

3. Ask Higher Order Questions and Work to Elicit Thoughtful Responses

Rather than asking simple questions focused on recall and comprehension, challenge your students by posing questions that require them to analyze, synthesize, and evaluate. Pose a challenging question to the whole class and provide some thinking time before you begin to call on students. After a student offers a response, you have options: Probe the student further (using questions like, "Why do you think so?" and "Could there be another explanation?"), ask another student to restate what the respondent said using his/her own words, invite someone to ask the respondent a follow-up question, or see if any student disagrees or would like to pose an alternative response. Students should come to expect that they will be asked to explain their thinking or justify their reasoning.

4. Add a Related Non-Fiction Text to the Lesson

Students build content knowledge and academic language through engagement with and conversations about informational text. Whenever possible, create space for reading aloud and discussing non-fiction books. Encourage students to make connections between the text and their prior knowledge or to other texts they've read. Welcome them to ask questions when you read a word that's unfamiliar. Helping students to build rich, nuanced, flexible vocabularies will support their academic success in all content areas.

Are These Suggestions Developmentally Appropriate?

The emphasis on rigor; complexity; academic language; higher order thinking; and providing a rationale, explanation, or justification that characterizes most conversations the CCSS can be distressing to early childhood educators. We survived NCLB's accountability apocalypse and now we fear that new storm clouds are brewing overhead. Should we be worried?

Honestly, I'm not worried at all. Here's why:

- Open your copy of the CCSS-ELA and look closely at the standards for the grade level you teach. As you can see, they are age appropriate. The same goes for the CCSS-M: the standards for the grade level you teach are age appropriate too.
- Every conversation about rigor in the CCSS should be interpreted in relation to the age of the students under discussion. Kindergartners will engage in challenging, achievable lessons characterized by the level of rigor that is

appropriate for a five-year-old child. Perhaps, for example, something like this: How many words can we think of that mean the same thing as "cold"?

• The authors of the CCSS-ELA wrote, "The use of play with young children is not specified by the standards, but it is welcome as a valuable activity in its own right and as a way to help students meet the expectations in this document" (CCSS-ELA, pg. 9). The individual authors might not truly understand the role of play in childhood or recognize the difficulties teachers experienced in the past decade justifying our block corners, our sociodramatic play areas, and our puppet theaters. However, their willingness to speak out in favor of play as a means by which young students may meet the expectations in the CCSS-ELA suggests that they have the best interests of young children—and their teachers—in mind.

References

California Department of Education. (1998). *History-social science standards for California public schools.* Sacramento, CA: California Department of Education.

California Department of Education. (2012). *California English language development standards.* Sacramento, CA: California Department of Education.

Gray, N. (1991). *A country far away.* New York: Scholastic.

Keenan, S. (2004). *O, say can you see? America's symbols, landmarks, and inspiring words.* New York: Scholastic.

Morris, A. (1993). *Bread, bread, bread.* New York: HarperCollins.

Morris, A. (1995). *Houses and homes.* New York: HarperCollins.

Morris, A. (1998). *Shoes, shoes, shoes.* New York: HarperCollins.

National Council for the Social Studies. (2013). *College, career, and civic life framework for Social Studies state standards (C3): Guidance for enhancing the rigor of K–12 Civics, Economics, Geography, and History.* Silver Spring, MD: NCSS.

New York State Education Department. (2011). *New York State prekindergarten foundation for the Common Core.* Albany, NY: New York State Education Department.

NGSS Elementary Standards. (2013). *Next generation science standards: For states, by states.* Retrieved from http://www.nextgenscience.org/

Easterling, L. (2007). *Families.* Portsmouth, NH: Heinemann.

Scillian, D. (2002). *One nation: America by the numbers.* Farmington, MI: Thomsen Gale.

7

SPOTLIGHT SKILL

Educating Families About the CCSS

The Common Core State Standards are still new. On the implementation time-lines of most states that adopted the CCSS, 2014–15 was identified as the first academic year in which all the content taught to students would be fully aligned with the Common Core and all students would be assessed using standardized tests fully aligned with the CCSS. Further, 2014–15 was also the point at which all the instructional materials and practices used to teach students were expected to reflect the CCSS' underlying priorities and values, which include:

- Providing instruction that features heightened complexity and greater cognitive demand
- Expecting students to learn and to use precise academic language
- Teaching students to offer evidence to support their opinions and explain their solutions
- Fostering students' deep conceptual understanding of all content taught

The current experiences of prekindergarten–Grade 3 teachers in states that have adopted the CCSS vary widely depending, in part, on the age of the children with whom they work and on the settings in which they teach. However, at least one issue is shared by all early childhood teachers implementing the Common Core: a critical need to play a leadership role in educating parents about the curricular and instructional switch that have accompanied the change.

The adoption of the Common Core State Standards has been a somewhat rocky process that has been playing out in public and highly visible ways. The ups and downs of their adoption and their implementation continue to make headlines in reports from the news media (Associated Press, 2014) and the popular press (Finn & Brickman, 2014). Parents, aware of the rumble of dissent, may be skeptical, concerned, or confused about the CCSS. On the other hand, parents may know very little about the CCSS: In a recent poll, 79% of the voting public admitted to knowing "not much" or "nothing at all" about these standards (Achieve, 2012). Teachers must be prepared to explain the classroom-level impact of the CCSS to their students' parents and family members.

What Do Parents Need to Know?

Although "the Common Core" is a familiar phrase to most adults in the United States, the popular media's presentation of the CCSS—focused mainly on whether these new standards are "good" or "bad"—has been superficial. Because the CCSS documents are written in the specialized professional language used by K–12 educators, rather than in a register aimed at the general public, there has been little discussion about the actual content of the Common Core.

Because parents often consider their children's teachers to be a source of reliable information about learning and development, many early childhood teachers are accustomed to supporting the learning of both young students and their parents. This chapter offers answers to some of the questions parents are likely to ask, describes one possible challenge that might present itself, and suggests excellent resources available online that can be used for your parent education efforts.

Parents' Frequently Asked Questions

1. **Why were the Common Core State Standards necessary? Doesn't every state already have its own content standards?**

Every state did have its own content standards. This is one of the problems the CCSS is intended to solve. Presently, each state's content standards are different—sometimes just a little, and sometimes a lot—from the standards used in other states. Further, each state established its own understanding of what a child would need to know and be able to do in order to be considered as working "at grade level." This created a great deal of inconsistency from one state to another. For example, a child working at grade level in one state could relocate to a neighboring state and—if the new state had higher standards and expectations for each grade level than her old state did—suddenly find herself working below grade level. States that have chosen to implement the CCSS will have more stable and consistent expectations and greater clarity about learning goals and student outcomes.

2. **How are the Common Core State Standards different from the previous standards?**

The CCSS were designed with the intent of ensuring all students will complete high school prepared for success in college and/or in a career. This provides K–12 education with a fresh focus and different types of learning outcomes. The CCSS—both for ELA and math—continually draw students' attention to the reasons they are learning certain knowledge and skills and to the ways in which they can apply what they learn to achieve their own goals.

The authors of the two CCSS documents started their work by identifying the probable demands of the 21st century workplace. They determined success in college and a career of the future would require high levels of literacy and numeracy; strong skills for collaboration and problem solving; well-developed abilities in reasoning and communication; and creativity, initiative, and persistence. Thus, the CCSS are intended to develop not only facility with academic content knowledge in mathematics and English language arts, but also capability to reason and explain complex ideas, to use precise and specific language, to listen thoughtfully, and to pose good questions that deepen understanding and clarity.

The CCSS' expectations for student learning are not only higher than those of the old standards, but they also pose greater cognitive demand. Students must learn to think more deeply, understand more fully, explain their ideas more clearly, and apply their new knowledge to routine and unfamiliar challenges.

Finally, in keeping with their desire to prepare today's students for successful futures in an increasingly globalized world, the CCSS' authors benchmarked these new standards internationally. Consideration of the expected student learning outcomes, curriculum materials, and instructional practices used in the nations whose children are currently demonstrating the highest levels of academic achievement also contributed to the formation of the CCSS.

3. How will implementation of the CCSS change classroom learning experiences for young children?

The skills in the CCSS for a given grade level can be engaged with at different levels and in different ways, depending on the needs and interests of the students. An activity's complexity, pace, and expectations for completion can be adjusted easily—thus allowing every student to engage in work that is challenging, achievable, and interesting.

Parents who have older children may notice some differences between the academic work that was typically done by their older children and the academic work done in classrooms informed by the CCSS. These include:

- **More engagement with complex informational text.**

Rather than relying mostly on storybooks and fiction, the CCSS directs teachers of young children to emphasize the reading and discussion of non-fiction texts. Learning is what young children do best, and engaging with academic content drawn from the sciences and social sciences help students build a strong knowledge base. A strong knowledge base is an ideal foundation for future learning.

- **Emphasis on the development and use of precise academic language.**

Young children have limited vocabularies and an almost unlimited capacity to learn. In the day-to-day experience of their classroom lives, teachers have many opportunities to use rich and nuanced vocabulary, to help their young students learn sophisticated, accurate, age-appropriate terminology drawn from different academic disciplines, and to encourage the use of that language in and outside of class. Some students will remember and use those exciting words in conversation with classmates—and soon everyone's vocabulary has expanded.

- **Expectation that children will be able to explain their thinking.**

The CCSS aren't exclusively focused on getting the correct answer and moving on. Teachers know that hearing and discussing a student's interesting but incorrect response can be more beneficial to the class' understanding of a concept than hearing from a student who got the correct answer right away. Learning how to approach a challenging task—be it solving a mathematics problem or grasping the meaning a poem—is difficult if no one ever talks about how they decided what to do and where to begin, or when and how they realized that they were not going to be successful unless they changed their approach. The CCSS in both ELA and math emphasize the need for children to be able to explain their thinking to the teacher and to their classmates. This begins in the kindergarten standards and continues all the way through Grade 12.

- **Equal attention to conceptual understanding, procedural skill and fluency, and application.**

The CCSS balance three different types of equally important knowledge:

Conceptual understanding: knowledge of how and why a process works
Procedural skill/fluency: facility with the processes rooted in conceptual understanding
Application: ability to take understanding and skills and use them in the real world

These types of knowledge co-exist in every academic discipline. Awareness that "its" and "it's" are different because one is possessive pronoun (his, hers, its, no apostrophe) and the other is a contraction of "it" and "is" is conceptual knowledge; explaining when to use "its" and when to use "it's" is procedural skill/fluency; and using "its" and "it's" correctly in a thank you note written to a guest speaker is application. Previous state standards, focused mainly on outcomes, emphasized procedural skill and fluency: Can a student correctly solve double-digit subtraction problems? Application was rarely seen, and conceptual understanding was often considered unnecessary. The CCSS strives to keep these three types of knowledge in balance.

5. **What can I do at home to help my child succeed in learning the content in the CCSS?**

Parents set the family's priorities: They determine how time is spent and control the experiences and opportunities available to their children. Making children's academic success a family priority does not require the purchase of supplemental workbooks and enforced hours of practice at home. Rather, families can develop a few new, enjoyable routines that will offer young students opportunities to develop and practice the skills necessary to succeed with the CCSS.

- **Consider reading a simple novel, rather than an illustrated storybook, aloud at bedtime.**

Novels are meatier than storybooks. The length of a novel allows for a more complex plot and richer character development, both of which create higher interest and greater suspense about the outcomes for the characters. Novels also use more sophisticated vocabulary and, because they are longer than storybooks, offer children more opportunity for children to learn new words.

Parents can read one chapter before bed each night and discuss the chapter over breakfast or on the way to school the next morning. Asking questions about details that aren't made explicit in the novel—the reasons behind a character's actions and decisions or the possibility of alternative solutions to a character's problem, for example—is an excellent way to help children develop the skills necessary to explain their thinking and support their ideas with evidence from the text.

- **Spend time engaging your child in substantive conversations.**

Children learn to communicate by talking and listening and by posing and answering questions. However, to develop conversation skills and build richness into their vocabularies, children must engage in conversations with older and more experienced companions. Rather than just asking a child, "What happened at school today?" parents can make the conversation more engaging by homing in on something specific: "Since Hunter and Harper are identical twins, how can your kindergarten teacher tell which boy is Hunter and which boy is Harper? How do you know which boy is which? Do you think they ever trade places and pretend to be their brother? Do they dress alike? Would you like to have an identical twin? Why or why not?"

Conversations with a young child (or children) work best when:

- The child has solid foundational knowledge about and interest in the topic:

  Baseball
  Star Wars
  Halloween costumes

- The conversation's focus is narrow and specific:

  Last night's baseball game
  Where Jedi live
  Buying a costume versus making a costume

- There are no right or wrong answers:

  Emphasize personal opinions, preferences, and experiences
  Stay away from verifiable facts and details

- **Look for opportunities to ask your child questions like "What makes you think that?" or "How did you figure that out?" or "How do you know that?" and wait for a complete explanation.**

In both mathematics and English language arts, the Common Core State Standards emphasize the need for students to use evidence to support their opinions and responses. The CCSS require students to provide more than the solution to a problem: Students are expected to explain the process by which they arrived at their solution and why they believe their solution is correct. Awareness of one's own thinking and reasoning—a phenomenon educators and psychologists call "metacognition"—helps students recognize the thinking skills and strategies they use to answer complex questions or complete multi-step procedures. Conversations in which a child discusses his or her reasoning with an interested adult can become opportunities for sharing and developing new metacognitive strategies.

- **Watch age-appropriate science and history documentaries with your child; pause regularly to talk about what you just watched.**

Children need opportunities to learn, hear, and use academic language, particularly in the content areas that receive the least instructional time in the early grades: science and social studies. Watching documentary films, television programs, or videos with your child—in addition to being fun and interesting—builds academic content knowledge and discipline-specific vocabulary. Choosing topics that are aligned with the science or social studies content specified for the child's grade level is unnecessary: the most important factor in choosing documentaries to watch with your young child is the child. For example, a sensitive eight-year-old with a passion for penguins might become very upset by the few penguin deaths that occur naturally in a documentary about Antarctica, while a knowledgeable four-year-old obsessed with outer space might enjoy an astronomy documentary aimed at an adult audience because of her extensive prior knowledge and high interest in the topic.

Other factors to consider when choosing documentaries to watch with children include attention to age-appropriate content and language. History is full of grisly, horrific events: beheading, war, plague, genocide, slavery, and much, much more. Some documentaries present these horrors in ways that might be palatable for young children—listening to a passage from the Iliad while images of battles from ancient Greek vase paintings are shown on the screen, for example—while other documentaries stage re-enacted battles with lots of bloodshed. Unless a history documentary is clearly marked as appropriate for children, prescreen your choices before watching them with your child.

Science documentaries—particularly those about the end of the universe, global warming, endangered animals, and other frightening topics—can also be problematic for young viewers. In addition, many science documentaries assume that viewers have a deep and wide knowledge base in the sciences: The specialized vocabulary and complex language used in those documentaries may be too sophisticated for young science lovers. Again, unless a science documentary is clearly appropriate for children (such as *The Magic Schoolbus* series), prescreening videos is a wise practice.

The length of a history or science documentary might also pose a problem. Consider watching videos in 10–15 minute segments. Taking a conversation break to talk about what you just watched is a good way to judge your child's focus and mental stamina. Stop as soon as the child begins to lose interest.

- **Teach your children about money—how to count it, how to pay for things with coins and bills, how to make change, and how to count change—and create opportunities for them to purchase things.**

Most young children have few opportunities to apply their mathematics skills outside of the classroom. However, once children learn how to count money, how to pay for purchases with coins and bills, and how to ensure they receive the correct change, they are ready to begin purchasing goods or services from a store, a restaurant, an ice cream truck, or a vending machine. Facility with money—holding it, counting it, using it, saving it, and even earning it—enables children not only to use their math skills for a tangible purpose but also to get a taste of competence and independence in the real world.

- **Help your child develop a growth mindset.**

Imagine a child attempting to assemble a new toy using the diagram provided in the package. The child's first attempt was unsuccessful. And the second attempt was also unsuccessful. Now the child feels stuck. In this situation, some children think, "I don't know how to build this toy," and move on to a different activity. However, other children think, "I don't know how to build this toy yet," and then continue working on it—using different strategies and learning from their mistakes—until they are successful.

Psychologist Carol Dweck (2006) would describe the first group of children as having a "fixed mindset." These children believe their capabilities are static and unchangeable: Because they weren't able to build the toy after two tries, they'll never be able to build the toy. The second group of children, the ones who felt they didn't know how to build the toy *yet*, is described by Dweck as having a "growth mindset." These children believe that the concerted application of effort, patience, persistence, and other factors within their own control will ultimately result in success. For children with a growth mindset, anything is within their reach if they are willing to work hard enough to attain it.

According to Dweck, when parents compliment children on their intelligence or talent, they are contributing to the development of a fixed mindset. Although children love to be praised, they also pick up an implicit (but unintentional) message hiding within their parents' compliments: You possess special abilities other children don't have, and those exceptional abilities enable to you be more successful than others. These children learn that intelligence is something inherent to a person—like blue eyes—something that you either have or don't have. When children who have learned these messages encounter difficulty learning something new, they are taken aback: They have learned that smart people learn things easily, so they perceive their difficulty as evidence that they are not smart (Dweck, 2006, p. 175). This type of thinking can damage children's motivation to learn and their willingness to try new things.

A growth mindset, by contrast, is much more conducive to learning and success than a fixed mindset. Children with a growth mindset believe they can learn anything if they are willing to invest time and effort, to study and practice persistently, and to develop good strategies for success in this endeavor. When these children are successful they attribute their success to their own actions, the things they did—worked hard, maintained a positive attitude, focused on their goal, practiced every day—rather than to their innate intelligence. They believe anyone can learn a new skill if they are willing to put in the sustained effort.

Happily, a growth mindset is something that all children can develop. Parents and teachers, the most powerful influences on a child's mindset, need to reframe the compliments they pay to the young learners in their care. Rather than praising children's intelligence, talent, or giftedness—or any other traits that children possess—adults should praise children for their efforts, ideas, and persistence—the direct result of choices they make, the focus they demonstrate, and the time they invested in mastering something new and difficult.

Potential Challenge

The Common Core State Standards are relatively straightforward. Each document lays out the knowledge and skills students are expected to master at each grade level by the end of the academic year in English Language Arts and in Mathematics. The CCSS do not indicate how the specified content should be taught: Decisions about instructional materials and practices are the responsibility of the administrators and teachers in each school district and school in every state that has adopted the CCSS.

Some of the instructional materials currently in use in early childhood classrooms—particularly in mathematics—are framed using procedures, processes, and terminology that are new and unfamiliar. In the early grades, CCSS mathematics instruction may look and sound very different from the mathematics instruction provided in previous years. For example, many of us learned to solve equations with a missing addend in a format something like this:

$$6 + \square = 9$$

When first graders learn this concept as part of the Common Core, the instructional materials they use might represent the relationships between the numbers in a different way. For example, the widely used EngageNY mathematics curriculum (New York State Education Department, n.d.) uses the concept of a "number bond" to describe relationships between certain numbers. The worksheet presented below (which I have separated into two separate segments) requires first graders to solve a math story by doing three things:

1. Completing the number bond
2. Completing the number sentences
3. Coloring the unknown number yellow

These connected rectangles do not look like an equation. Many of the key structural features and landmarks of early mathematics learning—numbers arranged in a horizontal line, a plus sign, an equal sign—are missing. How does someone complete a number bond?

Part Two of this mathematics worksheet requires first graders to complete the following "number sentences."

The parents of your students might find it easier to complete these number sentences than it was to complete the number bonds. Number sentences are organized in a format that reflects the mathematical thinking patterns of most adults educated in the United States.

Parents probably do not anticipate having trouble understanding the homework assignments they pull out of their young children's backpacks. However, now that children are learning how to do mathematics using strategies and techniques that may be very unfamiliar to their parents, this jarring experience is becoming common occurrence in states implementing the CCSS-Math.

This is a situation in which teachers should be proactive. Rather than waiting for parent concerns to reach a boiling point before offering support, teachers can reach out to parents and work on closing this knowledge gap quickly. Further,

Name _____   Date _____

Solve the math story. Complete the number bond and number sentences. Color the unknown number yellow.

Rich bought 6 cans of soda on Monday.

He bought some more on Tuesday.

Now, he has 9 cans of soda.

How many cans did Rich buy on Tuesday?

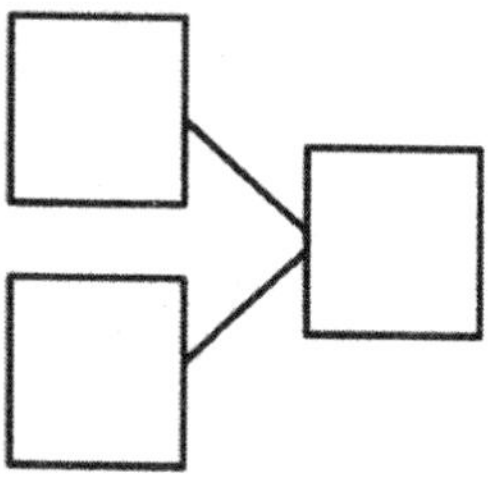

FIGURE 7.1 Representing basic addition and subtraction within a CCSS-aligned mathematics curriculum: completing a number bond

Rich bought _____ cans.

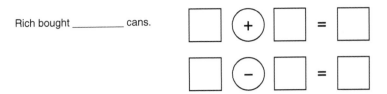

FIGURE 7.2 Representing basic addition and subtraction within a CCSS-aligned mathematics curriculum: completing number sentences

it would be ideal to provide many different avenues by which parents can access information about the CCSS-M. Some strategies for this include:

• **Organize a variety of evening events centered around mathematics instruction.**

Parent Mathematics Night. Parents, many of whom feel confused by the procedures, processes, or visual representations used in the instructional materials adopted by your district, may actually need less support than they think. Invite parents to your classroom for a 30-minute overview of the instructional materials—with a special focus on the ways in which the presentation and preferred practices depart from the familiar procedures parents were expecting to see—and 15 minutes of Q & A. This might be enough to allay their concerns.

Family Mathematics Night. Invite one parent or guardian from each family to experience a mini mathematics lesson introduced by the teacher and then "taught" one-on-one to parents by their children. This experience lets parents see how mathematics content is introduced and practiced in a typical lesson and—as a delightful bonus—provides an opportunity for children to demonstrate their understanding of the math concepts they have been learning as they "teach" and explain the content to their parent. This type of event also allows the parents and their children to develop shared language for talking about mathematics, which can help close the gap between the parents' mathematical thinking the children's mathematical thinking.

• **Invite parents to observe in your classroom during mathematics instruction so they can see and hear what their kids are learning and how the concepts are being taught.**

Inviting parents to observe a mathematics lesson is a great way to communicate that (1) parents are welcome in their children's classroom; (2) you have the confidence needed to teach with parents in the room; (3) you want to support the parents' learning and deepen their understanding of the mathematics their children are learning and how they are learning it.

• **Contact mathematics teacher educators (the professors in teacher education programs who teach early childhood and elementary**

mathematics methods courses) at local universities and invite them to speak to your PTA about the CCSS-M.

Professors' schedules are often flexible enough to allow them to accommodate requests of this type. And many professors enjoy supporting the work of local teachers. (This is especially true if the professors' children are current students or graduates of the school.)

- **Look for support provided by your district—such as a teacher on special assignment, a coach, or a mentor who specializes in mathematics—to help the parent community understand the new instructional materials.**

Ideally, districts should be providing assistance of this type to support the smooth implementation of the CCSS. If your district does not have an assigned support provider, check with your county office of education or your state Department of Education.

- **Seek out parent education materials developed by different states, school districts, and textbook publishers that might be helpful in clarifying the new procedures and terminology or in making connections between the current instructional methods and the methods that are more familiar to parents.**

Every state offers an assortment of CCSS-related materials designed to assist parents; some of these materials were developed by the National Parent Teacher Association, others were developed by the Council of the Great City Schools, and others were created by the states themselves. The links below have been carefully curated to take you directly to materials that are

- thorough and useful
- generalizable to every state
- available in English and Spanish (some are available in additional languages)
- unique (e.g., Hawai'i's freestanding preK document)

Selected Resources for Parents

California's Common Core Standards Parent Handbook, K–8

(Created by the California County Superintendents Educational Services Association)
    Available in Arabic, Armenian Eastern, Armenian Western, Chinese (Simplified), Chinese (Traditional), Farsi, Hmong, Japanese, Khmer, Korean, Punjabi, Russian, Somali, Spanish, Tagalog, Ukrainian, Vietnamese.
    http://ccsesa.org/special-projects/common-core-standards-communication-tools/

Parent Roadmaps to the Common Core State Standards, K–12

(Created by The Council of the Great City Schools)
  Available in English and Spanish
  Parent Roadmap to the CCSS in English Language Arts in Kindergarten
  Parent Roadmap to the CCSS in English Language Arts in Grade 1
  Parent Roadmap to the CCSS in English Language Arts in Grade 2
  Parent Roadmap to the CCSS in English Language Arts in Grade 3
  Parent Roadmap to the CCSS in Mathematics in Kindergarten
  Parent Roadmap to the CCSS in Mathematics in Grade 1
  Parent Roadmap to the CCSS in Mathematics in Grade 2
  Parent Roadmap to the CCSS in Mathematics in Grade 3
  http://www.cgcs.org/Page/328

Parents' Guide to Student Success, K–12

(Created by the National PTA)
  Two-page and four-page versions available in English and Spanish
  Parents' Guide to Student Success in Kindergarten
  Parents' Guide to Student Success in 1st Grade
  Parents' Guide to Student Success in 2nd Grade
  Parents' Guide to Student Success in 3rd Grade
  *http://www.pta.org/parents/content.cfm?ItemNumber=2583&navItemNum
ber=3363*

Pre-Kindergarten Parent Guide

(Created by the Hawai'i Department of Education)
  *http://165.248.30.40/hcpsv3/files/pre-kparentguide(final-4edit)_commoncore
docs_370.pdf*

Common Core Overview

(Created by the New York City Department of Education)
  Available in English, Arabic, Bengali, Chinese, French, Haitian Creole, Korean,
Russian, Spanish, Urdu
  *http://schools.nyc.gov/Academics/CommonCoreLibrary/ForFamilies/Understanding
CC/default.htm*

Expect Success Guide for Parents, PreK–8

(Created by the New York City Department of Education)
  Available in English, Arabic, Bengali, Chinese, French, Haitian Creole, Korean,
Russian, Spanish, Urdu

http://schools.nyc.gov/Academics/CommonCoreLibrary/ForFamilies/Understanding CC/default.htm

Shifts for Students and Parents

(Created by EngageNY)

Available in English, Spanish, Arabic, Bengali, Haitian Creole
https://www.engageny.org/resource/shifts-for-students-and-parents/

Parents' Backpack Guide to the Common Core
Frequently Asked Questions
What Parents Can Do to Help Their Children Learn
Common Core Resources for Parents to Learn More

(Created by EngageNY)

https://www.engageny.org/resource/planning-a-parent-workshop-toolkit-for-parent-engagement

References

Achieve. (2012). *Survey shows strong support for CCSS*. Retrieved from http://www.achieve.org/survey-shows-strong-support-ccss

Associated Press. (2014, April 28) Indiana: Common core replaced with state standards. *New York Times*. Retrieved from http://www.nytimes.com/2014/04/29/us/indiana-common-core-replaced-with-state-standards.html?_r=0

Dweck, C. S. (2006). *Mindset: The new psychology of success*. New York: Ballantine Books.

Finn, C. E., & Brickman, M. (2014, August 11). Beyond the Common Core. *National Review, 66* (14), 21–22.

New York State Education Department. (n.d.) *EngageNY Common Core Curriculum modules*. Albany, NY: NYSED.

PART III

Understanding the Common Core State Standards Documents

INTRODUCTION TO PART III

The generic Common Core State Standards documents can be downloaded at

| Mathematics: | http://www.corestandards.org/Math/ |
| English Language Arts: | http://www.corestandards.org/ELA-Literacy/ |

The CCSS were designed to comprise 85% of the content taught at each grade level (Gewertz, 2010). This gives states the opportunity to add high-priority academic content of their own choosing to the CCSS. As a result, many states have their own, state-specific CCSS-ELA and CCSS-M documents available online through the state's Department of Education. If your state has its own CCSS documents, be sure to use those CCSS-ELA and CCSS-M documents rather than the ones available through the general Common Core website that is cited above.

Contradictions Between the CCSS and PreK–3 Practices

The two Common Core State Standards documents were conceptualized, developed, and written without significant input from practicing preschool, kindergarten, or primary grade teachers or from researchers or scholars with expertise in child development or early childhood education. Therefore, as you read through the CCSS-M and the CCSS-ELA, you are likely to find elements that strike you as developmentally inappropriate.

For example, the CCSS-M were written to reflect the assumption that all children beginning a given grade level have already demonstrated mastery of the standards from the preceding year(s) (Reeves, Wiggs, Lassiter, Piercy, Ventura, & Bell, 2011, p. 44). Thus, CCSS-M assumes all students about to begin first grade have mastered all the standards related to Counting and Cardinality, a mathematical domain that is addressed only in kindergarten. Of course, this is an unrealistic expectation.

Since kindergarten attendance is mandatory in only 15 U.S. states, there is a strong possibility that first grade teachers will encounter students who have not had sufficient exposure to the all knowledge and skills contained in the Counting and Cardinality domain. In addition, due to the developmental realities of early childhood, first grade teachers may have students who simply forgot some of their mathematical know-how during the long summer vacation, or who weren't ready to learn about counting and cardinality when they were five years old, or whose inconsistent kindergarten attendance created gaps in their knowledge and skills in every content area. Early childhood educators know this, and are accustomed to finding and filling their students' knowledge gaps as they present themselves.

Assuming that every student mastered all the content they were exposed to each academic year—especially during kindergarten—is a bad idea. Common sense suggests that, even though the Counting and Cardinality domain begins and ends in kindergarten, primary grade teachers should continue to teach and review the skills and knowledge related to counting and cardinality until every one of their students has them locked into place. As you read through the CCSS documents, you may wish to make note of all the troubling or problematic elements you find. I suggest that you revisit those elements, discuss them with your colleagues and administrators, and determine how those elements will be managed at your school.

Relationship Between the CCSS-M and the CCSS-ELA

The CCSS for Mathematics and the CCSS for English Language Arts and Literacy in Social Studies, Science, and Technical Subjects were conceptualized and crafted by two separate teams of content-area experts. This quickly becomes apparent to anyone attempting to use the two CCSS documents: the CCSS-M and CCSS-ELA are structured and organized differently, use different language and terminology, and neither makes any reference to the other CCSS document. This can make it difficult to work with both documents side by side. However, these documents do reflect a shared understanding of the values, practices, and skills that will best prepare students for productive adult lives.

The CCSS-M presents a set of Standards for Mathematical Practice that describe the "processes and proficiencies" (CCSS-M, p. 6) that students should employ when they approach and engage with mathematics. And the CCSS-ELA includes a list of characteristics demonstrated by students who are college and career ready (CCSS-ELA, p. 7). Although the Standards for Mathematic Practice focus on habits of mind and flexible application of mathematics skills and the traits of college and career ready students focus on student learning outcomes, a comparison of the two lists of characteristics reveals a great deal of similarity between the two sets of standards.

Despite the apparent lack of connection between the CCSS-M document and the CCSS-ELA document, the development teams who wrote the standards seem to have had similar goals for students. Comprehension, construction, and critique; argument and evidence; strategic use of appropriate tools and skills; and a mindset

Standards for Mathematical Practice	Traits of College /Career Ready Students
• Make sense of problems and persevere in solving them. • Reason abstractly and quantitatively. • Construct viable arguments and critique the reasoning of others. • Model with mathematics. • Use appropriate tools strategically. • Attend to precision. • Look for and make use of structure. • Look for and express regularity in repeated reasoning.	• Demonstrate independence. • Build strong content knowledge. • Respond to the varying demands of audience, task, purpose, and discipline. • Comprehend as well as critique. • Value evidence. • Use technology and digital media strategically and capably. • Come to understand other perspectives and cultures.

FIGURE PART 3.1 Alignment of the core values of the CCSS-M and the CCSS ELA

that supports ongoing learning feature prominently in both lists. This alignment—based in a similar understanding of the approaches to learning and to experience that will lead to productive adulthoods—unites the two CCSS documents.

References

Gewertz, C. (2010, February 2). States can't pick and choose among Common Standards. *Education Week*. Retrieved from http://blogs.edweek.org/edweek/curriculum/2010/02/states_cant_pick_and_choose_am.html

Reeves, D. B., Wiggs, M. D., Lassiter, C. J., Piercy, T. D., Ventura, S., & Bell, B. (2011). *Navigating the implementation of the Common Core State Standards*. Englewood, CO: Lead + Learn Press.

8

UNDERSTANDING THE CCSS-MATHEMATICS STANDARDS DOCUMENT

The Common Core State Standards for Mathematics present two different types of standards: standards for mathematical practice and standards for mathematical content.

The Standards for Mathematical Practice (SMP), unlike lists of mathematics standards that focus exclusively on academic knowledge and skills, emphasize the need for students learn and to employ the habits of mind, approaches to learning, and adaptive reasoning skills that foster deep mathematical understanding. Since the terminology used in the Standards for Mathematical Practice may be unfamiliar to adults—and is too abstract for children—I've augmented the SMP by including a "student friendly" version (White & Dauksas, 2012) to make the practices clearer and more accessible.

The Standards for Mathematical Content, like most other lists of academic content standards, specify what students should understand and be able to do in mathematics at each grade level, K–12.

These two sets of standards—Mathematical Practice and Mathematical Content—coalesce around the central importance of *understanding* mathematics. Students who learn a step-by-step procedure for solving a particular type of mathematics problem can execute the procedure and get the correct answer: This is how many of us were taught to do math when we were youngsters. However, knowing only one procedure to use for solving a specific type of mathematics problem—rather than reading and making sense of the problem and choosing the best approach for solving it—limits students' abilities to engage with novel mathematics problems, to transfer skills from one math domain (adding numbers) to another (finding the perimeter of a geometric shape), and to build a base of mathematical knowledge and skill that will allow them to reason their way through almost any age-appropriate mathematical challenge. Taken as a whole, the

TABLE 8.1 The CCSS Standards for Mathematical Practice Described for Adults and for Children

CCSS STANDARDS FOR MATHEMATICAL PRACTICE (SMP)	SMP IN STUDENT-FRIENDLY LANGUAGE (White & Dauksas, 2012)
Make sense of problems and persevere in solving them.	I can try many times to understand and solve a math problem.
Reason abstractly and quantitatively.	I can think about the math problem in my head first.
Construct viable arguments and critique the reasoning of others.	I can make a plan, called a strategy, to solve the problem, and discuss other students' strategies too.
Model with mathematics.	I can use math symbols and numbers to solve the problem.
Use appropriate tools strategically.	I can use math tools, pictures, drawings, and objects to solve the problem.
Attend to precision.	I can check to see if my strategy and calculations are correct.
Look for and make use of structure.	I can use what I already know about math to solve the problem.
Look for and express regularity in repeated reasoning.	I can use a strategy that I used to solve another math problem.

CCSS-Math is designed to help students develop deep, conceptual understanding of mathematics and to know how to use their understanding to think and reason mathematically in the real world.

Quick Start With the CCSS-Mathematics Content Standards

The CCSS Mathematical Content Standards for grades K–3 are structured and organized using these categories:

TABLE 8.2 Structure of the CCSS-M Document

Grade Level	K, 1, 2, 3, . . . etc.
Domain	Larger group of related standards. Standards from different domains may sometimes be closely related.
Cluster	Smaller group of related standards within the same domain. Standards from different clusters may sometimes be closely related because mathematics topics are closely connected.
Standard	Defines what students should understand and be able to do.

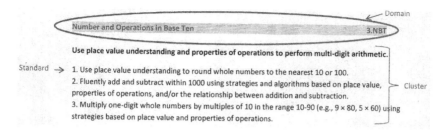

FIGURE 8.1 Reading the CCSS-M standards document

In the image above (*How to Read the Common Core State Standards for Mathematics*, n.d.), the domain entitled "Number and Operations in Base Ten" is abbreviated as NBT. The numeral 3 that appears before NBT in the gray domain box indicates this is a standard for Grade 3 (CCSS-M, p. 5).

As students grow and mature, the math concepts and skills presented in each domain increase in complexity. The trajectory of learning can mapped out at every grade level and across all the mathematical domains.

TABLE 8.3 Counting and Cardinality

Kindergarten	• Know number names and the count sequence. • Count to tell the number of objects. • Compare numbers.
Grade 1	(This domain ends in Kindergarten).
Grade 2	(This domain ends in Kindergarten).
Grade 3	(This domain ends in Kindergarten).

TABLE 8.4 Operations and Algebraic Thinking

Kindergarten	• Understand addition as putting together and adding to, and understand subtraction as taking apart and taking from.
Grade 1	• Represent and solve problems involving addition and subtraction. • Understand and apply properties of operations and the relationship between addition and subtraction. • Add and subtract within 20. • Work with addition and subtraction equations.
Grade 2	• Represent and solve problems involving addition and subtraction. • Add and subtract within 20. • Works with equal groups of objects to gain foundations for multiplication.
Grade 3	• Represent and solve problems involving multiplication and division. • Understand properties of multiplication and the relationship between multiplication and division. • Multiply and divide within 100. • Solve problems involving the four operations, and identify and explain patterns in arithmetic.

TABLE 8.5 Number and Operations in Base Ten

Kindergarten	• Work with numbers 11–19 to gain foundations for place value.
Grade 1	• Extend the counting sequence. • Understand place value. • Use place value understanding and properties of operations to add and subtract.
Grade 2	• Understand place value. • Use place value understanding and properties of operations to add and subtract.
Grade 3	• Use place value understanding and properties of operations to perform multi-digit arithmetic.

TABLE 8.6 Number and Operations—Fractions

Kindergarten	(Domain begins in Grade 3.)
Grade 1	(Domain begins in Grade 3.)
Grade 2	(Domain begins in Grade 3.)
Grade 3	• Develop understanding of fractions as numbers.

TABLE 8.7 Measurement and Data

Kindergarten	• Describe and compare measurable attributes. • Classify objects and count the number of objects in categories.
Grade 1	• Measure lengths indirectly and by iterating length units. • Tell and write time. • Represent and interpret data.
Grade 2	• Measure and estimate lengths in standard units. • Relate addition and subtraction to length. • Work with time and money. • Represent and interpret data.
Grade 3	• Solve problems involving measurement and estimation of intervals of time, liquid volumes, and masses of objects. • Represent and interpret data. • Geometric measurement: understand concepts of area and relate area to multiplication and to addition. • Geometric measurement: recognize perimeter as an attribute of plane figures and distinguish between linear and area measures.

TABLE 8.8 Geometry

Kindergarten	• Identify and describe shapes. • Analyze, compare, create, and compose shapes.
Grade 1	• Reason with shapes and their attributes.
Grade 2	• Reason with shapes and their attributes.
Grade 3	• Reason with shapes and their attributes.

Using the Mathematical Content Standards

The standards for each grade level begin with an introductory statement that highlights the most significant content to be taught and mastered during that year. Although the standards at each grade level include domains and content standards beyond those designated as the most significant, skills singled out in the introductory statement are clearly presented as the teacher's main priority.

At each grade level, the introductory page is followed by an overview page that provides a quick snapshot of the domains and clusters specified for that grade. The overview page is followed by the detailed grade-specific standards grouped into clusters.

The mathematics content standards were informed by research on the learning progressions through which children develop mathematical knowledge, skills, and understanding over time (CCSS-M, p. 4). The table below illustrates the broad, general learning progressions that comprise the mathematics standards in the primary grades.

TABLE 8.9 CCSS-M Learning Progressions for Each Domain

Learning Progressions for Each Domain of the Standards for Mathematical Content, Grades K–3				
Mathematical Domains	Kindergarten	Grade 1	Grade 2	Grade 3
Counting & Cardinality (CC)	✓			
Operations & Algebraic Thinking (OA)	✓	✓	✓	✓
Number & Operations in Base Ten (NBT)	✓	✓	✓	✓
Number & Operations in Fractions (NF)				✓
Measurement and Data (MD)	✓	✓	✓	✓
Geometry (G)	✓	✓	✓	✓

Realistic?

The Common Core State Standards for each grade level document the specific knowledge and skills every student is expected to attain by the end of the academic year in that grade level. Although it is possible that every kindergartner achieved mastery of counting and cardinality by June, my experience as a K–2 teacher indicates that a fair number of typically developing young children arrive at school at the start of first grade without complete mastery of counting and cardinality.

The Learning Progressions table seems to suggest that once a student completes kindergarten there is no turning back: Counting and cardinality is gone. Of course, that is definitely not the case. Students who don't conserve number consistently might not be ready to tackle some of the more complex mathematical calculations required by the first grade standards. Although you probably won't find counting and cardinality activities in a CCSS-aligned first grade math textbook, there are many other ways to provide students with the experiences they need to get themselves back on track and to catch up to their classmates.

As teachers, we are responsible for building bridges that connect the children we teach to the curriculum for our grade level. We aim to ensure that every one of our students is learning every day, and we are willing to do whatever is necessary to make that happen. If some first graders need to go back and review kindergarten mathematics content in order to be successful with the first grade curriculum, we go back and reteach kindergarten math content to those children. The students' needs—not the content standards' demands—are always the first priority of early childhood teachers.

Overview of the Standards for Mathematical Content, Grades K–3

An overview of the Standards for Mathematical Content is presented below, organized by domain. The standards within each domain are sequenced by grade level to show the student learning trajectories within the domain. Each individual mathematical content standard is typically followed by a cluster of substandards essential to students' full understanding of the main standard. For a comprehensive presentation of the standards and substandards in each mathematical domain for grades K–3, please see Chapters 12–15. (All standards cited below have been taken verbatim from the CCSS-M document.)

TABLE 8.10 Domain: Counting and Cardinality

Kindergarten	• Know number names and the count sequence. • Count to tell the number of objects. • Compare numbers.
Grade 1	(This domain ends in Kindergarten).
Grade 2	(This domain ends in Kindergarten).
Grade 3	(This domain ends in Kindergarten).

TABLE 8.11 Domain: Operations and Algebraic Thinking

Kindergarten	• Understand addition as putting together and adding to, and understand subtraction as taking apart and taking from.
Grade 1	• Represent and solve problems involving addition and subtraction. • Understand and apply properties of operations and the relationship between addition and subtraction. • Add and subtract within 20. • Work with addition and subtraction equations.
Grade 2	• Represent and solve problems involving addition and subtraction. • Add and subtract within 20. • Work with equal groups of objects to gain foundations for multiplication.
Grade 3	• Represent and solve problems involving multiplication and division. • Understand properties of multiplication and the relationship between multiplication and division. • Multiply and divide within 100. • Solve problems involving the four operations, and identify and explain patterns in arithmetic.

TABLE 8.12 Domain: Number and Operations in Base Ten

Kindergarten	• Work with numbers 11–19 to gain foundations for place value.
Grade 1	• Extend the counting sequence. • Understand place value. • Use place value understanding and properties of operations to add and subtract.
Grade 2	• Understand place value. • Use place value understanding and properties of operations to add and subtract.
Grade 3	• Use place value understanding and properties of operations to perform multi-digit arithmetic.

TABLE 8.13 Domain: Number and Operations—Fractions

Kindergarten	(Domain begins in Grade 3.)
Grade 1	(Domain begins in Grade 3.)
Grade 2	(Domain begins in Grade 3.)
Grade 3	• Develop understanding of fractions as numbers.

TABLE 8.14 Domain: Measurement and Data

Kindergarten	• Describe and compare measurable attributes. • Classify objects and count the number of objects in categories.
Grade 1	• Measure lengths indirectly and by iterating length units. • Tell and write time. • Represent and interpret data.
Grade 2	• Measure and estimate lengths in standard units. • Relate addition and subtraction to length. • Work with time and money. • Represent and interpret data.
Grade 3	• Solve problems involving measurement and estimation of intervals of time, liquid volumes, and masses of objects. • Represent and interpret data. • Geometric measurement: understand concepts of area and relate area to multiplication and to addition. • Geometric measurement: recognize perimeter as an attribute of plane figures and distinguish between linear and area measures.

TABLE 8.15 Domain: Geometry

Kindergarten	• Identify and describe shapes. • Analyze, compare, create, and compose shapes.
Grade 1	• Reason with shapes and their attributes.
Grade 2	• Reason with shapes and their attributes.
Grade 3	• Reason with shapes and their attributes.

As you may have noticed, some of the standards for mathematical content—"reason with shapes and their attributes" or "represent and interpret data," for example—reappear in multiple grade levels. Although the standard itself is repeated, the specific academic knowledge and skills associated with that standard, which are called "clusters" in the CCSS-M document, increase in complexity and sophistication across the grade levels. The clusters associated with each standard are presented in Part IV of this book: Implementing the Common Core State Standards in Early Childhood Settings, Grade by Grade.

The Standards for Mathematical Practice

The Standards for Mathematical Practice (SMP), which are described in great detail on pages 6–8 of the CCSS-M document, are listed below. In all likelihood, the descriptions of each element of the SMP will feel familiar: The SMP seem like a mathematics-centered interpretation of the student dispositions, behaviors, and attitudes early that childhood educators typically refer to as the child's approaches to learning. *Approaches to learning* is a broad term that aims to capture the ways in which a child enters an environment; engages with new materials, activities, or experiences; develops relationships with others; gets his needs met; and so on. Knowing students' approaches to learning allows teachers to customize the activities and learning opportunities they present to their class.

The SMP are intended to help students develop three types of traits that will help them become successful mathematics thinkers, learners, and users: mathematical imagination, determination, and positivity. *Mathematical imagination* allows a child to notice interesting mathematical puzzles and questions in the course of her daily life, keeps her wondering about the puzzles and questions even after a few days, and pushes her to sit down and try to figure out the answers. *Determination* is what keeps her at the kitchen table until bedtime, focused on drawing diagrams and making computations. And *positivity*—confidence in her ability to find a solution if she keeps working at it, even if it means making a lot of mistakes or having to ask someone for help—plays a large role in reaching a successful outcome.

TABLE 8.16 Traits of Successful Mathematics Learners

Imagination	Determination	Positivity
Curiosity	Persistence	Self-confidence
Creativity	Stamina	Optimism
Openness	Focus	Initiative
Flexibility	Grit	Growth mindset
Invention	Effort	Self-awareness
Motivation	Self-regulation	Willingness to make mistakes

I'm pleased the authors of the CCSS-M acknowledge the importance of affect, confidence, and self-efficacy in learning new knowledge and skills. This is a big step toward more age-appropriate, child-friendly, and meaningful mathematics learning experiences for our students.

The Standards for Mathematical Practice are presented below. (They are also listed on each grade level's overview page in the Standards for Mathematical Content as a reminder of the interconnection of the two sets of standards.) I've provided an early-childhood interpretation of each practice standard.

Common Core State Standards-Mathematics Standards for Mathematical Practice

1. Make Sense of Problems and Persevere in Solving Them

This practice standard emphasizes the importance of developing young children's metacognitive awareness and encourages teachers to help their students engage thoughtfully in mathematical problem solving. Mathematically proficient students pay attention as they work, and "continually ask themselves, 'Does this make sense?'" (CCSS-M, p. 6). When the answer to that question is "no," mathematically proficient students will go back through their work, look for the error that got them off track, and then continue moving forward. Providing access to interesting, engaging, open-ended mathematics activities—for enrichment, extension, or just for fun—is a great way to keep students' minds continually engaged with math content and mathematical thinking.

2. Reason Abstractly and Quantitatively

When students are working on mathematics exercises, they must attend to and think about the meaning of what they are doing. Quantitative reasoning requires learners to construct a coherent representation of the problem in their mind and ensure that their solution makes sense.

Here is an example of a student developing her proficiency with this practice standard. When I was teaching second grade, I gave my students this word problem:

Seven children are going on a field trip to a farm. A minivan can seat five children. How many minivans will be needed to get all the children to the farm?

Heather, one of my strongest math students, gave this answer: 1 ⅖

In a way, Heather was thinking along the right lines: one minivan would have 5 children in it and the other would have 2 children in it. However, it's very hard to drive ⅖ of a minivan! The correct answer would have to be "two minivans." Heather focused on the mathematical calculation, but forgot to consider the real-world context within which the problem was framed.

3. Construct Viable Arguments and Critique the Reasoning of Others

Initially, this practice standard sounds like a poor fit for a preK–3 classroom: We work assiduously to rein in and redirect young students who argue and criticize their peers' ideas. However, a close read of the standard clarifies its intent. This mathematical practice standard revisits the emphasis on metacognition introduced in Standard One. The goals, at least in a preschool or primary grade classroom, would be that students will be able to (a) explain both how they solved a mathematical problem and how they know they arrived at the correct answer; (b) recognize and explain errors identified in other students' work; and (c) ask useful questions that can help clarify and improve everyone's understanding of the problem, procedure, and solution.

This mathematical practice standard also encourages teachers to create opportunities for children to have substantive conversations about mathematics using accurate mathematical terminology—for example, a student who explained that he plussed 24 and 5 and got 29 would be assisted in restating his procedure using the word "added."

4. Model With Mathematics

Modeling with mathematics involves students applying mathematics to real world problems and communicating with others about their reasoning, procedures, and solutions to the problems under consideration. In addition, modeling with mathematics engages young students in the use of manipulatives, drawings, tables, charts, or role-play as a way to make their thinking visible and to communicate with peers about mathematical processes.

5. Use Appropriate Tools Strategically

Like modeling with mathematics, this practice standard encourages young children to use appropriate tools—paper and pencil; counting bears; a digital camera; base ten blocks; a personal whiteboard; a calculator; the smart board; a ruler, yardstick, or tape measure; a document camera; handmade charts or tables—to help them solve mathematical problems, make their thinking visible to their peers, and prompt discussions about mathematical problem solving. Students will have additional tools at their disposal as they mature; their use of these tools will feel more natural because they are already accustomed to using tools for mathematical purposes.

6. Attend to Precision

Although young children may have age-appropriate difficulty with certain types of precision—measurement, writing numbers in neat alignment on blank paper, counting a large quantity of small objects—there are other types of mathematical precision that are attainable by students in grades preK–3. They can learn to use precise mathematical language, such as "greater than" and "minus" rather than "bigger than" and "take away," consistently. Young children can learn to specify units of measure and to label charts, tables, and diagrams to make them clearer and easier for others to understand. And they can learn to calculate accurately and efficiently, and to check their work.

7. Look for and Make Use of Structure

Helping young children look for, identify, and recognize mathematical patterns and structures can easily begin in prekindergarten classrooms: Hang up a 100s chart and ask a small group what they notice about the numbers on the chart. The rhythm and repetition in each row and column will catch the eye of students who are able to recognize and identify numerals. Likewise, give young children "treasure boxes" that contain multiple examples of a single type of object—one box might have a variety of international coins, another could have assorted buttons, mixed sea shells or bottle caps, a third box could contain nuts and bolts of different sizes—that are similar in some ways and different in other ways. These boxes offer students opportunities to identify the relevant attributes of the materials in each box and to sort and categorize the items using various attributes and to create patterns of their own.

8. Look for and Express Regularity in Repeated Reasoning

Young children often have difficulty shifting perspective: Either they look at the problem with a bird's eye view and ignore the details or focus tightly on the details and lose the big picture. This practice standard presses teachers to encourage students "to maintain oversight of the process while attending to the details" (CCSS-M, p. 8). Along similar lines—especially as the numbers utilized in math problems increase in size as they move up toward third grade—children should be reminded to step back and evaluate whether or not their solutions to mathematics problems appear reasonable. One or two zeroes carelessly omitted or accidentally included in a calculation can have a significant impact on a student's solution.

Tips for Working With the CCSS-Math Standards

1. Get to Know the Language Used by the CCSS-M Authors

Some of the language used in the CCSS-M may feel unfamiliar. For example, the CCSS-M specifies that, by the end of third grade, students should be able to "recognize perimeter as an attribute of plane figures" and to "distinguish between linear and area measures." Most third grade teachers are very comfortable teaching concepts from geometric measurement such as perimeter and area, but may be uncertain about the intentions and expectations laid out in the standards document due to the unfamiliar terminology. Reading the substandards listed beneath the grade level standards may also provide helpful details.

2. Mathematics Instruction Should Be Informed by Both the Standards for Mathematical Practice and the Standards for Mathematical Content

The CCSS-M were designed to ensure that all students would successfully master the skills necessary to solve a range of mathematical problems and to understand not only the processes and procedures they are using but also why and how those processes and procedures work. The authors of the CCSS-M indicate that all the expectations in the Standards for Mathematical Content that "begin with the word 'understand' are especially good opportunities to connect the practices to the content" (CCSS-M, p. 8).

3. The Grade Level Content Standards Do Not Need To Be Covered in a Particular Sequence

The content and concepts presented in the CCSS-M for a given grade level are meant to be revisited and explored in greater depth throughout the year. Teachers are expected to move around within the grade-level practice and content standards to balance the introduction of new material with the review (and, perhaps, intensification) of material covered earlier.

4. The Standards for Each Grade Level Were Designed to Comprise 85% of the Mathematics Curriculum for Each Grade

This wiggle room provides opportunities for teachers to adjust the pace of instruction and revisit skills that need reinforcement while covering all the curriculum content within the prescribed amount of time.

5. The CCSS-M for Each Grade Present the Knowledge and Skills Students Should Master by the End of the Academic Year

Our knowledge of young children's development teaches us that students learn and grow at different rates. And the age of the students in a classroom impacts the developmental variance: Younger children's capabilities generally vary more widely than would be found among a class of older students. First graders who were not developmentally ready for double digit addition and subtraction in November of the academic year are likely to have stronger cognitive and self-regulation skills in April of the academic year and might be able to engage with double digit addition and subtraction with greater success at this point in time.

References

How to read the Common Core State Standards for Mathematics. (n.d.) Retrieved from http://ped.state.nm.us/ped/CCDocuments/CCSSO_Quick_Guide_to_Standards.pdf

National Governors Association Center for Best Practices, Council of Chief State School Officers. (2010). *Common Core State Standards for mathematics.* Washington, DC: National Governors Association Center for Best Practices, Council of Chief State School Officers.

White, J., & Dauksas, L. (2012). CCSSM: Getting started in K–Grade 2. *Teaching Children Mathematics, 1* (7), 440–445.

9

UNDERSTANDING THE CCSS-ENGLISH LANGUAGE ARTS AND LITERACY IN SOCIAL STUDIES, SCIENCE, AND TECHNICAL SUBJECTS STANDARDS DOCUMENT

The Common Core State Standards are intended to ensure all U.S. students will complete high school "college and career ready." So, before the CCSS-ELA standards-writing team could begin developing the Common Core State Standards for English Language Arts and Literacy, they first had to develop a set of College and Career Readiness (CCR) standards. The CCR document—focused tightly on reading, writing, speaking, listening, and language—includes 32 traits that characterize someone who is ready for college and/or a career.

In addition to describing the student learning outcomes for K–12 education under the Common Core, the 32 CCR standards also serve as the **anchor standards** that frame and organize the CCSS-ELA. The 32 CCR standards are grouped into four English Language Arts strands:

> Reading = 10 anchor standards (plus Foundational Skills in grades K–5)
> Writing = 10 anchor standards
> Speaking and Listening = 6 anchor standards
> Language = 6 anchor standards

Within each strand, the same anchor standards are used for every grade level from kindergarten through Grade 12. At each grade level, however, the anchor standards are interpreted and framed in ways that are age-appropriate, challenging, and achievable for children in that grade.

Quick Start: Using the CCSS-ELA Document

Each domain of the CCSS-ELA—Reading, Writing, Speaking and Listening, and Language—begins with a list of the CCR Anchor Standards for that domain. Typically, several anchor standards are clustered together under a common heading; these same headings are used to organize the content standards in that section.

Individual CCR anchor standards are identified by their strand (Reading, Writing, Speaking and Listening, or Language), CCR status, and number. Three CCR anchor standards are presented in the graphic below:

> **R.CCR.1** (Reading, College and Career Ready Standard 1) = Read closely to determine what the text says explicitly and to make inferences from it; cite specific textual evidence when writing or speaking to support conclusions drawn from the text.
>
> **R.CCR.2** (Reading, College and Career Ready Standard 2) = Determine central ideas of themes of a text and analyze their development; summarize the key supporting details and ideas.
>
> **R.CCR.3** (Reading, College and Career Ready Standard 3) = Analyze how and why individuals, events and ideas develop and interact over the course of a text.

Individual grade-specific content standards are identified by their strand, grade, and number (or number and letter, where applicable): RL.1.1, as seen in the example below, stands for Reading Literature (strand), grade 1 (grade), standard (number) 1.

> **RL.1.1** (Reading Literature, Grade 1, Standard 1) = Ask and answer questions about key details in a text.
>
> **RL.1.2** (Reading Literature, Grade 1, Standard 2) = Retell stories, including key details, and demonstrate understanding of their central message or lesson.
>
> **RL.1.3** (Reading Literature, Grade 1, Standard 3) = Describe characters, settings, and major events in a story, using key details.

Figure 9.1 presents three CCR anchor standards (left) and the three Reading Literature content standards for Grade 1 linked directly to those three CCR anchor standards (right).

The four Reading strands (plus Foundational Skills) are presented in the following sections (*How to read the Common Core State Standards for English Language Arts*, n.d.).

The presentation of each strand follows the same structure:

- Strand title
- Anchor standards for the strand
- Theme of the strand
- Key features of the strand
- Comprehensive skills trajectory (K–3) for all the standards in the strand

English Language Arts Standards » Anchor Standards » College and Career Readiness Anchor Standards for Reading

The K–5 standards on the following pages define what students should understand and be able to do by the end of each grade. They correspond to the College and Career Readiness (CCR) anchor standards below by number. The CCR and grade-specific standards are necessary complements—the former providing broad standards, the latter providing additional specificity—that together define the skills and understandings that all students must demonstrate.

Key Ideas and Details

1. Read closely to determine what the text says explicitly and to make logical inferences from it; cite specific textual evidence when writing or speaking to support conclusions drawn from the text.
2. Determine central ideas or themes of a text and analyze their development; summarize the key supporting details and ideas.
3. Analyze how and why individuals, events, and ideas develop and interact over the course of a text.

English Language Arts Standards » Reading: Literature » Grade 1

Standards in this strand:

| RL.1.1 | RL.1.2 | RL.1.3 | RL.1.4 | RL.1.5 | RL.1.6 | RL.1.7 | RL.1.8 | RL.1.9 | RL.1.10 |

Key Ideas and Details

RL.1.1. Ask and answer questions about key details in a text.

RL.1.2. Retell stories, including key details, and demonstrate understanding of their central message or lesson.

RL.1.3. Describe characters, settings, and major events in a story, using key details.

THESE ARE THOSE CCR ANCHOR STANDARDS INTERPRETED FOR USE IN GRADE 1

THESE ARE THE CCR ANCHOR STANDARDS

FIGURE 9.1 Guide to reading the CCSS-ELA document

The CCSS-English Language Arts Skills Trajectory tables document the expectations for each standard and highlight the pace at which the complexity and cognitive demand of the standards increase over time as children move from kindergarten to Grade 3. (All of the content standards are reproduced verbatim from the CCSS-ELA document.)

CCSS-ELA STRAND: Reading

Anchor Standards for Reading

Key Ideas and Details

1. Read closely to determine what the text says explicitly and to make logical inferences from the text; cite specific textual evidence when writing or speaking to support conclusions drawn from the text.
2. Determine central ideas of themes of a text and analyze their development; summarize the key supporting details and ideas.
3. Analyze how and why individuals, events, and ideas develop and interact over the course of a text.

Craft and Structure

4. Interpret words and phrases as they are used in a text, including determining technical and connotative and figurative meanings, and analyze how specific word choices shape meaning or tone.
5. Analyze the structure of texts, including how specific sentences, paragraphs, and larger portions of the text (e.g., a section, chapter, scene, or stanza) relate to each other and the whole.
6. Assess how point of view or purpose shapes the content and style of a text.

Integration of Knowledge and Ideas

7. Integrate and evaluate content presented in diverse media and formats, including visually and quantitatively, as well as in words.
8. Delineate and evaluate the argument and specific claims in a text, including the validity of the reasoning as well as the relevance and sufficiency of the evidence.
9. Analyze how two or more texts address similar themes or topics in order to build knowledge or to compare the approaches the authors take.

Range of Reading and Level of Text Complexity

10. Read and comprehend complex literary and informational texts independently and proficiently.

Reading's Theme: Text Complexity and the Growth of Comprehension

The CCSS-ELA reading standards balance attention to the sophistication and complexity of the students' reading material and to the skill with which they read these texts. Students should be reading, listening to, and interpreting both literary and informational text beginning in kindergarten. As they mature, students will be expected to demonstrate increased capacity for delving deeply into text and for using texts more fully.

In preschool and the primary grades, teachers are expected to establish a strong foundation for their students' future success with complex reading behaviors such as making connections within texts and between texts, noticing similarities in the ideas or characteristics of different texts, looking for textual evidence to support their own opinions, and recognizing inconsistencies or ambiguities in texts.

Although the youngest students are likely to make text-to-self connections, the CCSS-ELA downplays the value of this type of response. Rather, the CCSS-ELA emphasizes the importance of relying on the text itself—such as going back into the text to find evidence to support or refute an opinion—and on the value of comparing one text to another.

FIGURE 9.2

Key Features of the Reading Strand

- Equal emphasis is placed on the complexity of what students read and on how well they read it.
- Students must glean more meaning and make fuller use of the text they read, including
    - Making an increasing number of connections among ideas in the text
    - Making an increasing number of connections between texts
    - Considering a wider range of textual evidence
    - Becoming more aware of inconsistencies and poor reasoning in texts
- In grades K–5, the reading standards are organized into three strands:
    - Reading: Literature
    - Reading: Informational Text
    - Reading: Foundational Skills

At each grade level, the Reading: Literature and Reading: Informational Text standards are aligned to the same set of CCR Anchor Standards and are organized under the same headings used in the anchor standards.

English Language Arts Skills Trajectories, Grades K–3

Reading Skill Trajectories for Literature and Informational Text

Anchor Standard 1. Read closely to determine what the text says explicitly and to make logical inferences from the text; cite specific textual evidence when writing or speaking to support conclusions drawn from the text.

How does this standard look in the Reading Standards for Literature from Kindergarten to Grade 3?	
Kindergarten	With prompting and support, ask and answer questions about key details in a text.
Grade 1	Ask and answer questions about key details in a text.
Grade 2	Ask and answer such questions as *who, what, where, when, why,* and *how* to demonstrate understanding of key details in a text
Grade 3	Ask and answer questions to demonstrate understanding of a text, referring explicitly to the text as the basis for the answers.

How does this standard look in the Reading Standards for Informational Text from Kindergarten to Grade 3?	
Kindergarten	With prompting and support, ask and answer questions about key details in a text.
Grade 1	Ask and answer questions about key details in a text.
Grade 2	Ask and answer such questions as *who, what, where, when, why,* and *how* to demonstrate understanding of key details in a text
Grade 3	Ask and answer questions to demonstrate understanding of a text, referring explicitly to the text as the basis for the answers.

Anchor Standard 2. Determine central ideas of themes of a text and analyze their development; summarize the key supporting details and ideas.

How does this standard look in the Reading Standards for Literature from Kindergarten to Grade 3?	
Kindergarten	With prompting and support, retell familiar stories, including key details.
Grade 1	Retell stories, including key details, and demonstrate understanding of their central message or lesson.
Grade 2	Recount stories, including fables and folktales from diverse cultures, and determine their central message, lesson, or moral.
Grade 3	Recount stories, including fables, folktales, and myths from diverse cultures; determine their central message, lesson, or moral, and explain how it is conveyed through key details in the text.

How does this standard look in the Reading Standards for Informational Text from Kindergarten to Grade 3?	
Kindergarten	With prompting and support, identify the main topic and retell key details of a text.
Grade 1	Identify the main topic and retell key details of a text.
Grade 2	Identify the main topic of a multiparagraph text as well as the focus of the specific paragraphs within the text.
Grade 3	Determine the main idea of a text; recount the key details and explain how they support the main idea.

Anchor Standard 3. Analyze how and why individuals, events, and ideas develop and interact over the course of a text.

How does this standard look in the Reading Standards for Literature from Kindergarten to Grade 3?	
Kindergarten	With prompting and support, identify characters, settings, and major events in a story.
Grade 1	Describe characters, settings, and major events in a story, using key details.
Grade 2	Describe how characters in a story respond to major events and challenges.
Grade 3	Describe characters in a story (e.g., their traits, motivations, or feelings) and explain how their actions contribute to the sequence of events.

How does this standard look in the Reading Standards for Informational Text from Kindergarten to Grade 3?	
Kindergarten	With prompting and support, describe the connection between two individuals, events, ideas, or pieces of information in a text.
Grade 1	Describe the connection between two individuals, events, ideas, or pieces of information in a text.
Grade 2	Describe the connection between a series of historical events, scientific ideas or concepts, or steps in technical procedures in a text.
Grade 3	Describe the connection between a series of historical events, scientific ideas or concepts, or steps in technical procedures in a text, using language that pertains to time, sequence, and cause/effect.

Anchor Standard 4. Interpret words and phrases as they are used in a text, including determining technical and connotative and figurative meanings, and analyze how specific word choices shape meaning or tone.

How does this standard look in the Reading Standards for _Literature_ from Kindergarten to Grade 3?	
Kindergarten	Ask and answer questions about unknown words in a text.
Grade 1	Identify words and phrases in stories or poems that suggest feelings or appeal to the senses.
Grade 2	Describe how words and phrases (i.e., regular beats, alliteration, rhymes, repeated lines) supply rhythm and meaning in a story, poem, or song.
Grade 3	Determine the meaning of words and phrases as they are used in a text, distinguishing literal from non-literal language.

How does this standard look in the Reading Standards for _Informational Text_ from Kindergarten to Grade 3?	
Kindergarten	With prompting and support, ask and answer questions about unknown words in a text.
Grade 1	Ask and answer questions to help determine or clarify the meaning of words and phrases in a text.
Grade 2	Determine the meaning of words and phrases in a text relevant to _a grade 2 topic or subject area._
Grade 3	Determine the meaning of general academic and domain-specific words and phrases in a text relevant to a _grade 3 topic or subject area._

Anchor Standard 5. Analyze the structure of texts, including how specific sentences, paragraphs, and larger portions of the text (e.g., a section, chapter, scene, or stanza) relate to each other and the whole.

How does this standard look in the Reading Standards for _Literature_ from Kindergarten to Grade 3?	
Kindergarten	Recognize common types of texts (e.g., storybooks, poems).
Grade 1	Explain major differences between books that tell stories and books that give information, drawing on a wide reading of a range of text types.
Grade 2	Describe the overall structure of a story, including describing how the beginning introduces the story and the ending concludes the action.
Grade 3	Refer to parts of stories, dramas, and poems when writing or speaking about a text, using terms such as chapter, scene, and stanza; describe how each successive part builds on earlier sections.

How does this standard look in the Reading Standards for Informational Text from Kindergarten to Grade 3?	
Kindergarten	Identify the front cover, back cover, and title pages of a book.
Grade 1	Know and use various text features (e.g., headings, tables of contents, glossaries, electronic menus, icons) to locate key facts or information in a text.
Grade 2	Know and use various text features (e.g., captions, bold print, subheadings, glossaries, indexes, electronic menus, icons) to locate key facts or information in a text efficiently.
Grade 3	Use text features and search tools (e.g., key words, sidebars, hyperlinks) to locate information relevant to a given topic efficiently.

Anchor Standard 6. Assess how point of view or purpose shapes the content and style of a text.

How does this standard look in the Reading Standards for Literature from Kindergarten to Grade 3?	
Kindergarten	With prompting and support, name the author and illustrator of a story and define the role of each in telling the story.
Grade 1	Identify who is telling the story at various points in the text.
Grade 2	Acknowledge differences in the points of view of characters, including by speaking in a different voice for each character when reading a dialogue aloud.
Grade 3	Distinguish their own point of view from that of the narrator or those of the characters.

How does this standard look in the Reading Standards for Informational Text from Kindergarten to Grade 3?	
Kindergarten	Name the author and illustrator of a text and define the role of each in presenting the ideas or information in a text.
Grade 1	Distinguish between information provided by pictures or other illustrations and information provided by the words in a text.
Grade 2	Identify the main purpose of a text, including what the author wants to answer, explain, or describe.
Grade 3	Distinguish their own point of view from that of the author of a text.

Anchor Standard 7. Integrate and evaluate content presented in diverse media and formats, including visually and quantitatively, as well as in words.

How does this standard look in the Reading Standards for *Literature* from Kindergarten to Grade 3?	
Kindergarten	With prompting and support, describe the relationship between illustrations and the story in which they appear (e.g., what moment in a story an illustration depicts).
Grade 1	Use illustrations and details in a story to describe its characters, setting, or events.
Grade 2	Use information gained from the illustrations and words in a print or digital text to demonstrate understanding of its characters, setting, or plot.
Grade 3	Explain how specific aspects of a text's illustrations contribute to what is conveyed by the words in a story (e.g., create mood, emphasize aspects of a character or setting.

How does this standard look in the Reading Standards for *Informational Text* from Kindergarten to Grade 3?	
Kindergarten	With prompting and support, describe the relationship between illustrations and the story in which they appear (e.g., what person, place, thing, or idea in the text an illustration depicts).
Grade 1	Use the illustrations and details in a text to describe its key ideas.
Grade 2	Explain how specific images (e.g., a diagram showing how a machine works) contribute to and clarify a text.
Grade 3	Use information gained from illustrations (e.g., maps, photographs) and the words in a text to demonstrate understanding of the text (e.g., where, when, why, and how key events occur).

Anchor Standard 8. Delineate and evaluate the argument and specific claims in a text, including the validity of the reasoning as well as the relevance and sufficiency of the evidence.

How does this standard look in the Reading Standards for *Literature* from Kindergarten to Grade 3?
This anchor standard is not applicable to literature.

How does this standard look in the Reading Standards for *Informational Text* from Kindergarten to Grade 3?	
Kindergarten	With prompting and support, identify the reasons an author gives to support points in a text.
Grade 1	Identify the reasons an author gives to support points in a text.
Grade 2	Describe how reasons support specific points the author makes in a text.
Grade 3	Describe the logical connection between particular sentences and paragraphs in a text (e.g., comparison, cause/effect, first/second/third in a sequence).

Anchor Standard 9. Analyze how two or more texts address similar themes or topics in order to build knowledge or to compare the approaches the authors take.

How does this standard look in the Reading Standards for *Literature* from Kindergarten to Grade 3?	
Kindergarten	With prompting and support, compare and contrast the adventures and experiences of characters in familiar stories.
Grade 1	Compare and contrast the adventures and experiences of characters in stories.
Grade 2	Compare and contrast two or more versions of the same story (e.g., Cinderella stories) by different authors or from different cultures.
Grade 3	Compare and contrast the themes, settings, and plots of stories written by the same author about the same or similar characters (e.g., in books from a series).

How does this standard look in the Reading Standards for *Informational Text* from Kindergarten to Grade 3?	
Kindergarten	With prompting and support, identify basic similarities in and differences between two texts on the same topic (e.g., in illustrations, descriptions, or procedures).
Grade 1	Identify basic similarities in and differences between two texts on the same topic (e.g., in illustrations, descriptions, or procedures).
Grade 2	Compare and contrast the most important points presented by two texts on the same topic.
Grade 3	Compare and contrast the most important points and key details presented in two texts on the same topic.

Anchor Standard 10. Read and comprehend complex literary and informational texts independently and proficiently.

How does this standard look in the Reading Standards for Literature from Kindergarten to Grade 3?	
Kindergarten	Actively engage in group reading activities with purpose and understanding.
Grade 1	With prompting and support, read prose and poetry of appropriate complexity for grade 1.
Grade 2	By the end of the year, read and comprehend literature, including stories and poetry, in the grades 2–3 text complexity band proficiently, with scaffolding as needed at the high end of the range.
Grade 3	By the end of the year, read and comprehend literature, including stories, dramas, and poetry, at the high end of the grades 2–3 text complexity band independently and proficiently.

How does this standard look in the Reading Standards for Informational Text from Kindergarten to Grade 3?	
Kindergarten	Actively engage in group reading activities with purpose and understanding.
Grade 1	With prompting and support, read informational texts appropriately complex for grade 1.
Grade 2	By the end of the year, read and comprehend informational texts, including history/social studies, science, and technical texts, in the grades 2–3 text complexity band proficiently, with scaffolding as needed at the high end of the range.
Grade 3	By the end of the year, read and comprehend informational texts, including history/social studies, science, and technical texts, at the high end of the grades 2–3 text complexity band independently and proficiently.

Reading Standards for Foundational Skills

The competencies presented in Reading: Foundational Skills, a strand only for students in Grades K–5, are not aligned with the CCR Anchor Standards. These standards are included in the Reading domain to ensure that young students develop a thorough understanding and working knowledge of concepts of print, the alphabetic principle, and other basic elements and conventions of English reading and writing.

Reading Skill Trajectories for Foundational Skills

1. Print Concepts: Demonstrate understanding of the organization and basic features of print.	
Kindergarten	a. Follow words from left to right, top to bottom, and page by page. b. Recognize that spoken words are represented in written language by specific sequences of letters. c. Understand that words are separated by spaces in print. d. Recognize and name all upper- and lowercase letters of the alphabet.
Grade 1	a. Recognize the distinguishing features of a sentence (e.g., first word, capitalization, ending punctuation).
Grade 2	(Stops with Grade 1)
Grade 3	(Stops with Grade 1)

2. Phonological Awareness: Demonstrate understanding of spoken words, syllables, and sounds.	
Kindergarten	a. Recognize and produce rhyming words. b. Count, pronounce, blend, and segment syllables in spoken words. c. Blend and segment onsets and rimes of single syllable spoken words. d. Isolate and pronounce the initial, medial vowel, and final sounds (phonemes) in three-phoneme (consonant-vowel-consonant or CVC words). (This does not include CVCs ending with /l/, /r/, or /x/.) e. Add or substitute individual sounds (phonemes) in simple, one-syllable words to make new words.
Grade 1	a. Distinguish long from short vowel sounds in spoken single-syllable words. b. Orally produce single-syllable words by blending sounds (phonemes), including consonant blends. c. Isolate and pronounce the initial, medial vowel, and final sounds (phonemes) in spoken single-syllable words. d. Segment spoken single-syllable words into their complete sequence of individual sounds (phonemes).
Grade 2	(Stops with Grade 1)
Grade 3	(Stops with Grade 1)

3. Phonics and Word Recognition: Know and apply grade-level phonics and word analysis skills in decoding words.

Kindergarten	a. Demonstrate basic knowledge of one-to-one letter-sound correspondence by producing the primary or many of the most frequent sound for each consonant b. Associate the long and short vowel sounds with common spellings (graphemes) for the five major vowels. c. Read common high-frequency words by sight (e.g., the, of, to, you, she, my, is, are, do, does). d. Distinguish between similarly spelled words by identifying the sounds of the letters that differ.
Grade 1	a. Know the spelling-sound correspondences for common consonant digraphs. b. Decode regularly spelled one-syllable words. c. Know final -e and common vowel team conventions for representing long vowel sounds. d. Use knowledge that every syllable must have a vowel sound to determine the number of syllables in a printed word. e. Decode two-syllable words following basic patterns by breaking the words into syllables. f. Read words with inflectional endings. g. Recognize and read grade-appropriate irregularly spelled words.
Grade 2	a. Distinguish long and short vowels when reading regularly spelled one-syllable words. b. Know spelling-sound correspondences for additional common vowel teams. c. Decode regularly spelled two-syllable words with long vowels. d. Decode words with common prefixes and suffixes. e. Identify words with inconsistent but common spelling-sound correspondences. f. Recognize and read grade-appropriate irregularly spelled words.
Grade 3	a. Identify and know the meaning of the most common prefixes and derivational suffixes. b. Decode words with common Latin suffixes. c. Decode multisyllable words. d. Read grade-appropriate irregularly spelled words.

4. Fluency: Read with sufficient accuracy and fluency to support comprehension.	
Kindergarten	Read emergent-reader texts with purpose and understanding.
Grade 1	a. Read on-level text with purpose and understanding. b. Read on-level text orally with accuracy, appropriate rate, and expression on successive readings. c. Use context to confirm or self-correct word recognition and understanding, rereading as necessary.
Grade 2	a. Read on-level text with purpose and understanding. b. Read on-level text orally with accuracy, appropriate rate, and expression on successive readings. c. Use context to confirm or self-correct word recognition and understanding, rereading as necessary.
Grade 3	a. Read on-level text with purpose and understanding. b. Read on-level text orally with accuracy, appropriate rate, and expression on successive readings. c. Use context to confirm or self-correct word recognition and understanding, rereading as necessary.

Tips for Working With the CCSS-ELA Reading Standards

1. Start With Your Students, Not With the Standards

If your class of second graders came to school in August and quickly made it clear that they hadn't mastered the first grade content standards, would you ignore the evidence the children provided and insist on teaching the second grade standards? Of course you wouldn't: Your job is to teach academic content to the children who are members of your second grade class; not to teach second grade academic content regardless of whether or not the children have the foundational skills they need to learn that content.

Early childhood teachers always meet their children where they are. This approach safeguards children from developing gaps in their academic skills, keeps you and the kiddos on the same page, and—in the long run—enables your students to achieve academic success at their own pace.

2. Don't Get Overwhelmed by the Amount of Content You Are Expected to Cover

The CCSS-ELA includes a lot of content: They're both deep and wide. But each standard and sub-standard don't warrant the same amount of focused attention and effort. Zero in on (a) the standards that your students are struggling to master and (b) the "power standards" that will build mental muscle. Also, remember that you have the option of using like-ability groups—either within your own classroom or in collaboration with another teacher at your grade level—so that all students will be engaging with academic content that is both challenging and achievable for them. This doesn't have to be a permanent arrangement: It just needs to last long enough for everyone to master the content that is right for them.

3. Identify the Big Themes and Be Sure to Hit Those on a Weekly Basis

You are likely to have a specific focus within your ELA program that reflects your understanding of the central curricular "push" in the grade level you are teaching. For example, first grade teachers almost always emphasize reading skill development; second grade teachers might zero in on strengthening content area vocabulary and academic language; and third grade teachers often focus on writing to begin to get students prepared for success in fourth grade. Whatever you've chosen as your curricular "push" area, keep your students engaged with and connected to that content by making it a special part of each week.

CCSS-ELA STRAND: Writing

Anchor Standards for Writing

Text Types and Purposes

1. Write arguments to support claims in an analysis of substantive topics or texts, using valid reasoning and relevant and sufficient evidence.
2. Write information/explanatory texts to examine and convey complex ideas and information clearly and accurately through the effective selection, organization, and analysis of content.
3. Write narratives to develop real or imagined experiences or events using effective technique, well-chosen details, and well-structured event sequences.

Production and Distribution of Writing

4. Produce clear and coherent writing in which the development, organization, and style are appropriate to task, purpose, and audience.
5. Develop and strengthen writing as needed by planning, revising, editing, rewriting, or trying a new approach.
6. Use technology, including the Internet, to produce and publish writing and to interact and collaborate with others.

Research to Build and Present Knowledge

7. Conduct short as well as more sustained research projects based on focused questions, demonstrating understanding of the subject under investigation.

8. Gather relevant information from multiple print and digital sources, assess the credibility and accuracy of each source, and integrate the information while avoiding plagiarism.
9. Draw evidence from literary or informational texts to support analysis, reflection, and research. (Begins in grade 4)

Range of Writing

10. Write routinely over extended time frames (time for research, reflection, and revision) and shorter time frames (a single sitting or a day or two) for a range of tasks, purposes, and audiences.

Writing's Theme: Text Types, Responding to Reading, and Research

Writing is framed in two different ways in the CCSS-ELA:

1. A set of general skills useful in many different types of writing
   - *Planning, writing, revising, editing, publishing*

2. A variety of specific writing types or genres
   - *Arguments, informative/explanatory texts, and narratives*

The writing standards emphasize the reading-writing connection by expecting that students will draw information from literary or informational texts to buttress an argument and to provide supporting evidence. And, because writing is central to most forms of inquiry, research standards are foregrounded in this strand. (Research skills are also infused throughout the CCSS-ELA.)

FIGURE 9.3

Key Features of the Writing Standards

- Students engage in writing arguments, informative/explanatory texts, and narratives.
- Students draw upon and write about evidence from literary and informational texts.
- Students plan, write, revise, edit, and publish their writing and write for research purposes.

Writing Skills Trajectories, K–3

Anchor Standard 1. Write arguments to support claims in an analysis of substantive topics or texts, using valid reasoning and relevant and sufficient evidence.

How does this look in the Writing Standards from Kindergarten to Grade 3?	
Kindergarten	Use a combination of drawing, dictating and writing to compose opinion pieces in which they tell a reader the topic or the name of the book they are writing about and state an opinion or preference about the topic or book (e.g., My favorite book is . . .).
Grade 1	Write opinion pieces in which they introduce the topic or name of the book they are writing about, state an opinion, supply a reason for the opinion, and provide some sense of closure.
Grade 2	Write opinion pieces in which they introduce the topic or book they are writing about, state an opinion, supply reasons that support the opinion using linking words (e.g., because, and, also) to connect opinion and reasons, and provide a concluding statement or section.
Grade 3	Write opinion pieces on topics or texts, supporting a point of view with reasons. (a) Introduce the topic or text they are writing about, state an opinion, and create an organizational structure that lists reasons. (b) Provide reasons that support the opinion. (c) Use linking words and phrases (e.g., because, therefore, since, for example) to connect opinion and reasons. (d) Provide a concluding statement or section.

Anchor Standard 2. Write information/explanatory texts to examine and convey complex ideas and information clearly and accurately through the effective selection, organization, and analysis of content.

How does this look in the Writing Standards from Kindergarten to Grade 3?	
Kindergarten	Use a combination of drawing, dictating, and writing to compose informative/explanatory texts in which they name what they are writing about and supply some information about the topic.
Grade 1	Write informative/explanatory texts in which they name a topic, supply some facts about the topic, and provide some sense of closure.
Grade 2	Write informative/explanatory texts in which they introduce a topic, use facts and definitions to develop points, and provide a concluding statement or section.
Grade 3	Write informative/explanatory texts to examine a topic and convey ideas and information clearly. (a) Introduce a topic and group related information together; include illustrations when useful to aiding comprehension. (b) Develop the topic with facts, definitions, and details. (c) Use linking words and phrases (e.g., also, another, and, more, but) to connect ideas within categories of information. (d) Provide a concluding statement or section.

Anchor Standard 3. Write narratives to develop real or imagined experiences or events using effective technique, well-chosen details, and well-structured event sequences.

How does this look in the Writing Standards from Kindergarten to Grade 3?	
Kindergarten	Use a combination of drawing, dictating, and writing to narrate a single event or several loosely linked events, tell about the events in the order in which they occurred, and provide a reaction to what happened.
Grade 1	Write narratives in which they recount two or more appropriately sequenced events, include some details regarding what happened, use temporal words to signal event order, and provide some sense of closure.
Grade 2	Write narratives in which they recount a well-elaborated event or short sequence of events, include details to describe actions, thoughts, and feelings, use temporal words to signal even order, and provide a sense of closure.
Grade 3	Write narratives to develop real or imagined experiences of events using effective technique, descriptive details, and clear event sequences. (a) Establish a situation and introduce a narrator and/or characters; organize an event sequence that unfolds naturally. (b) Use dialogue and descriptions of actions, thoughts, and feelings to develop experiences and events or show the response of characters to situations. (c) Use temporal words and phrases to signal event order. (d) Provide a sense of closure

Anchor Standard 4. Produce clear and coherent writing in which the development, organization, and style are appropriate to task, purpose, and audience.

How does this look in the Writing Standards from Kindergarten to Grade 3?	
Kindergarten	(Begins in grade 3)
Grade 1	(Begins in grade 3)
Grade 2	(Begins in grade 3)
Grade 3	With guidance and support from adults, produce writing in which the development and organization are appropriate to task and purpose.

Anchor Standard 5. Develop and strengthen writing as needed by planning, revising, editing, rewriting, or trying a new approach.

How does this look in the Writing Standards from Kindergarten to Grade 3?	
Kindergarten	With guidance and support from adults, respond to questions and suggestions from peers and add details to strengthen writing as needed.
Grade 1	With guidance and support from adults, focus on a topic, respond to questions and suggestions from peers, and add details to strengthen writing as needed.
Grade 2	With guidance and support from adults and peers, focus on a topic and strengthen writing as needed by revising and editing.
Grade 3	With guidance and support from peers and adults, develop and strengthen writing as needed by planning, revising, and editing.

Anchor Standard 6. Use technology, including the Internet, to produce and publish writing and to interact and collaborate with others.

How does this look in the Writing Standards from Kindergarten to Grade 3?	
Kindergarten	With guidance and support from adults, use a variety of digital tools to produce and publish writing, including in collaboration with peers.
Grade 1	With guidance and support from adults, use a variety of digital tools to produce and publish writing, including in collaboration with peers.
Grade 2	With guidance and support from adults, use a variety of digital tools to produce and publish writing, including in collaboration with peers.
Grade 3	With guidance and support from adults, use technology to produce and publish writing (using keyboarding skills) as well as to interact and collaborate with others.

Anchor Standard 7. Conduct short as well as more sustained research projects based on focused questions, demonstrating understanding of the subject under investigation.

How does this look in the Writing Standards from Kindergarten to Grade 3?	
Kindergarten	Participate in shared research and writing projects (e.g., explore a number of books by a favorite author and express opinions about them).
Grade 1	Participate in shared research and writing projects (e.g., explore a number of "how-to" books on a given topic and use them to write a sequence of instructions).
Grade 2	Participate in shared research and writing projects (e.g., read a number of books on a single topic to produce a report; record science observations).
Grade 3	Conduct short research projects that build knowledge about a topic.

Anchor Standard 8. Gather relevant information from multiple print and digital sources, assess the credibility and accuracy of each source, and integrate the information while avoiding plagiarism.

How does this look in the Writing Standards from Kindergarten to Grade 3?	
Kindergarten	With guidance and support from adults, recall information from experience or gather information from provided sources to answer a question.
Grade 1	With guidance and support from adults, recall information from experience or gather information from provided sources to answer a question.
Grade 2	Recall information from experiences or gather information from provided sources to answer a question.
Grade 3	Recall information from experiences or gather information from print or digital sources; take brief notes on sources and sort evidence into provided categories.

Anchor Standard 9. Draw evidence from literary or informational texts to support analysis, reflection, and research. (This standard begins in Grade 4)

Anchor Standard 10. Write routinely over extended time frames (time for research, reflection, and revision) and shorter time frames (a single sitting or a day or two) for a range of tasks, purposes, and audiences.

How does this look in the Writing Standards from Kindergarten to Grade 3?	
Kindergarten	Begins in grade 3
Grade 1	Begins in grade 3
Grade 2	Begins in grade 3
Grade 3	Write routinely over extended time frames (time for research, reflection and revision) and shorter time frames (a single sitting or a day or two) for a range of discipline-specific tasks, purposes, and audiences.

Tips for Working With the CCSS-ELA Writing Standards

1. Begin Teaching Keyboarding Skills in Kindergarten to Ensure That All Students Become Proficient Typists by the Beginning of Grade 3

Most teachers of young children know the standardized tests students take in third grade are completed entirely online. Of course this means no Number 2 pencils, no test booklets, and no scratch paper. But it also means third graders who are proficient keyboard users may earn scores that are artificially elevated due only to their heightened ability to operate the equipment provided to test-takers. And the inverse is true as well: If the most eloquent and thoughtful third grade writers lack keyboard skills, they may earn scores that are artificially depressed.

A focus on keyboarding skills first appears in the CCSS-ELA in third grade. Six months of keyboarding might enable third graders to get past the "hunt and peck" stage, but it is unlikely that they will become proficient keyboardists. Starting keyboarding in kindergarten—and working at it regularly for three years—will help children develop keyboarding skills that would ease some of the anxiety around standardized testing.

2. Establish and Maintain a Strong, Consistent Focus on Writing

The CCSS' expectations for writing ramp up quickly, and learning to write well takes time, effort, and lots of practice. Making free-choice writing a daily classroom habit gives young children the opportunity to see their growth and to learn that improvement comes through daily effort. Have fun with this daily writing: Introduce new genres and new purposes for writing, change out the writing materials available to the students (every student can write enough to fill one post-it note!), and create special times and spaces in which to share work.

3. Use Technology to Increase Reluctant Writers' Engagement in the Writing Process

Would your reluctant writers consider crafting 30-second "news briefs" to be read aloud, video-recorded, and posted on a password-protected class website for all the families to see? Might some students want to write and present a bite-sized book reviews? Technology creates exciting possibilities that can be realized easily with devices already in your classroom. The keys to success with this approach are (a) keeping the students' reports brief—no more than four or five sentences—and (b) recording them immediately after they are written. This keeps things fresh and prevents students from getting bogged down and never finishing their reports.

CCSS-ELA STRAND: Speaking and Listening

Anchor Standards for Speaking and Listening

Comprehension and Collaboration

1. Prepare for and participate effectively in a range of conversations and collaborations with diverse partners, building on others' ideas and expressing their own clearly and persuasively.
2. Integrate and evaluate information presented in diverse media and formats, including visually, quantitatively, and orally.
3. Evaluate a speaker's point of view, reasoning, and use of evidence and rhetoric.

Presentation of Knowledge and Ideas

4. Present information, findings, and supporting evidence such that listeners can follow the line of reasoning and the organization, development, and style are appropriate to the task, purpose, and audience.
5. Make strategic use of digital media and visual displays of data to express information and enhance understanding of presentation.
6. Adapt speech to a variety of contexts and communicative tasks, demonstrating command of formal English when indicated or appropriate.

**Speaking and Listening's Theme:
Flexible Communication and Collaboration**

The conception of speaking and listening presented in the CCSS-ELA goes far beyond learning the skills needed to make formal presentations. This domain intertwines oral communication and interpersonal skills in ways that emphasize the importance of collaborative work. Skills presented in this domain include:

Expressing and listening carefully to ideas
Integrating information from oral, visual, quantitative, and media sources
Evaluating what they hear
Using media and visual displays strategically to achieve communicative purposes
Adapting speech to context and task

When teaching and practicing the important skills presented in this domain, teachers will need to attend thoughtfully to the learning experiences of students who are English Learners to ensure that they are making adequate progress.

FIGURE 9.4

Key Features of the Speaking and Listening Standards

*   Students develop a broad range of useful oral communication and interpersonal skills.
*   Students express and listen carefully to ideas, integrate information from varied sources, evaluate what they hear, and communicate using thoughtful media and visual displays.

Speaking and Listening Skill Trajectories, K–3

Anchor Standard 1. Prepare for and participate effectively in a range of conversations and collaborations with diverse partners, building on others' ideas and expressing their own clearly and persuasively.

How does this look in the Listening and Speaking Standards from Kindergarten to Grade 3?	
Kindergarten	Participate in collaborative conversations with diverse partners about kindergarten topics and texts with peers and adults in small and larger groups. (a) Follow agreed-upon rules for discussions (e.g., listening to others and taking turns speaking about the topics and texts under discussion). (b) Continue a conversation through multiple exchanges.
Grade 1	Participate in collaborative conversations with diverse partners about grade 1 topics and texts with peers and adults in small and larger groups. (a) Follow agreed-upon rules for discussions (e.g., listening to others with care, speaking one at a time about the topics and texts under discussion). (b) Build on others' talk in conversations by responding to the comments of others through multiple exchanges. (c) Ask questions to clear up any confusion about the topics and texts under discussion.
Grade 2	Participate in collaborative conversations with diverse partners about grade 2 topics and texts with peers and adults in small and larger groups. (a) Follow agreed-upon rules for discussions (e.g., gaining the floor in respectful ways, listening to others with care, speaking one at a time about the topics and texts under discussion).
Grade 3	Engage effectively in a range of collaborative discussions (one-on-one, in groups, and teacher-led) with diverse partners on grade 3 topics and texts, building on others' ideas and expressing their own clearly. (a) Come to discussions prepared, having read or studied the required material; explicitly draw on that preparation and other information known about the topic to explore ideas under discussion. (b) Follow agreed-upon rules for discussions (e.g., gaining the floor in respectful ways, listening to others with care, speaking one at a time about the topics and texts under discussion). (c) Ask questions to check understanding of information presented, stay on topic, and link their comments to the remarks of others. (d) Explain their own ideas and understanding in light of the discussion.

Anchor Standard 2. Integrate and evaluate information presented in diverse media and formats, including visually, quantitatively, and orally.

How does this look in the Listening and Speaking Standards from Kindergarten to Grade 3?	
Kindergarten	Confirm understanding of a text read aloud or information presented orally or through other media by asking and answering questions about key details and requesting clarification if something is not understood.
Grade 1	Ask and answer questions about key details in a text read aloud or information presented orally or through other media.
Grade 2	Recount or describe key ideas or details from a text read aloud or information presented orally or through other media.
Grade 3	Determine the main ideas and supporting details of a text read aloud or information presented in diverse media and formats, including visually, quantitatively, and orally.

Anchor Standard 3. Evaluate a speaker's point of view, reasoning, and use of evidence and rhetoric.

How does this look in the Listening and Speaking Standards from Kindergarten to Grade 3?	
Kindergarten	Ask and answer questions in order to seek help, get information, or clarify something that is not understood.
Grade 1	Ask and answer questions about what a speaker says in order to gather additional information or clarify something that is not understood.
Grade 2	Ask and answer questions about what a speaker says in order to clarify comprehension, gather additional information, or deepen understanding of a topic or issue.
Grade 3	Ask and answer questions about information from a speaker, offering appropriate elaboration and detail.

Anchor Standard 4. Present information, findings, and supporting evidence such that listeners can follow the line of reasoning and the organization, development, and style are appropriate to the task, purpose, and audience.

How does this look in the Listening and Speaking Standards from Kindergarten to Grade 3?	
Kindergarten	Describe familiar people, places, things, and events and, with prompting and support, provide additional detail.
Grade 1	Describe people, places, things, and events with relevant details, expressing ideas and feelings clearly.
Grade 2	Tell a story or recount an experience with appropriate facts and relevant descriptive details, speaking audibly in coherent sentences.
Grade 3	Report on a topics or text, tell a story, or recount an experience with appropriate facts and relevant, descriptive details, speaking clearly at an understandable pace.

Anchor Standard 5. Make strategic use of digital media and visual displays of data to express information and enhance understanding of presentation.

How does this look in the Listening and Speaking Standards from Kindergarten to Grade 3?	
Kindergarten	Add drawings or other visual displays to descriptions as desired to provide additional detail.
Grade 1	Add drawings or other visual displays to descriptions when appropriate to clarify ideas, thoughts, and feelings.
Grade 2	Create audio recordings of stories or poems, add drawings or other visual displays to stories or recounts of experiences when appropriate to clarify ideas, thoughts, and feelings.
Grade 3	Create audio recordings of stories or poems that demonstrate fluid reading at an understandable pace; add visual displays when appropriate to emphasize or enhance certain facts or details.

Anchor Standard 6. Adapt speech to a variety of contexts and communicative tasks, demonstrating command of formal English when indicated or appropriate.

How does this look in the Listening and Speaking Standards from Kindergarten to Grade 3?	
Kindergarten	Speak audibly and express thoughts, feelings, and ideas clearly.
Grade 1	Produce complete sentences when appropriate to task and situation.
Grade 2	Produce complete sentences when appropriate to task and situation in order to provide requested detail or clarification.
Grade 3	Speak in complete sentences when appropriate to task and situation in order to provide requested detail or clarification.

Tips for Working With the CCSS-ELA Listening and Speaking Standards

1. Think About the Speaking and Listening Standards as "Communication Standards"

To me, "speaking and listening" evokes the image of a room full of people sitting and listening to a single speaker. The speaker may be active and engaged, but the listeners are passive. By the time they reach school age, most children have already developed the skills necessary to be passive listeners: They are frequently cast in that role in their classrooms, school assemblies, religious services, and other "children should be seen and not heard" settings.

Young children need to develop the ability to communicate effectively: to exchange information with others in order to learn, solve problems, get information, make connections with people, and build friendships. In conversations, participants play listening and speaking roles simultaneously and monitor their own participation and contribution to the group. These are the skills worth developing when guiding your students toward mastery of these standards.

2. Integrate Social-Emotional Learning Into the Speaking and Listening Strand

Learning to communicate with different types of people, to enter and exit conversations smoothly, to express difficult emotions in appropriate ways, and to receive constructive criticism from others can be enormously challenging for young children. An explicit focus on developing effective communication strategies is made even more powerful when social relationships, uncomfortable emotions, and strategies for managing complex interactions are woven into these lessons. Social-emotional learning is crucial to young children's development of ethical perspectives and responsibility for themselves and others.

CCSS-ELA STRAND: Language

Anchor Standards for Language

Conventions of Standard English

1. Demonstrate command of the conventions of standard English grammar and usage when writing or speaking.
2. Demonstrate command of the conventions of standard English capitalization, punctuation, and spelling when writing.

Knowledge of Language

3. Apply knowledge of language to understand how language functions in different contexts, to make effective choices for meaning or style, and to comprehend more fully when reading or listening.

Vocabulary Acquisition and Use

4. Determine or clarify the meaning of unknown and multiple-meaning words and phrases by using context clues, analyzing meaningful word parts, and consulting general and specialized reference materials as appropriate.
5. Demonstrate understanding of figurative language, word relationships, and nuances in word meanings.
6. Acquire and use accurately a range of general academic and domain-specific words and phrases sufficient for reading, writing, speaking, and listening at the college and career readiness level; demonstrate independence in gathering

Language's Theme: Conventions, Effective Use, and Vocabulary
Although the language domain includes the essential "rules" of standard written and spoken English, it also approaches language as a matter of choice and context: Students must learn to adapt their voices to the demands of the setting, medium, and audience. The vocabulary standards focus on developing students' understanding of words, their relationships, and their nuances, as well as on acquiring new vocabulary, particularly general academic language and content-specific academic language.

FIGURE 9.5

vocabulary knowledge when encountering an unknown term important to comprehension or expression.

Key Features of the Language Standards

- Students master the rules of standard written English and learn to approach language as a craft that involves making informed choices among alternatives.
- Students understand the nuances and relationships among words and phrases.
- Students acquire new vocabulary, particularly academic and domain-specific words and terms.

Language Skills Trajectories, K–3

Anchor Standard 1. Demonstrate command of the conventions of standard English grammar and usage when writing or speaking.

How does this look in the Language Standards from Kindergarten to Grade 3?	
Kindergarten	Demonstrate command of the conventions of standard English grammar and usage when writing or speaking. (a) Print many upper- and lowercase letters. (b) Use frequently occurring nouns and verbs. (c) Form regular plural nouns orally by adding /s/ or /es/ (e.g., *dog, dogs; wish, wishes*). (d) Understand and use question words (interrogatives) (e.g., *who, what, where, when, why, how*). (e) Use the most frequently occurring prepositions (e.g., *to, from, in, out, on, off, for, of, by, with*). (f) Produce and expand complete sentences in shared language activities.

Grade 1	Demonstrate command of the conventions of standard English grammar and usage when writing or speaking.
	(a) Print all upper- and lowercase letters.
	(b) Use common, proper, and possessive nouns.
	(c) Use singular and plural nouns with matching verbs in basic sentences (e.g., *He hops; We hop*).
	(d) Use personal possessive and indefinite pronouns (e.g., *I, me, my; they, them, their; anyone, everything*).
	(e) Use verbs to convey a sense of past, present, and future (e.g., *Yesterday I walked home; Today I walk home; Tomorrow I will walk home*).
	(f) Use frequently occurring adjectives.
	(g) Use frequently occurring conjunctions (e.g., *and, but, or, because*).
	(h) Use determiners (e.g., *articles, demonstratives*).
	(i) Use frequently occurring prepositions (e.g., *during, beyond, toward*).
	(j) Produce and expand complete simple and compound declarative, interrogative, imperative, and exclamatory sentences in response to prompts.
Grade 2	Demonstrate command of the conventions of standard English grammar when writing or speaking.
	(a) Use collective nouns (e.g., *group*).
	(b) Form and use frequently occurring irregular plural nouns (e.g., *feet, children, teeth, mice, fish*).
	(c) Use reflexive pronouns (e.g., *myself, ourselves*).
	(d) Form and use the past tense of frequently occurring irregular verbs (e.g., *sat, hid, told*).
	(e) Use adjectives and adverbs, and choose between them depending on what is to be modified.
	(f) Produce, expand, and rearrange complete simple and compound sentences (e.g., *The boy watched the movie; The little boy watched the movie; The action movie was watched by the little boy*).
Grade 3	Demonstrate command of the conventions of standard English grammar when writing or speaking.
	(a) Explain the function of nouns, pronouns, verbs, adjectives, and adverbs in general and their function in particular sentences.
	(b) Form and use regular and irregular plural nouns.
	(c) Use abstract nouns (e.g., *childhood*).
	(d) Form and use regular and irregular verbs.
	(e) Form and use the simple (e.g., *I walked; I walk; I will walk*) verb tenses.
	(f) Ensure subject-verb agreement and pronoun-antecedent agreement.
	(g) Form and use comparative and superlative adjectives and adverbs, and choose between them depending on what is to be modified.
	(h) Use coordinating and subordinating conjunctions.
	(i) Produce simple, compound, and complex sentences.

Anchor Standard 2. Demonstrate command of the conventions of standard English capitalization, punctuation, and spelling when writing.

How does this look in the Language Standards from Kindergarten to Grade 3?	
Kindergarten	Demonstrate command of the conventions of standard English capitalization, punctuation, and spelling when writing. (a) Capitalize the first word in a sentence and the pronoun *I*. (b) Recognize and name end punctuation. (c) Write a letter or letters for most consonant and short-vowel sounds (phonemes). (d) Spell simple words phonetically, drawing on knowledge of sound-letter relationships.
Grade 1	Demonstrate command of the conventions of standard English capitalization, punctuation, and spelling when writing. (a) Capitalize dates and names of people. (b) Use end punctuation for sentences. (c) Use commas in dates and to separate single words in a series. (d) Use conventional spelling for words with common spelling patterns and for frequently occurring irregular words. (e) Spell untaught words phonetically, drawing on phonemic awareness and spelling conventions.
Grade 2	Demonstrate command of the conventions of standard English capitalization, punctuation, and spelling when writing. (a) Capitalize holidays, product names, and geographic names. (b) Use commas in greetings and closings of letters. (c) Use an apostrophe to form contractions and frequently occurring possessives. (d) Generalize learned spelling patterns when writing words (e.g., cage→badge; boy→boil). (e) Consult reference materials, including beginning dictionaries, as needed to check and correct spellings.
Grade 3	Demonstrate command of the conventions of standard English capitalization, punctuation, and spelling when writing. (a) Capitalize appropriate words in titles. (b) Use commas in addresses. (c) Use commas and quotation marks in dialogue. (d) Form and use possessives. (e) Use conventional spelling for high-frequency and other studied words and for adding suffixes to base words (e.g., *sitting, smiled, cries, happiness*). (f) Use spelling patterns and generalizations (e.g., word families, position-based spellings, syllable patterns, ending rules, meaningful word parts) in writing words. (g) Consult reference materials, including beginning dictionaries, as needed to check and correct spellings.

Anchor Standard 3. Apply knowledge of language to understand how language functions in different contexts, to make effective choices for meaning or style, and to comprehend more fully when reading or listening.

What does this look like in the Language Standards from Kindergarten to Grade 3?	
Kindergarten	(Begins in grade 2)
Grade 1	(Begins in grade 2)
Grade 2	Use knowledge of language and its conventions when writing, speaking, reading, or listening. (a) Compare formal and informal uses of English.
Grade 3	Use knowledge of language and its conventions when writing, speaking, reading, or listening. (a) Choose words and phrases for effect. (b) Recognize and observe differences between the conventions of spoken and written standard English.

Anchor Standard 4. Determine or clarify the meaning of unknown and multiple-meaning words and phrases by using context clues, analyzing meaningful word parts, and consulting general and specialized reference materials as appropriate.

How does this look in the Language Standards from Kindergarten to Grade 3?	
Kindergarten	Determine or clarify the meaning of unknown and multiple-meaning words and phrases based on *kindergarten reading and content.* (a) Identify new meanings for familiar words and apply them accurately (e.g., knowing *duck* is a bird and learning the verb to *duck*). (b) Use the most frequently occurring inflections and affixes (e.g., *-ed,-s, re-, un-, pre-,-ful,-less*) as a clue to the meaning of an unknown word.
Grade 1	Determine or clarify the meaning of unknown and multiple-meaning words and phrases based on *grade 1 reading and content,* choosing flexibly from an array of strategies. (a) Use sentence-level context as a clue to the meaning of a word or phrase. (b) Use frequently occurring affixes as a clue to the meaning of a word. (c) Identify frequently occurring root words (e.g., *look*) and their inflectional forms (e.g., *looks, looked, looking*).

Grade 2	Determine or clarify the meaning of unknown and multiple-meaning words and phrases based on *grade 2 reading and content*, choosing flexibly from an array of strategies. (a) Use sentence-level context as a clue to the meaning of a word or phrase. (b) Determine the meaning of the new word formed when a known prefix is added to a known word (e.g., *happy/unhappy, tell/retell*). (c) Use a known root word as a clue to the meaning of an unknown word with the same root (e.g., *addition, additional*). (d) Use knowledge of the meaning of individual words to predict the meaning of compound words (e.g., *birdhouse, lighthouse, housefly; bookshelf, notebook, bookmark*). (e) Use glossaries and beginning dictionaries, both print and digital, to determine or clarify the meaning of words and phrases.
Grade 3	Determine or clarify the meaning of unknown and multiple-meaning words and phrases based on *grade 1 reading and content*, choosing flexibly from a range of strategies. (a) Use sentence-level context as a clue to the meaning of a word or phrase. (b) Determine the meaning of the new word formed when a known affix is added to a known word (e.g., *agreeable/disagreeable, comfortable/uncomfortable, care/careless, heat/preheat*). (c) Use a known root word as a clue to the meaning of an unknown word with the same root (e.g., *company, companion*). (d) Use glossaries or beginning dictionaries, both print and digital, to determine or clarify the precise meaning of key words and phrases.

Anchor Standard 5. Demonstrate understanding of figurative language, word relationships, and nuances in word meanings.

How does this look in the Language Standards from Kindergarten to Grade 3?
Kindergarten	With guidance and support from adults, explore word relationships and nuances in word meanings. (a) Sort common objects into categories (e.g., shapes, foods) to gain a sense of the concepts the categories represent. (b) Demonstrate understanding of frequently occurring verbs and adjectives by relating them to their opposites (antonyms). (c) Identify real-life connections between words and their use (e.g., note places at school that are colorful). (d) Distinguish shades of meaning among verbs describing the same general action (e.g., *walk, march, strut, prance*) by acting out the meanings.

Grade 1	With guidance and support from adults, demonstrate understanding of word relationships and nuances in word meanings. (a) Sort words into categories (e.g., colors, clothing) to gain a sense of the concepts the categories represent. (b) Define words by category and by one or more key attributes (e.g., a *duck* is a bird that swims; a *tiger* is a large cat with stripes). (c) Identify real life connections between words and their use (e.g., note places at home that are *cozy*). (d) Distinguish shades of meaning among verbs differing in manner (e.g., *look, peek, glance, stare, glare, scowl*) and adjectives differing in intensity (e.g., *large, gigantic*) by defining or choosing them or by acting out the meanings.
Grade 2	Demonstrate understanding of word relationships and nuances in word meanings. (a) Identify real-life connections between words and their use (e.g., describe foods that are *spicy* or *juicy*). (b) Distinguish shades of meaning among closely related verbs (e.g., *toss, throw, hurl*) and closely related adjectives (e.g., *thin, slender, skinny, scrawny*).
Grade 3	Demonstrate understanding of word relationships and nuances in word meanings. (a) Distinguish the literal and no-literal meanings of words and phrases in context (e.g., *take steps*). (b) Identify real-life connections between words and their use (e.g., describe people who are *friendly or helpful*). (c) Distinguish shades of meaning among related words that describe states of mind or degrees of certainty (e.g., *knew, believed, suspected, heard, wondered*).

Anchor Standard 6. Acquire and use accurately a range of general academic and domain-specific words and phrases sufficient for reading, writing, speaking, and listening at the college and career readiness level; demonstrate independence in gathering vocabulary knowledge when encountering an unknown term important to comprehension or expression.

How does this look in the Language Standards from Kindergarten to Grade 3?	
Kindergarten	Use words and phrases acquired through conversations, reading and being read to, and responding to texts.
Grade 1	Use words and phrases acquired through conversations, reading and being read to, and responding to texts, including using frequently occurring conjunctions to signal simple relationships (e.g., *because*).
Grade 2	Use words and phrases acquired through conversations, reading and being read to, and responding to texts, including using adjectives and adverbs to describe (e.g., *When other kids are happy, that makes me happy*).

Grade 3	Acquire and use accurately grade-appropriate conversational, general academic, and domain-specific words and phrases, including those that signal spatial and temporal relationships (e.g., *After dinner that night we went looking for them*).

Tips for Working With the CCSS-ELA Language Standards

1. Ensure That All Languages, Not Only English, Are Treated With Respect in Your Classroom

Although the CCSS-ELA language standards focus exclusively on developing proper English grammar, usage, and vocabulary, it is critical for children—especially monolingual English-speaking children—to understand that all languages are complex and beautiful. Young children should also learn that mastering grammar, usage, and vocabulary is an essential aspect of learning to speak and understand any language. Children should recognize and respect the knowledge and cultural capital possessed by their multilingual peers.

2. Help Your Students Develop a Love of Words and Wordplay

Puns and riddles, rhyme and rhythm, Bananagrams and Boggle, the imaginary wocket in Dr. Seuss' pocket, and terrifically tantalizing tongue-twisters: Words are an endless source of delight to those who recognize and respond to their playful power. If you're a teacher who loves words, don't be shy about letting your students know. Create word contests (what's the silliest word in the English language?), find out who knows the meanings of words that they have read but can't pronounce, ask everyone to choose a favorite word . . . the possibilities are endless. Your positivity and passion for words will be contagious and your students will never forget some of the words they learned the year they were in your class.

What About the CCSS-ELA Appendices?

Appendix A contains

- Research supporting key elements of the standards
- Supplementary material on reading, writing, speaking and listening, and language
- Glossary of key terms used in the standards document

Appendix B contains

- Text exemplars that illustrate the complexity, quality, and range of reading appropriate for the "grade bands" that frame the CCSS-ELA: K–1, 2–3, 4–5, 6–8
- Sample performance tasks linked to the text exemplars

Appendix C contains

- Annotated student writing samples demonstrating a performance of adequate or better at various grade levels

What About Literacy in History/Social Studies, Science, and Technical Subjects?

The full title of the CCSS-ELA is *Common Core State Standards for English Language Arts and Literacy in History/Social Studies, Science, and Technical Subjects*. But there are no history, social studies, science, or technical subjects content standards in the K–5 section of the CCSS-ELA. According to the authors of the CCSS-ELA, "a single K–5 section lists standards for reading, writing, speaking, listening, and language across the curriculum, reflecting the fact that most or all of the instruction students in these grades receive comes from one teacher" (CCSS-ELA, p. 8).

Presumably, the authors concluded that elementary school teachers would (1) pull academic content from their state's history/social studies and science/technical subjects content standards documents and (2) teach the subject matter content in a manner that engages the students' knowledge and skills in reading, writing, listening and speaking, and language.

The CCSS-ELA for Grades 6–12 are presented in two separate sections—one section is designed for the English language arts teacher and the other section is designed for the social studies and science teachers. Both sections use the same CCR anchor standards, but also include grade-specific standards "tuned to the literacy requirements of the particular disciplines" (CCSS-ELA, p. 8).

References

How to read the Common Core State Standards for English Language Arts. (n.d.) Retrieved from http://ped.state.nm.us/ped/CCDocuments/CCSSO_Quick_Guide_to_Standards.pdf

National Governors Association Center for Best Practices, Council of Chief State School Officers. (2010). *Common Core State Standards for English language arts and literacy in history/social studies, science, and technical subjects*. Washington, DC: National Governors Association Center for Best Practices, Council of Chief State School Officers.

PART IV

Using DAP to Teach the Common Core in Early Childhood Settings, Grade by Grade

INTRODUCTION TO PART IV

The old state standards—the ones implemented in response to No Child Left Behind—created a stampede of preK–3 teachers running to buy books of blackline masters for use in their "skill and drill practice" centers. In the period from 2002–2013, developmentally appropriate practice was either pushed out of young children's classrooms or engaged in surreptitiously.

After a decade, it is clear that NCLB's approach to boosting student achievement was not highly successful. Perhaps NCLB-based policies created unspectacular outcomes for students and made little progress closing the achievement gap because those policies encouraged paper-and-pencil work and discouraged (or eliminated) developmentally appropriate teaching practice in the early years of schooling. Had young children been allowed—encouraged!—to learn through the methods that have been empirically proven to be most effective, perhaps the outcomes of NCLB would have been more favorable.

Now we have been given new sets of standards: the CCSS-ELA and the CCSS-Math. Teachers and administrators have heard a lot of talk about rigor, cognitive demand, heightened expectations for writing across all curricular areas and other aspects of the CCSS that might make them challenging for students to master.

Currently, the CCSS are in the early days of implementation. It's not yet clear how difficult it will be to ensure that all students master the standards set for their grade level. But, at all grade levels—in early childhood and beyond—providing students with developmentally appropriate learning experiences is the best way support their ongoing academic success:

Attend to each learner as a whole child
Nurture students' growth and progress across all developmental domains
☐ *Cognitive*   ☐ *Academic*   ☐ *Social*
☐ *Emotional*   ☐ *Physical*   ☐ *Behavioral*

Meet children at their current developmental levels and help them all to move forward. Develop all students' English vocabulary, academic language, and content knowledge.

In this book I argue that the knowledge and skills presented in the CCSS-ELA and the CCSS-M can be easily and effectively taught to children using developmentally appropriate practices. But, in reality, the question of whether or not developmentally appropriate practices can be used effectively to teach the CCSS can only be answered by practicing early childhood teachers and, perhaps, by the administrators who guide the teachers' work.

In the following part, you will find six chapters—one for prekindergarten, one for transitional/junior kindergarten, and one for each grade level from kindergarten to Grade 3. These chapters are designed for teachers working with students in these grades; however, much of the information might be interesting to parents as well.

- Prekindergarten and transitional kindergarten

The Common Core State Standards do not include specifications for prekindergarten or transitional kindergarten. However, every state and U.S. territory has adopted a set of Early Learning Standards (ELS) for children from ages 3 to 5. I recommend that preK and TK teachers download the ELS for their state and use them to build their programs around the state-approved student learning outcomes.

The prekindergarten and kindergarten chapters share the same format:

- Typical age range for the grade level
- Working metaphor representing the children in the grade level
- Developmental traits typically seen in classrooms of children in the grade level
- Specific information relevant to the grade level
- Key elements of developmentally appropriate practice
- What are children expected to know and be able to do when they begin kindergarten?
- Kindergarten Through Grade 3

Each chapter for grades K–3 is structured using the same format:

- Typical age range for the grade level
- Working metaphor representing the children in the grade level
- Developmental traits typically seen in classrooms of children in the grade level
- Discussion of a focus topic relevant to the grade level
- Complete CCSS-Math Standards for the grade level
- Annotated CCSS-Math Standards for the grade level
  - All standards fully unpacked
- Complete CCSS-ELA Standards for the grade level

- Annotated CCSS-ELA Standards for the grade level
  - All standards fully unpacked
- Three tips for teachers working with students at that grade level

What Does It Mean to "Unpack" Academic Content Standards?

The Common Core State Standards are not a curriculum. The CCSS are academic content standards: They state explicitly what students in a given grade level should know and be able to do by the end of the academic year. Academic content standards provide no information other than that. Classroom teachers must sit down with the CCSS for their grade level and develop an intentional, effective, realistic plan for guiding their students to mastery of the specified content.

Unpacking the standards is the first step in this process. Teachers—working collaboratively or on their own—look at each individual standard to figure out what it actually means in relation to young children in classrooms, how it builds on what students learned in the previous year, how it fits with the other standards for the grade level, how it might be taught successfully, whether or not it has elements that might be tricky for some students, determine if there are any "power standards" important enough to return to again and again throughout the year, and so on. Some teachers might organize the standards into learning progressions or trajectories; others could look for meaningful interdisciplinary connections to other topics they are expected to teach.

Standards must be unpacked before the content they contain can be taught or learned. The process is the same regardless of whether you are unpacking your state's Early Learning Standards or the Common Core State Standards. The following chapters will jumpstart your own efforts—especially for teachers of children in grades K–3—because I have already started unpacking the standards for you.

As you continue to unpack the CCSS or ELS for your grade level, I am certain you will ask different questions than I asked as I went through the process, notice different details than I did, and have your own unique brainstorms and insights about the content standards, your students, and your curriculum. That's one of the joys of teaching: We bring everything we know and every aspect of who we are into our classrooms, and we are willing to use everything we've got if it helps our students learn.

10

USING DAP TO TEACH THE CCSS IN PREKINDERGARTEN

Typical age range for prekindergarten: 3–5½ years old
   Working metaphor for prekindergarten students: Prekindergartners are **bold explorers.**
   Prekindergartners are eager, fearless explorers on an adventure into the future. They know their destination—kindergarten—but they can't begin to imagine the many wondrous things they will see and do along the way. And they have no idea how much they will learn and change and grow. The beauty—and the challenge—of prekindergarten is that each child begins the journey from a different starting point and forges a uniquely personal path to reach the same finish line. Teachers need to keep a close watch on their bold explorers to make sure that everyone keeps their hands inside the jeep and continues to move forward and make progress.

Focus Topic: What Are Children Expected Know and Be Able to Do When They *Begin* Kindergarten?

The Common Core State Standards begin with kindergarten. But the kindergarten CCSS-ELA and the CCSS-M present the knowledge and skills expected of kindergartners at the end of their kindergarten year. This leaves teachers of children in prekindergarten and transitional/junior kindergarten to make curricular decisions without "official" guidance regarding the knowledge and skills to be taught. This is both a blessing and a burden. It is a blessing to have the freedom to shape a developmentally appropriate learning environment and to provide developmentally appropriate learning experiences without compromise. But it is a burden to be responsible for determining how best to prepare a diverse group of young children for success in kindergarten and beyond.

TABLE 10.1 Developmental Traits of Prekindergartners Typically Seen in Classrooms

Physical	Gross motor skills are dominant, so prekindergartners enjoy physical activity—climbing, running, jumping—although they have a tendency to be clumsy. Most can sit still for brief periods of time.
Social-Emotional	Prekindergartners are eager to have responsibilities (passing out snacks, collecting all the scissors). They're friendly and very talkative. They enjoy working/playing with friends, though they also engage frequently in parallel play. They move quickly from one activity or interest to the next because they have short attention spans.
Cognitive	Prekindergartners learn best through whole-body activities, like easel painting and building with large blocks, rather than with pencil and paper tasks. They enjoy manipulating materials—sand and water play, using magnets—and learning by doing. Imaginative dress-up and pretend play is another favorite activity that supports their language development. Prekindergartners also love listening to stories and show a keen interest in learning and using new words.

Happily, you don't have to make these decisions without guidance. There are other sources of practical information, support, and consultation readily available to you. Here are three to get you started:

1. Your State's Department of Education

Virtually all of the U.S. states have adopted (or are in the process of adopting) early learning standards. These standards typically lay out young children's developmental trajectories in all domains (and sometimes within specific content areas) and establish target knowledge, skills, approaches to learning, and experiences that prepare students to enter kindergarten ready to succeed. If your state has early learning standards, be sure to direct your prekindergarten and transitional/junior kindergarten students toward the same student learning outcomes that your state has identified.

2. Kindergarten Teachers in the Districts and Schools Typically Attended by Graduates of Your Program

Kindergarten teachers have very clear expectations of what makes a student "ready" for kindergarten. Sometimes these expectations are tightly aligned to the state's early learning standards, but this is not always the case. If your program serves students from the neighborhoods near your center, you might reach out to the kindergarten teachers at the schools your current students will attend and find out if they would be interested in connecting with you to bridge the gap between preK and kindergarten. The kindergarten teachers have much to gain from establishing partnerships and collaboration with the local prekindergarten programs, especially the opportunity to "custom order" the skills and capabilities they hope their new students will have. And you have so much to gain by knowing that you're doing everything you can to maximize your students' opportunities for success.

3. Your Parent Community

The parents of your current students are a ready source of insight into the expectations, practices, and demands of the elementary schools in your local area. Their continual migration from the sidelines of soccer games, to the waiting areas of dance academies, to the parking lots of religious schools, to the bleachers of swim meets gives the parent community many opportunities to talk, exchange information, and share opinions. Ask your parents what they've heard about the academic demands and behavioral expectations held by the kindergarten and primary grade teachers in your local schools. You might hear something quite different from what the kindergarten teachers shared with you, but both perspectives are valid and worth hearing.

Working With Early Learning Standards

Early childhood education and care—a broad term I'm using to encompass all the settings into which young children go and all the things they do each day during the years before they begin kindergarten—serves so many children and includes many different types of learning environments, funding sources, caregivers and teachers, curriculum content, licensure, daily schedules, eligibility requirements, and so on; capturing every possible setting and situation is impossible. For the purposes of this chapter, I use the term "prekindergarten" to include settings that enroll children from the ages of 3–5 years of age and provide supervised play-based learning experiences and opportunities for social engagement with peers.

The Common Core State Standards do not include standards or guidelines for prekindergarten mathematics or prekindergarten English language arts. However, most states have developed a set of early learning standards (ELS) to guide the work of prekindergarten teachers. These ELS range from focusing almost exclusively on the domains of child development (as in New York State, Wisconsin, Hawai'i)—

Physical and motor development
Social and emotional development
Cognitive development and general knowledge
Language and communication development
Approaches to learning

—to focusing almost exclusively on academic content areas (as in Illinois, the District of Columbia, Alabama):

Approaches to learning/Logic and reasoning
Communication and language

Literacy
Mathematics
Scientific inquiry
Social studies
The arts
Social-emotional development
Physical development/Health and safety

Although each state's ELS are framed and organized differently, the actual standards themselves—the specific knowledge, skills, and dispositions children are expected to learn before beginning kindergarten—are very similar from one state to the next. So, regardless of whether your state's ELS are presented in the "developmentally focused" or the "academically focused" format, your implementation of the standards in your classroom will be the same: The most effective way to teach young children is through the use of developmentally appropriate practices.

(Please keep your state's Early Learning Standards, your students and their families, and your own classroom practices in mind as you read the remainder of this chapter.)

Key Elements of Developmentally Appropriate Practice

The National Association for the Education of Young Children (Copple et al., 2013) offers these recommendations for prekindergarten teachers who want to teach in developmentally appropriate ways and maximize their students' learning.

1. Be Intentional

Teachers make thoughtful decisions about what to teach and how to teach it. Further, teachers always have a reason for teaching a particular skill. Perhaps this skill builds on the students' prior knowledge? Maybe it prepares students to connect with new knowledge? Or did the teacher review Monday's math drawings and realize most of the students would benefit from a re-teach?

Teachers have short-range and long-range goals for their students, and are strategic and deliberate in their plans to move the students forward toward those goals. Something might look like goofy fun—using two pairs of tweezers, one for each hand—to pick up tangled rubber bands and drop them into a jar—but you can be sure the teacher put that activity out for a reason. Using tweezers requires precise movements of the thumb and forefinger; that silly game is probably an exercise aimed at strengthening students' pincer grasp.

2. Create a Caring Community of Learners

School is a place for learning. But learning new things can be difficult. Learners of all ages are more willing to take risks and try something new when they know they'll be encouraged, not laughed at, if they make a mistake. A caring classroom community is the foundation of an effective learning environment. A teacher and a group of children become a caring community when they share an ethos: a mutual understanding of how people should be treated, how problems should be solved, how to disagree without hurting any feelings, and how the community might grow and change over the course of the year. Membership in a caring classroom community supports young students—during their successes and their struggles—as they do the challenging work of learning, growing, and getting ready for kindergarten.

3. Teach to Enhance Development and Learning

Teachers want all their students to learn every day. They get to know each of their students—their likes and dislikes, their strengths and areas for growth, their hopes for the future—and they identify the ways each student learns best. Then, when making instruction plans, developing center activities, or trying to decide how to refresh the house corner to make it more inviting and exciting, teachers think about their students' needs. *The four English Language Learners need more practice with academic language . . . could the house corner become a school? If I moved the old overhead projector into that space, every child would want to participate.*

Effective teachers choose the instructional strategies they believe will be most effective with this particular group of students at this particular point in time. These aren't life-and-death decisions: Teachers present about 40 lessons each week and a handful of those lessons will be ineffective, too long, too complicated for the kids. If the kids weren't enticed into playing school, the teacher can make a few changes once the kids have left for the day and turn that space into something else. She hasn't abandoned her plan to give her ELLs more opportunity to practice academic language just because the school idea was unsuccessful: She'll be back in her classroom tomorrow morning with new ideas to entice her ELLs into academic conversations in English.

4. Plan Curriculum That Will Enable Students to Achieve Important Goals

Your state's early learning standards are just a list of skills to be mastered. One of the teacher's responsibilities is to weave those standards into coherent, purposeful, engaging curriculum units that will engage the students in learning the standards. Your curriculum units could involve students in projects (Helm & Beneke, 2003), or in aesthetically rich activities inspired by Reggio Emilia (Wurm, 2005), or they could emerge from areas of interest demonstrated by the students (Krogh & Morehouse, 2014; Wien, 2008). Here again, intentionality is critical. What do you want the students to learn from the unit? How will you be sure all the students learned it? As a teacher, you always need a clear purpose for everything you do with your students.

5. Assess Children's Development and Learning

To be an effective teacher, you have to know your students as learners. And, the more thoroughly you know your students, the more effective you will be. Assessing students' learning is a daily, ongoing practice for most early childhood teachers. Jotting down an anecdotal observation, scanning a few work samples to put in students' files, audio-taping a conversation about a scary dog outside the play yard fence, taking a series of photos of Sophie and Anna swinging across the monkey bars are all part of teaching young children.

The learning of very young children is challenging to document: They grow and change quickly, their development is uneven across the various domains, and they have limited patience for sitting still. However, assessment documentation plays a critically important role in fine-tuning your instructional plans so they fit your students like a glove. For more detailed information about observing and documenting students' learning, please see the Chapter 4 SPOTLIGHT SKILL: Observing, Documenting, and Assessing Students' Learning.

6. Establish Reciprocal Relationships With Your Students' Families

If you truly care about your young students, you must also care about your students' families. The health, happiness, and success of your students is inextricably interwoven with the health, happiness, and success of your students' parents, grandparents, aunts and uncles, siblings, cousins, and the network of families and friends whom they know and trust and love. Developing and maintaining reciprocal relationships with the significant adults in your students' lives is critically important.

A student's adult family members generally know more about the student than you do: They've known her since she was born, and they've seen her in many different contexts. Their knowledge and insights are a critically important source of information about the student, and it is crucial that you let the family know how much you value their input. Work to establish and maintain positive, effective communication with the families, such as inviting them to participate in classroom activities. And, if the parents do not respond to your calls or emails, always try to attribute positive intent: They might be busy, working multiple jobs, uncomfortable in school settings because of their own childhood experiences, caring for other children or for aging parents. Never give up on your efforts to make contact with your students' families.

Three Tips for Teachers of Prekindergarten Bold Explorers

1. Do Not Look to the Kindergarten CCSS for Guidance With Curriculum Content

The knowledge and skills listed in the kindergarten CCSS documents are the academic goals students are expected to meet *at the end of kindergarten*. In other words, the kindergarten standards represent the academic expectations for students who are beginning Grade 1. These standards are not developmentally appropriate for prekindergartners.

2. Include the CCSS-Mathematics Standards for Mathematical Practice in Your Mathematics Curriculum

The CCSS do not include content standards for prekindergarten. However, the CCSS mathematics standards include a second type of standards—the Standards for Mathematical Practice (as opposed to the more typical Standards for Mathematical Content)—that are readily applicable to the mathematics teaching and learning that occur in prekindergarten settings. The Standards for Mathematical Practice are performance standards that describe the approaches to mathematics, the mathematical habits of mind, and the attitudes about mathematics that are demonstrated by outstanding mathematical thinkers/learners. Helping young students develop these ways of approaching and thinking about mathematics before they enter kindergarten will prepare them for success in kindergarten.

TABLE 10.2 CCSS-M Standards for Mathematical Practice

CCSS Standards For Mathematical Practice (SMP)	SMP in Student-Friendly Language (White & Dauksas, 2012)
Make sense of problems and persevere in solving them.	I can try many times to understand and solve a math problem.
Reason abstractly and quantitatively.	I can think about the math problem in my head first.
Construct viable arguments and critique the reasoning of others.	I can make a plan, called a strategy, to solve the problem, and discuss other students' strategies too.
Model with mathematics.	I can use math symbols and numbers to solve the problem.
Use appropriate tools strategically.	I can use math tools, pictures, drawings, and objects to solve the problem.
Attend to precision.	I can check to see if my strategy and calculations are correct.
Look for and make use of structure.	I can use what I already know about math to solve the problem.
Look for and express regularity in repeated reasoning.	I can use a strategy that I used to solve another math problem.

3. Help Your Children Develop Productive Approaches to Learning

Along with the developmental domains one would expect to see—physical/motor, socio-emotional, and cognitive—many states' Early Learning Standards include "approaches to learning" as a separate domain. A child's approaches to learning include characteristics and behaviors such as

Engagement in activities
Creativity
Imagination
Curiosity
Initiative
Persistence
Planning and reflection
Problem solving skills

Children with positive, productive approaches to learning are open to new experiences, confident about their ability to learn how to do things, and able to ask for assistance when they need it. Encouraging and developing children's skills in these areas might be better preparation for success in kindergarten than teaching them academic skills.

References

Copple, C., Bredekamp, S., Koralek, D., & Charner, K. (Eds.). (2013). *Developmentally appropriate practice: Focus on preschoolers.* Washington, DC: National Association for the Education of Young Children.

Helm, J. H., & Beneke, S. (Eds.). (2003). *The power of projects.* New York: Teachers College Press.

Krogh, S. L., & Morehouse, P. (2014). *The early childhood curriculum: Inquiry learning through integration.* New York: Routledge.

White, J., & Dauksas, L. (2012). CCSSM: Getting started in K–grade 2. *Teaching Children Mathematics, 1* (7), 440–445.

Wien, C. A. (Ed.). (2008). *Emergent curriculum in the primary classroom.* New York: Teachers College Press.

Wurm, J. P. (2005). *Working the Reggio way.* St. Paul, MN: Redleaf Press.

11

USING DAP TO TEACH THE CCSS IN TRANSITIONAL KINDERGARTEN

Typical age range for transitional kindergartners: 4½–5¾ years old

Working metaphor for transitional kindergartners: Transitional kindergartners are **ligers**.

A liger is a big cat hybrid that is half lion and half tiger. Like ligers, TK students are a hybrid: half prekindergartner/half kindergartner. Also like ligers—who are alleged to have the strength of a lion and the speed of a tiger—children enrolled in Transitional/Junior Kindergarten are quite spectacular. Despite being so close to kindergarten age, these children are not yet interested in settling down and embracing the demands and expectations of kindergarten. Ligers are strong, quick, and ready to learn—but on their own terms, in their own way, and at their own pace.

Focus Topic: What Is Transitional Kindergarten and Whom Does It Serve?

Transitional kindergartens typically enroll children whose fifth birthday occurs after their state's cutoff date for kindergarten entry (some point between July 31 and October 15) but before mid-December. Transitional kindergarten is intended to be a learning environment appropriate for children who are young, either chronologically—those five-year-olds with late autumn birthdays—or developmentally—children old enough to enter kindergarten but whose behavior and learning needs suggest they are not yet ready to engage with kindergarten curriculum and experiences.

Transitional kindergarten offers this second group of children, the developmentally young, what teachers often call "the gift of time": Allowing these students another year of maturation before beginning kindergarten increases the likelihood that they will be successful upon entry to kindergarten. Children who complete

TABLE 11.1 Developmental Traits of Transitional Kindergartners Typically Seen in Classrooms

Physical	Gross motor skills are developing quickly, so TK students enjoy physical activity: climbing, running, jumping. Some may be able to sit at a table and work quietly for short bursts of time (10–15 minutes).
Social-Emotional	Younger TK students can be friendly and talkative. Dramatic play is important for all TKs' language development, although their difficulty seeing things from a point of view other than their own can create disruptions to the pretend scenarios. Older TK students like rules, routines, and adult approval.
Cognitive	A structured day characterized by repetition and routine, such as re-reading stories and poems, doing patterning activities, and following a schedule, creates a safe and comfortable environment that supports TK students' learning. They may be eager to please and dislike making mistakes; some TK students will repeat the same type of drawing or journal entry in order to feel successful. TK students learn best by doing, rather than by listening or watching.

a year of transitional/junior kindergarten may either begin "regular" kindergarten the following academic year or move directly from TK to Grade 1.

When California mandated a statewide implementation of transitional kindergarten in all public schools in the 2012–13 academic year, "nearly two thirds of principals and teachers reported that they received guidance from the[ir] district that TK should resemble kindergarten" (Quick et al., 2014, p. 8). However, the self-reports of TK teachers indicated that—at the classroom level—TK did not resemble kindergarten. In fact, California's TK teachers had different priorities, taught different academic content, and used different instructional methods than their kindergarten colleagues. The researchers found that

1. TK teachers spent *significantly less time* than kindergarten teachers

   - Providing instruction in English Language Arts
   - Providing instruction in mathematics

2. TK teachers spent *significantly more time* than kindergarten teachers

   - Teaching social studies and science
   - Teaching art and music
   - Using small-group and child-directed instruction
   - Focusing on activities aimed at social-emotional skill development

TK teachers have flexibility in their decisions regarding curriculum content because, as with prekindergarten, there are no content standards for transitional kindergarten in the Common Core State Standards. And, according to the report documenting the first year of California's TK implementation, the TK teachers used that curricular freedom to restore much-needed balance to the academic offerings in their classrooms. Science and social studies, art and music, learning experiences focused on social-emotional learning—content which had been central to kindergarten before the implementation of No Child Left Behind in 2001—all were reinstated in California's transitional kindergartens. California's TK classrooms seem to bear more resemblance to kindergarten classrooms in the late 1990s than to the kindergarten classrooms of the present day (Quick et al., 2014, p. 84).

(Please keep your state's Early Learning Standards, your students and their families, and your own classroom practices in mind as you read the remainder of this chapter.)

Working With State Early Learning Standards

The Common Core State Standards do not include English Language Arts or Mathematics content standards for students enrolled in transitional/junior kindergartens. However, most states have developed a set of early learning standards (ELS) to guide the work of prekindergarten teachers. These ELS range from focusing almost exclusively on the domains of child development (as in New York State, Wisconsin, Hawai'i)—

> Physical and motor development
> Social and emotional development
> Cognitive development and general knowledge
> Language and communication development
> Approaches to learning

—to focusing almost exclusively on academic content areas (as in Illinois, the District of Columbia, Alabama):

> Approaches to learning/Logic and reasoning
> Communication and language
> Literacy
> Mathematics
> Scientific inquiry
> Social studies
> The arts
> Social-emotional development
> Physical development/Health and safety

Although each state's ELS are framed and organized differently, the actual standards themselves—the specific knowledge, skills, and dispositions children are expected to learn before beginning kindergarten—are very similar from one state to the next. So, regardless of whether your state's ELS are presented in the "developmentally focused" format or in the "academically focused" format, the your plans for operationalizing the standards in your classroom would not change: The most effective way to teach young children is through the use of developmentally appropriate practices.

Working With Parents of Transitional Kindergartners

Parents often look to teachers—even teachers who do not have their own children—for guidance and advice about childrearing. This is particularly true for parents of children in TK classrooms. Parents of TK students who are chronologically young may have concerns about their children's social interactions, their academic skill development in relation to the older students, and whether or not they are being adequately challenged/stimulated/supported. Parents of TK students who are developmentally young may be worried that their children might have a learning disability or might choke on a bite of hot dog in the lunchroom. They have concerns about friendships, behavior, and moving on to kindergarten next year. Sometimes the parents will have more concerns and worries than you can manage.

It makes sense to familiarize yourself with all the services that are available to children and families through your school district, your county, and in your community. Parents may want referrals to physical and mental health providers, dentists and orthodontists, vision and hearing screening, neuropsychologists and clinicians who evaluate children's learning needs, tutors and speech-language pathologists, and so on; the easiest way to manage these requests is with a simple handout listing a few providers in each category that can be given to parents as needed.

Three Tips for Teachers of TK Ligers

1. Your Students Are Enrolled in Transitional Kindergarten— Not Regular Kindergarten—Because They're Young, Chronologically and/or Developmentally

Don't be surprised when TK students burst into tears of frustration, make bad choices, leave their coats behind in the classroom every day for a week, and accidentally drop stacks of carefully alphabetized papers in the hallway 30 seconds before the dismissal bell rings. These are age-appropriate behaviors for young five-year-olds. Expect that you will be providing each of your students with scaffolds and additional support as needed throughout your year together.

2. Your TK Students Are Young, but They Are Not Babies

Five-year-olds are capable of learning how to do many things for themselves. Teach your students the skills they need to become more independent, to take initiative, and to solve their own problems. Developing autonomy and accomplishing tasks successfully will enable your young students to build self-confidence and a sense of competence that will help them to succeed more easily next year in kindergarten.

TABLE 11.2 CCSS-M Standards for Mathematical Practice

CCSS Standards For Mathematical Practice (SMP)	SMP in Student-Friendly Language (White & Dauksas, 2012)
Make sense of problems and persevere in solving them.	I can try many times to understand and solve a math problem.
Reason abstractly and quantitatively.	I can think about the math problem in my head first.
Construct viable arguments and critique the reasoning of others.	I can make a plan, called a strategy, to solve the problem, and discuss other students' strategies too.
Model with mathematics.	I can use math symbols and numbers to solve the problem.
Use appropriate tools strategically.	I can use math tools, pictures, drawings, and objects to solve the problem.
Attend to precision.	I can check to see if my strategy and calculations are correct.
Look for and make use of structure.	I can use what I already know about math to solve the problem.
Look for and express regularity in repeated reasoning.	I can use a strategy that I used to solve another math problem.

3. Include the CCSS-Mathematics Standards for Mathematical Practice in Your Mathematics Curriculum

The CCSS do not include content standards for prekindergarten. However, the CCSS mathematics standards include a second type of standards—the Standards for Mathematical Practice (as opposed to the Standards for Mathematical Content)—that are readily applicable to the mathematics teaching and learning that occur in prekindergarten settings. The Standards for Mathematical Practice are performance standards that describe the approaches to mathematics, the mathematical habits of mind, and the attitudes about mathematics that are demonstrated by outstanding mathematical thinkers/learners. Helping young students develop these ways of approaching and thinking about mathematics before they enter kindergarten will prepare them for success in kindergarten.

References

Quick, H., Manship, K., Gonzalez, R., Holod, A., Cadigan, M., Anthony, J., Hauser, A., Madsen, S., Blum, J., & Mercado-Garcia, D. (2014). *Study of California's transitional kindergarten program: Report on the first year of implementation.* San Mateo, CA: American Institutes for Research.

White, J., & Dauksas, L. (2012). CCSSM: Getting started in K–grade 2. *Teaching Children Mathematics, 1* (7), 440–445.

12

USING DAP TO TEACH THE CCSS IN KINDERGARTEN

Typical age range for kindergarten: 5–6 years old

Working metaphor for kindergartners: Kindergartners are **actors starring in a production called** ***Kindergarten: The Musical.***

After years of working in obscurity in preschools, day camps, and their parents' minivans, these five-year-olds have finally made it to the big time: kindergarten! They're at "real school" now and they're ready to shine. Each actor in *Kindergarten: The Musical* has a different constellation of talents—including (but not limited to) singing, dancing, juggling, making silly faces, reciting poetry, baton twirling, improvisational comedy—and they are always ready to claim center stage and show everyone what they can do. In this brand new world, every day brings unexpected challenges and wonderful surprises. Disappointment, hiding in the wings but prepared to strike at any time, is also part of the actors' new lives. They rely on their relationships with their cast-mates and YOU, their "director," to support them through those difficult times and help them regain their sparkle.

Focus Topic: Kindergarten Is Not "The New First Grade"

After taking a closer look at the specific academic knowledge and skills presented in the kindergarten CCSS for ELA and Math, many pundits, policymakers, politicians have been discussing the same question: whether or not kindergarten has become "the new first grade." Many of these people believe—mistakenly—that the academic intensification of kindergarten is a result of the Common Core. But that is not the case.

In truth, kindergarten became "the new first grade" circa 2002–2006, the early years of the implementation of No Child Left Behind. States and school districts, desperate to ensure their schools would make Adequate Yearly

TABLE 12.1 Developmental Traits of Kindergartners Typically Seen in Classrooms

Physical	To be able to control their physical behavior when learning new content or completing an activity, kinders need a lot of physical activity indoors and outdoors each day. Their fine motor skills are developing and they can focus on a pencil-and-paper task for short periods of time.
Social- Emotional	Kindergartners thrive on adult encouragement and approval and they dislike making mistakes and breaking rules. They are cooperative and often want to help the teacher. Kindergartners enjoy playing and working with their classmates, especially when everyone adheres to the established classroom procedures and rules.
Cognitive	Structure and routine are important to kindergartners' feelings of safety and success. They learn best through exploration and play, using concrete materials like sand and water, blocks, and other manipulatives. Pretend play has an important role in kindergartners' language development and should be encouraged.

Progress (AYP), cracked down hard on kindergarten. As a researcher studying kindergarten teachers' curricular and instructional decision making in a highly prescriptive school district in Texas during those years, I watched as workbooks replaced socio-dramatic play, seatwork replaced outdoor activities, and blocks were boxed up and moved into closets to create more space for desks and tables where children could sit and do their "work jobs" (Goldstein, 2007a, 2007b, 2008b). Teachers and student teachers, school administrators and parents, teacher educators and scholars were aware of these enormous changes in kindergarten, but our conversations and publications didn't attract much popular attention.

The CCSS' expectations for kindergarten ELA and Mathematics are certainly focused more strongly on academic skills than any state's expectations for kindergarten would have been in 1990. But the downward creep of academic skills into kindergarten (and preschool) is just one of many things that have changed in public schooling over the past 25 years. The CCSS is a hot-button issue for a lot of people in the United States, so it can easily become a scapegoat for anything the general public finds unsatisfactory about public education.

The CCSS's expectations for kindergarten learners are high because child development research indicates that young children are extremely good at learning new things (Copple et al., 2013, ix). Are the expectations too high? Yes, they're too high for some children. But they are also too low for other children, and just right for the rest. However, young children's growth and development do not occur at a consistently steady pace: Intellectual growth spurts and power surges are balanced by mental consolidation and integration, and a lot can change for a child over the 9 months of an academic year.

Unlike the content standards previously used by each state, the CCSS is sharply focused only on the most important skills (Common Core State Standards Initiative Standards-Setting Considerations, n.d.). Teachers are encouraged to revisit key concepts and skills repeatedly throughout the year to allow students to reengage with material they had not fully mastered the first time around: This is the case in both ELA and Math. Kindergartners will have the opportunity to learn fewer things more thoroughly and to apply what they've learned to real world tasks and challenges.

In the remainder of this chapter you will find the following:

- Complete CCSS-Math Standards for kindergarten
- *Annotated* CCSS-Math Standards for kindergarten
  - All standards fully unpacked
- Complete CCSS-ELA Standards for kindergarten
- *Annotated* CCSS-ELA Standards for kindergarten
  - All standards fully unpacked
- Three tips for teachers working with the cast of *Kindergarten: The Musical*

The text for the kindergarten standards for mathematical content and for English Language Arts is quoted verbatim from the CCSS-M and CCSS-ELA Standards documents. The annotations to the standards provided in each content area are my efforts to help get you started on unpacking the standards. The ideas and observations I present are nothing more than one person's interpretation of the knowledge and skills included in the standards. I wish it were possible for me to hear your interpretations!

Kindergarten Standards for Mathematical Content

- In kindergarten, instructional time should focus on *two critical areas*:
  - (1) representing, relating, and operating on whole numbers, initially with sets of objects;
  - (2) describing shapes and space.

The majority of kindergarten mathematics learning time should be devoted to number.

Kindergarten Mathematics Standards by Domain

Counting and Cardinality (CC)

- **Know number names and the count sequence.**
  K.CC.1   Count to 100 by ones and tens.

K.CC.2 Count forward beginning from a given number within the known sequence (instead of having to begin at 1).

K.CC.3. Write numbers from 0 to 20. Represent a number of objects with a written numeral from 0–20 (with 0 representing a count of no objects).

- **Count to tell the number of objects.**

K.CC.4 Understand the relationship between numbers and quantities; connect counting to cardinality.

    a. When counting objects, say the number names in the standard order, pairing each object with one and only one number name and each number name with one and only one object.

    b. Understand that the last number name said tells the number of objects counted. The number of objects is the same regardless of their arrangement or the order in which they were counted.

    c. Understand that each successive number name refers to a quantity that is one larger.

K.CC.5 Count to answer "how many?" questions about as many as 20 things arranged in a line, a rectangular array, or a circle, or as many as 10 things in a scattered configuration; given a number from 1–20, count out that many objects.

- **Compare numbers.**

K.CC.6 Identify whether the number of objects in one group is greater than, less than, or equal to the number of objects in another group, e.g., by using matching and counting strategies (includes groups with up to ten objects).

K.CC.7 Compare two numbers between 1 and 10 as written numbers.

Operations and Algebraic Thinking (OA)

- **Understand addition as putting together and adding to, and understand subtraction as taking apart and taking from.**

K.OA.1 Represent addition and subtraction with objects, fingers, mental images, drawings, sounds (e.g., claps), acting out situations, verbal explanations, expressions, or equations.

K.OA.2 Solve addition and subtraction word problems, and add and subtract within 10, e.g., by using objects of drawings to represent the problem.

K.OA.3 Decompose numbers less than or equal to 10 into pairs in more than one way, e.g., by using objects of drawings, and record each decomposition by drawing or equation (e.g., $5 = 2 + 3$ and $5 = 4 + 1$).

K.OA.4 For any number from 1 to 9, find the number that makes 10 when added to the given number, e.g., by using objects or drawings, and record the answer with a drawing or equation.

K.OA.5 Fluently add and subtract within 5.

Number and Operations in Base Ten (NBT)

- **Work with numbers 11–19 to gain foundations for place value.**

    K.NBT.1 Compose and decompose numbers from 11 to 19 into ten ones
    and some further ones, e.g., by using objects or drawings, and
    record each composition or decomposition by drawing or equa-
    tion (e.g., 18 = 10 + 8); understand that these numbers are com-
    posed of ten ones and one, two, three, four, five, six seven, eight,
    or nine ones.

Measurement and Data (MD)

- **Describe and compare measurable attributes.**

    K.MD.1 Describe measurable attributes of objects, such as length or weight.
    Describe several measurable attributes as a single object.

    K.MD.2 Directly compare two objects with a measurable attribute in com-
    mon, to see which object has "more of"/"less of" the attribute, and
    describe the difference. *For example, directly compare the heights of
    two children and describe one child as taller/shorter.*

- **Classify objects and count the number of objects in each category.**

    K.MD.3 Classify objects into given categories; count the numbers of objects
    in each category and sort the categories by count.

Geometry (G)

- **Identify and describe shapes (squares, circles, triangles, rectangles,
  hexagons, cubes, cones, cylinders, and spheres).**

    K.G.1   Describe objects in the environment using names of shapes, and
    describe the relative positions of these objects using terms such as
    above, below, beside, in front of, behind, and *next to.*

    K.G.2   Correctly name shapes regardless of their orientations or overall
    size.

    K.G.3   Identify shapes as two-dimensional (lying in a plane, flat) or three-
    dimensional (solid).

- **Analyze, compare, create, and compose shapes.**

    K.G.4   Analyze and compare two-and three-dimensional shapes, in different
    sizes and orientations, using informal language to describe their simi-
    larities, differences, parts (e.g., number of sides and vertices/"corners")
    and other attributes (e.g., having sides of equal length).

    K.G.4   Model shapes in the world by building shapes from components
    (e.g., sticks and clay balls) and drawing shapes.

    K.G.6   Compose simple shapes to form larger shapes. *For example, "Can
    you join these two triangles with full sides touching to make a rect-
    angle?"*

TABLE 12.2 CCSS-M Standards for Mathematical Practice

CCSS STANDARDS FOR MATHEMATICAL PRACTICE (SMP)	SMP IN STUDENT-FRIENDLY LANGUAGE (White & Dauksas, 2012)
Make sense of problems and persevere in solving them.	I can try many times to understand and solve a math problem.
Reason abstractly and quantitatively.	I can think about the math problem in my head first.
Construct viable arguments and critique the reasoning of others.	I can make a plan, called a strategy, to solve the problem, and discuss other students' strategies too.
Model with mathematics.	I can use math symbols and numbers to solve the problem.
Use appropriate tools strategically.	I can use math tools, pictures, drawings, and objects to solve the problem.
Attend to precision.	I can check to see if my strategy and calculations are correct.
Look for and make use of structure.	I can use what I already know about math to solve the problem.
Look for and express regularity in repeated reasoning.	I can use a strategy that I used to solve another math problem.

ANNOTATED
Kindergarten Standards for Mathematical Content

MUCH OF THE LANGUAGE USED IN THE CCSS-MATHEMATICS DEPARTS FROM THE TYPICAL MATH TERMINOLOGY USED IN PAST STANDARDS. THE AUTHORS OF THE STANDARDS DELIBERATELY LIMIT THE USE OF GENERIC LANGUAGE IN ORDER TO INTRODUCE ACADEMIC LANGUAGE, E.G., THE LANGUAGE MATHEMATICIANS USE TO TALK ABOUT MATH.

- In Kindergarten, instructional time should focus on two *critical areas*:
  (1) representing, relating, and operating on whole numbers, initially with sets of objects;
  (2) describing shapes and space.

The majority of kindergarten mathematics learning time should be devoted to number.

Kindergarten Mathematics Standards by Domain

REMEMBER, THESE ARE THE EXPECTATIONS STUDENTS SHOULD BE ABLE TO MEET AT THE *END OF KINDERGARTEN.*

Counting and Cardinality (CC)

* Know number names and the count sequence.

    K.CC.1 Count to 100 by ones and tens.

    THIS STANDARD DOES NOT REQUIRE RECOGNITION OF NUMERALS. STUDENTS ARE EXPECTED TO COUNT BY ROTE FROM 1 TO 100 AND TO COUNT BY TENS TO 100 USING MULTIPLES OF 10.

    K.CC.2 Count forward beginning from a given number within the known sequence (instead of having to begin at 1).

    THIS STRATEGY IS OFTEN REFERRED TO AS "COUNTING ON." IT DOES NOT REQUIRE STUDENTS TO RECOGNIZE NUMERALS.

    K.CC.3 Write numbers from 0 to 20. Represent a number of objects with a written numeral from 0–20 (with 0 representing a count of no objects).

    REVERSAL OF WRITTEN NUMERALS IS EXPECTED; POINT OUT AND CORRECT THE ERROR. THE FOCUS OF THIS STANDARD IS USING NUMERALS TO REPRESENT QUANTITIES.

* Count to tell the number of objects.

    K.CC.4 Understand the relationship between numbers and quantities; connect counting to cardinality.
    a. When counting objects, say the number names in the standard order, pairing each object with one and only one number name and each number name with one and only one object.

    THIS SKILL IS OFTEN CALLED ONE-TO-ONE CORRESPONDENCE. FANS OF PIAGET KNOW THIS STANDARD AS "CONSERVATION OF NUMBER."

    b. Understand that the last number name said tells the number of objects counted. The number of objects is the same regardless of their arrangement or the order in which they were counted.

WHEN A STUDENT FINISHES COUNTING THE OBJECTS (". . . FIVE, SIX, SEVEN."), ASK HER "HOW MANY DO YOU HAVE?" IF THE STUDENT SAYS "SEVEN," SHE HAS MASTERED THIS STAN-DARD. IF SHE COUNTS THE OBJECTS AGAIN BEFORE SHE ANSWERS, SHE HAS NOT MASTERED THE STANDARD.

    c.   **Understand that each successive number name refers to a quantity that is one larger.**

THIS STANDARD REQUIRES STUDENTS TO UNDERSTAND THAT SOMEONE WHO HAS 5 OBJECTS ALSO HAS 4 OBJECTS, 3 OBJECTS, 2 OBJECTS, AND 1 OBJECT; IF SOMEONE HAD 5 OBJECTS AND WANTED TO HAVE 6, HE WOULD ONLY NEED TO ADD ONE MORE OBJECT, NOT 6 MORE. THE FOCUS IS ON PART-TO-WHOLE RELATIONSHIPS.

K.CC.5 **Count to answer "how many?" questions about as many as 20 things arranged in a line, a rectangular array, or a circle, or as many as 10 things in a scattered configuration; given a number from 1–20, count out that many objects.**

AN ARRAY IS AN ORDERLY ARRANGEMENT OF OBJECTS, SUCH AS ROWS, COLUMNS, OR A MATRIX. THIS STANDARD FOCUSES ON A STUDENT'S ABILITY TO KEEP TRACK AS SHE COUNTS OBJECTS.

• **Compare numbers.**

K.CC.6 **Identify whether the number of objects in one group is greater than, less than, or equal to the number of objects in another group, e.g., by using matching and counting strategies (includes groups with up to ten objects).**

SOME STUDENTS MIGHT USE MATCHING STRATEGIES (PAIR-ING UP OBJECTS TO SEE WHICH HAS MORE), COUNTING STRATEGIES (COUNTING EACH OBJECT AND COMPARING THE QUANTITIES), OR EQUAL SHARES (STARTING WITH A PILE AND TAKING OBJECTS AWAY) TO DETERMINE WHETHER ONE GROUP IS GREATER THAN, LESS THAN, OR EQUAL TO THE OTHER.

K.CC.7 **Compare two numbers between 1 and 10 as written numerals.**

NOTE: STANDARD #6 INVOLVES WORKING WITH *OBJECTS OR DRAWINGS* IN THE CONTEXT OF GREATER THAN/EQUALS/LESS THAN. STANDARD #7 INVOLVES PENCIL AND PAPER WITHOUT ANY MANIPULATIVES.

Operations and Algebraic Thinking (OA)

- Understand addition as putting together and adding to, and understand subtraction as taking apart and taking from.

  K.OA.1 Represent addition and subtraction with objects, fingers, mental images, drawings, sounds (e.g., claps), acting out situations, verbal explanations, expressions, or equations.

  > I RECOMMEND STAYING AWAY FROM USING ANY REPRESENTATIONAL FORM THAT THE STUDENTS CANNOT SEE OR TOUCH. SOUNDS AND MENTAL IMAGES ARE INVISIBLE AND INTANGIBLE AND THIS HAS THE POTENTIAL TO CONFUSE STUDENTS IN SIGNIFICANT, TIME-INTENSIVE WAYS.

  K.OA.2. Solve addition and subtraction word problems, and add and subtract within 10, e.g., by using objects or drawings to represent the problem.

  > THERE ARE FOUR TYPES OF PROBLEMS: RESULT UNKNOWN, ADD TO; RESULT UNKNOWN, TAKE FROM; PUT TOGETHER/TAKE APART, TOTAL UNKNOWN; AND PUT TOGETHER/TAKE APART, ADDEND UNKNOWN. STUDENTS MUST BE ABLE TO SOLVE AND EXPLAIN THEIR SOLUTIONS TO ALL FOUR TYPES OF PROBLEM.

  K.OA.3 Decompose numbers less than or equal to 10 into pairs in more than one way, e.g., by using objects or drawings, and record each decomposition by drawing or equation (e.g., 5 = 2 + 3 and 5 = 4 + 1).

  > STUDENTS NEED TO DEMONSTRATE UNDERSTANDING OF PART-WHOLE RELATIONSHIPS: A SET OF 5 OBJECTS CAN BE BROKEN INTO SUBSETS (IN MULTIPLE WAYS) AND STILL BE 5.

  K.OA.4 For any number from 1 to 9, find the number that makes 10 when added to the given number, e.g., by using objects or drawings, and record the answer with a drawing or equation.

  > THIS STRATEGY IS ALSO REFERRED TO AS "MAKING TEN."

  K.OA.5 Fluently add and subtract within 5.

  > STUDENTS ARE FLUENT WHEN THEY DISPLAY ACCURACY (CORRECT ANSWER), EFFICIENCY (A REASONABLE NUMBER OF STEPS IN 3–5 SECONDS WITHOUT RESORTING TO COUNTING), AND FLEXIBILITY (USING STRATEGIES).

  > PLEASE NOTE: THESE STANDARDS FOCUS ON UNDERSTANDING THE CONCEPTS OF ADDITION AND SUBTRACTION, NOT

ON READING AND SOLVING ADDITION AND SUBTRACTION EQUATIONS.

Number and Operations in Base Ten (NBT)

• Work with numbers 11–19 to gain foundations for place value.

K.NBT.1 Compose and decompose numbers from 11 to 19 into ten ones and some further ones, e.g., by using objects or drawings, and record each composition or decomposition by drawing or equation (e.g., 18 = 10 + 8); understand that these numbers are composed of ten ones and one, two, three, four, five, six seven, eight, or nine ones.

KINDERGARTNERS SHOULD NOT "UNITIZE" A TEN (E.G., THEY ARE NOT EXPECTED TO RECOGNIZE THAT A GROUP OF TEN OBJECTS IS A UNIT CALLED "A TEN" BECAUSE THAT IS A GRADE 1 STANDARD). RATHER, THEY KEEP COUNT OF THE OBJECTS AS SINGLE UNITS AS THEY EXPLORE A SET OF 10 OBJECTS AND "LEFTOVERS."

Measurement and Data (MD)

• Describe and compare measurable attributes.

K.MD.1 Describe measurable attributes of objects, such as length or weight. Describe several measurable attributes of a single object.

K.MD.2 Directly compare two objects with a measurable attribute in common, to see which object has "more of"/"less of" the attribute, and describe the difference. For example, directly compare the heights of two children and describe one child as taller/shorter.

STUDENTS MIGHT BE LIMITED TO DESCRIBING OBJECTS AS BIGGER THAN OR SMALLER THAN ANOTHER OBJECT. AN UNWRITTEN PART OF THIS STANDARD INVOLVES TEACHING STUDENTS TO USE PRECISE MATHEMATICAL TERMINOLOGY TO DESCRIBE THE DIFFERENCES: YES, THAT OBJECT IS BIGGER . . . BUT *HOW* IS IT BIGGER? IN WHAT WAY? IS IT TALLER? LONGER? HEAVIER? WIDER? DOES IT COVER MORE SPACE?

• Classify objects and count the number of objects in each category.

K.MD.3. Classify objects into given categories; count the numbers of objects in each category and sort the categories by count.

CLASSIFICATION IS THE SAME THING AS SORTING. STUDENTS SHOULD SORT OBJECTS INTO CATEGORIES, COUNT HOW

MANY OBJECTS ARE IN EACH CATEGORY, AND THEN ORGA-NIZE THE CATEGORIES BY THE QUANTITY OF OBJECTS THEY CONTAIN.

Geometry (G)

• Identify and describe shapes (squares, circles, triangles, rectangles, hexagons, cubes, cones, cylinders, and spheres).

K.G.1 Describe objects in the environment using names of shapes, and describe the relative positions of these objects using terms such as above, below, beside, in front of, behind, and next to.

STUDENTS ARE EXPECTED TO START OUT USING ORDINARY TERMS FOR THE SHAPES BUT SHOULD SHIFT TO USING ACCU-RATE MATHEMATICAL TERMINOLOGY.

K.G.2 Correctly name shapes regardless of their orientations or over-all size.

STUDENTS RECOGNIZE THE ATTRIBUTES THAT DEFINE WHAT A SHAPE IS CALLED AND IDENTIFY THE ATTRIBUTES THAT AREN'T REQUIRED TO NAME A SHAPE.

K.G.3. Identify shapes as two-dimensional (lying in a plane, flat) or three-dimensional (solid).

• Analyze, compare, create, and compose shapes.

K.G.4 Analyze and compare two-and three-dimensional shapes, in different sizes and orientations, using informal language to describe their similarities, differences, parts (e.g., number of sides and vertices/"corners") and other attributes (e.g., having sides of equal length).

K.G.5 Model shapes in the world by building shapes from compo-nents (e.g., sticks and clay balls) and drawing shapes.

STUDENTS DEMONSTRATE THEIR UNDERSTANDING OF GEO-METRIC ATTRIBUTES OF SHAPES BY CREATING OTHER SHAPES.

K.G.6 Compose simple shapes to form larger shapes. For example, "Can you join these two triangles with full sides touching to make a rectangle?"

STUDENTS MANIPULATE SIMPLE SHAPES BY MOVING, ROTAT-ING, FLIPPING, AND ARRANGING TO CREATE A NEW SHAPE.

Kindergarten Reading Standards

TABLE 12.3

Reading Standards: Literature	Reading Standards: Informational Text
Key Ideas and Details	
RL.K.1. With prompting and support, ask and answer questions about key details in a text.	RI.K.1. With prompting and support, ask and answer questions about key details in a text.
RL.K.2. With prompting and support, retell familiar stories, including key details.	RI.K.2. With prompting and support, identify the main topics and retell key details of a text.
RL.K.3. With prompting and support, identify characters, settings, and major events in a story.	RI.K.3. With prompting and support, describe the connection between two individuals, events, ideas, or pieces of information in a text.
Craft and Structure	
RL.K.4. Ask and answer questions about unknown words in a text.	RI.K.4. With prompting and support, ask and answer questions about unknown words in a text.
RL.K.5. Recognize common types of texts (e.g., storybooks, poems).	RI.K.5. Identify the front cover, back cover, and title page of a book.
RL.K.6. With prompting and support, name the author and illustrator of a story and define the role of each in telling the story.	RI.K.6. Name the author and illustrator of a text and define the role of each in presenting the ideas or information in a text.
Integration of Knowledge and Ideas	
RL.K.7. With prompting and support, describe the relationship between illustrations and the story in which they appear (e.g., what moment in a story an illustration appears).	RI.K.7. With prompting and support, describe the relationship between illustrations and the text in which they appear (e.g., what person, place, thing, or idea in the text an illustration depicts).

(Continued)

TABLE 12.3 (Continued)

8. (Not applicable to literature)	RI.K.8. With prompting and support, identify the reasons and author gives to support points in a text.
RL.K.9. With prompting and support, compare and contrast the adventures and experiences of characters in familiar stories.	RI.K.9. With prompting and support, identify basic similarities and differences between two texts on the same topic (e.g., illustrations, descriptions, or procedures).

Range of Reading and Level of Text Complexity

RL.K.10. Actively engage in group reading activities with purpose and understanding.	RI.K.10. Actively engage in group reading activities with purpose and understanding.

TABLE 12.4

Reading Standards: Foundational Skills

Print Concepts

RF.K.1. Demonstrate understanding of the organization and basic features of print.

  a. Follow words from left to right, top to bottom, and page by page.
  b. Recognize that spoken words are represented in written language by specific sequences of letters.
  c. Understand that words are separated by spaces in print.d. Recognize and name all upper- and lowercase letters of the alphabet.

Phonological Awareness

RF.K.2. Demonstrate understanding of spoken words, syllables, and sounds (phonemes).

  a. Recognize and produce rhyming words.
  b. Count, pronounce, blend, and segment syllables in spoken words.
  c. Blend and segment onsets and rimes of single syllable spoken words.
  d. Isolate and pronounce the initial, medial vowel, and final sounds (phonemes) in three-phoneme (consonant-vowel-consonant or CVC words). (This does not include CVCs ending with /l/, /r/, or /x/.)
  e. Add or substitute individual sounds (phonemes) in simple, one-syllable words to make new words.

Phonics and Word Recognition

RF.K.3. Know and apply grade-level phonics and word analysis skills in decoding words.
 	
   a. Demonstrate basic knowledge of one-to-one letter-sound correspondence by producing the primary or many of the most frequent sounds for each consonant.
 	
   b. Associate the long and short vowel sounds with common spellings (graphemes) for the five major vowels.
 	
   c. Read common high-frequency words by sight (e.g., the, of, to, you, she, my, is, are, do, does).
 	
   d. Distinguish between similarly spelled words by identifying the sounds of the letters that differ.

Fluency
RF.K.4. Read emergent-reader texts with purpose and understanding.

Kindergarten Writing Standards

TABLE 12.5

Text Types and Purposes
W.K.1. Use a combination of drawing, dictating, and writing to compose opinion pieces in which they tell a reader the topic or the name of the book they are writing about and state an opinion or preference about the topic or book (e.g., My favorite book is . . .).
W.K.2. Use a combination of drawing, dictating, and writing to compose informative/explanatory texts in which they name what they are writing about and supply some information about the topic.
W.K.3. Use a combination of drawing, dictating, and writing to narrate a single event or several loosely linked events, tell about the events in the order in which they occurred, and provide a reaction to what happened.
Production and Distribution of Writing
4. (Begins in grade 3)
W.K.5. With guidance and support from adults, respond to questions and suggestions from peers and add details to strengthen writing as needed.
W.K.6. With guidance and support from adults, use a variety of digital tools to produce and publish writing, including in collaboration with peers.

(Continued)

TABLE 12.5 (Continued)

Research to Build and Present Knowledge
W.K.7. Participate in shared research and writing projects (e.g., explore a number of books by a favorite author and express opinions about them).
W.K.8. With guidance and support from adults, recall information from experience or gather information from provided sources to answer a question.
9. (Begins in grade 4)
Range of Writing
10. (Begins in grade 3)

Kindergarten Speaking and Listening Standards

TABLE 12.6

Comprehension and Collaboration
SL.K.1. Participate in collaborative conversations with diverse partners about kindergarten topics and texts with peers and adults in small and larger groups.
a. Follow agreed-upon rules for discussions (e.g., listening to others and taking turns speaking about the topics and texts under discussion)   b. Continue a conversation through multiple exchanges.
SL.K.2. Confirm understanding of a text read aloud or information presented orally or through other media by asking and answering questions about key details and requesting clarification if something is not understood.
SL.K.3. Ask and answer questions in order to seek help, get information, or clarify something that is not understood.
Presentation of Knowledge and Ideas
SL.K.4. Describe familiar people, places, things, and events and, with prompting and support, provide additional detail.
SL.K.5. Add drawings or other visual displays to descriptions as desired to provide additional detail.
SL.K.6. Speak audibly and express thoughts, feelings, and ideas clearly.

Kindergarten Language Standards

TABLE 12.7

Conventions of Standard English
L.K.1. Demonstrate command of the conventions of standard English grammar and usage when writing or speaking. (a) Print many upper- and lowercase letters. (b) Use frequently occurring nouns and verbs. (c) Form regular plural nouns orally by adding /s/ or /es/ (e.g., dog, *dogs*; wish, *wishes*). L.K.2. Demonstrate command of the conventions of standard English capitalization, punctuation, and spelling when writing. (a) Capitalize the first word in a sentence and the pronoun *I*. (b) Recognize and name end punctuation. (c) Write a letter or letters for most consonant and short-vowel sounds (phonemes). (d) Spell simple words phonetically, drawing on knowledge of sound-letter relationships.

Knowledge of Language
3. (Begins in grade 2)

Vocabulary Acquisition and Use
L.K.4. Determine or clarify the meaning of unknown and multiple-meaning words and phrases based on *kindergarten reading and content*. (a) Identify new meanings for familiar words and apply them accurately (e.g., knowing *duck* is a bird and learning the verb *to duck*). (b) Use the most frequently occurring inflections and affixes (e.g., *-ed,-s, re-, un-, pre-,-ful,-less*) as a clue to the meaning of an unknown word. L.K.5. With guidance and support from adults, explore word relationships and nuances in word meanings. (a) Sort common objects into categories (e.g., shapes, foods) to gain a sense of the concepts the categories represent. (b) Demonstrate understanding of frequently occurring verbs and adjectives by relating them to their opposites (antonyms). (c) Identify real-life connections between words and their use (e.g., note places at school that are *colorful*). (d) Distinguish shades of meaning among verbs describing the same general action (e.g., *walk, march, strut, prance*) by acting out the meanings. L.K.6. Use words and phrases acquired through conversations, reading and being read to, and responding to texts.

ANNOTATED

Kindergarten Reading Standards

THESE STANDARDS INDICATE THE KNOWLEDGE AND SKILLS STUDENTS SHOULD MASTER BY THE *END OF KINDERGARTEN.*

TABLE 12.8

Reading Standards: Literature	Reading Standards: Informational Text
Key Ideas and Details	
RL.K.1. With prompting and support, ask and answer questions about key details in a text.	RI.K.1. With prompting and support, ask and answer questions about key details in a text.
RL.K.2. With prompting and support, retell familiar stories, including key details.	RI.K.2. With prompting and support, identify the main topics and retell key details of a text.
RL.K.3. With prompting and support, identify characters, settings, and major events in a story.	RI.K.3. With prompting and support, describe the connection between two individuals, events, ideas, or pieces of information in a text.
ANNOTATION	ANNOTATION
STUDENTS NEED TO KNOW WHAT MAKES SOMETHING A "KEY DETAIL" AND WHAT KINDS OF QUESTIONS COULD BE ASKED AND ANSWERED ABOUT A KEY DETAIL. THEY NEED TO PUT KEY DETAILS IN SEQUENTIAL ORDER TO RETELL A FAMILIAR STORY. THEY ALSO HAVE TO RECOGNIZE AND NAME ELEMENTS IN A STORY: CHARACTERS, PROBLEM, SETTING, ETC.	STUDENTS NEED TO BE ABLE TO • ASK QUESTIONS ABOUT KEY DETAILS AND IMPORTANT IDEAS IN A NON-FICTION TEXT • ANSWER QUESTIONS ABOUT IMPORTANT IDEAS AND KEY DETAILS IN A NON-FICTION TEXT • STATE THE MAIN IDEA OF THE TEXT IN THEIR OWN WORDS AND EXPLAIN THEIR THINKING • EXPLAIN HOW INDIVIDUALS, IDEAS, EVENTS, OR FACTS IN THE TEXT ARE CONNECTED

Craft and Structure

RL.K.4. Ask and answer questions about unknown words in a text.	RI.K.4. With prompting and support, ask and answer questions about unknown words in a text.
RL.K.5. Recognize common types of texts (e.g., storybooks, poems).	RI.K.5. Identify the front cover, back cover, and title page of a book.
RL.K.6. With prompting and support, name the author and illustrator of a story and define the role of each in telling the story.	RI.K.6. Name the author and illustrator of a text and define the role of each in presenting the ideas or information in a text.
ANNOTATION	ANNOTATION
QUESTIONS TO ASK STUDENTS: • WHAT CAN YOU DO WHEN YOU COME TO A WORD YOU DO NOT KNOW? • WHAT KIND OF BOOK IS THIS? DOES IT TELL A STORY? OR DOES IT TELL TRUE INFORMATION? WHAT CLUES DID YOU FIND IN THE TEXT THAT HELPED YOU FIGURE THIS OUT? • WHO IS THE AUTHOR OF THIS BOOK? WHAT DOES AN AUTHOR DO? • WHO IS THE ILLUSTRATOR OF THIS BOOK? WHAT DOES AN ILLUSTRATOR DO?	STUDENTS SHOULD UNDERSTAND: • HOW A PIECE OF INFORMATIONAL TEXT IS STRUCTURED AND HOW THAT STRUCTURE IS DIFFERENT FROM A STORY'S STRUCTURE • WHY AN AUTHOR MIGHT CHOOSE ONE ILLUSTRATION OVER ANOTHER

Integration of Knowledge and Ideas

RL.K.7. With prompting and support, describe the relationship between illustrations and the story in which they appear (e.g., what moment in a story an illustration appears).	RI.K.7. With prompting and support, describe the relationship between illustrations and the text in which they appear (e.g., what person, place, thing, or idea in the text an illustration depicts).

(Continued)

TABLE 12.8 (Continued)

8. (Not applicable to literature)	RI.K.8. With prompting and support, identify the reasons and author gives to support points in a text.
RL.K.9. With prompting and support, compare and contrast the adventures and experiences of characters in familiar stories.	RI.K.9. With prompting and support, identify basic similarities and differences between two texts on the same topic (e.g., illustrations, descriptions, or procedures).
ANNOTATION	ANNOTATION
ASK STUDENTS COMPLEX QUESTIONS, SUCH AS: • HOW DOES THE PICTURE HELP YOU TO UNDERSTAND THE STORY? CAN YOU SHOW ME AN EXAMPLE? • HOW ARE THE CHARACTERS IN THESE TWO STORIES SIMILAR/ ALIKE? HOW ARE THEY DIFFERENT FROM EACH OTHER? CAN YOU GIVE ME EXAMPLE FROM THE TWO STORIES WE READ? • HOW DID EACH OF THE CHARACTERS SOLVE THE PROBLEM IN THEIR STORY? HOW DO YOU KNOW THIS? CAN YOU GIVE A SPECIFIC EXAMPLE FROM ONE STORY? • DID THE TWO CHARACTERS SOLVE THEIR PROBLEMS IN THE SAME WAY? IN WHAT WAYS WERE THEY THE SAME? IN WHAT WAYS WERE THEY DIFFERENT? • WERE THEIR SOLUTIONS MORE SIMILAR TO EACH OTHER OR MORE DIFFERENT FROM EACH OTHER? CAN YOU EXPLAIN YOUR THINKING?	ASK THE ACADEMICALLY ADVANCED STUDENTS CHALLENGE QUESTIONS, LIKE: • HOW CAN YOU RECOGNIZE THE AUTHOR'S REASONING/ ARGUMENT? HOW CAN YOU FIND SUPPORT OR EVIDENCE WITHIN THE TEXT? • HOW DO PICTURES HELP CONVEY MEANING AND INFORMATION IN AN INFORMATIONAL TEXT? • WHY MIGHT TWO TEXTS ON THE SAME TOPIC INCLUDE DIFFERENT FACTS AND INFORMATION?

Range of Reading and Level of Text Complexity	
RL.K.10. Actively engage in group reading activities with purpose and understanding.	RI.K.10. Actively engage in group reading activities with purpose and understanding.
ANNOTATION	ANNOTATION
STUDENTS SHOULD INCREASINGLY . . . • BE ACTIVELY ENGAGED AND RESPONSIBLE FOR THEIR LEARNING • READ INDEPENDENTLY AND CLOSELY • READ APPROPRIATELY COMPLEX TEXTS TO LEARN NEW WORDS AND NEW IDEAS THAT ENRICH THEIR VOCABULARY AND THINKING.	SEE READING: LITERATURE COLUMN.

TABLE 12.9

Reading Standards: Foundational Skills
Print Concepts

RF.K.1. Demonstrate understanding of the organization and basic features of print.
   a. Follow words from left to right, top to bottom, and page by page.
   b. Recognize that spoken words are represented in written language by specific sequences of letters.
   c. Understand that words are separated by spaces in print.
   d. Recognize and name all upper- and lowercase letters of the alphabet.

ANNOTATION
STUDENTS ARE EXPECTED TO RECOGNIZE AND NAME ALL UPPER AND LOWERCASE LETTERS OF THE ALPHABET BY THE END OF KINDERGARTEN.

(*Continued*)

TABLE 12.9 (Continued)

Phonological Awareness

RF.K.2. Demonstrate understanding of spoken words, syllables, and sounds (phonemes).

   a. Recognize and produce rhyming words.
   b. Count, pronounce, blend, and segment syllables in spoken words.
   c. Blend and segment onsets and rimes of single syllable spoken words.
   d. Isolate and pronounce the initial, medial vowel, and final sounds (phonemes) in three-phoneme (consonant-vowel-consonant or CVC words). (This does not include CVCs ending with /l/, /r/, or /x/.)
   e. Add or substitute individual sounds (phonemes) in simple, one-syllable words to make new words.

ANNOTATION

USE QUESTIONS AND PROMPTS TO ELICIT STUDENTS' KNOWLEDGE OF SOUNDS. ASK FOR WORDS THAT RHYME WITH ANOTHER WORD, FOR THE SOUND AT THE BEGINNING OF A WORD (AND, IF POSSIBLE, THE NAME OF THE LETTER THAT MAKES THAT SOUND), CLAP THE SYLLABLES IN YOUR NAME, ETC.

Phonics and Word Recognition

RF.K.3. Know and apply grade-level phonics and word analysis skills in decoding words.

   a. Demonstrate basic knowledge of one-to-one letter-sound correspondence by producing the primary or many of the most frequent sound for each consonant
   b. Associate the long and short vowel sounds with common spellings (graphemes) for the five major vowels.
   c. Read common high-frequency words by sight (e.g., the, of, to, you, she, my, is, are, do, does).
   d. Distinguish between similarly spelled words by identifying the sounds of the letters that differ.

ANNOTATION

STUDENTS CONTINUE TO LEARN SPECIFIC STRATEGIES FOR DECODING WORDS IN TEXTS. LEARNING SOUND-SYMBOL CORRESPONDENCE, VOWEL PATTERNS, HIGH FREQUENCY WORDS, AND SIGHT WORDS STRENGTHENS DECODING, SPELLING, AND VOCABULARY DEVELOPMENT. AS STUDENTS READ, ASK QUESTIONS LIKE:

DOES THAT SOUND RIGHT?

DOES THAT LOOK RIGHT?

DOES THAT MAKE SENSE?

CAN YOU GET THE WORD STARTED? WHAT SOUND DOES THE FIRST LETTER MAKE?

Fluency
RF.K.4. Read emergent-reader texts with purpose and understanding.
ANNOTATION
FLUENCY ENABLES READERS TO FOCUS ON THE MEANING OF THE TEXT AND TO UNDERSTAND MORE OF WHAT THEY READ. ENCOURAGE EMERGENT READERS TO "MAKE THEIR VOICE SOUND LIKE TALKING" WHEN THEY READ ALOUD.

ANNOTATED

Kindergarten Writing Standards

TABLE 12.10

Text Types and Purposes
W.K.1. Use a combination of drawing, dictating and writing to compose opinion pieces in which they tell a reader the topic or the name of the book they are writing about and state an opinion or preference about the topic or book (e.g., My favorite book is . . .).
W.K.2. Use a combination of drawing, dictating, and writing to compose informative/ explanatory texts in which they name what they are writing about and supply some information about the topic.
W.K.3. Use a combination of drawing, dictating, and writing to narrate a single event or several loosely linked events, tell about the events in the order in which they occurred, and provide a reaction to what happened.
ANNOTATION
STUDENTS MUST LEARN TO EXPRESS THEIR OPINIONS AND SHARE THEIR OPINIONS WITH OTHERS; THIS MEANS THEY NEED MANY OPPORTUNITIES TO DEVELOP PRODUCTIVE WRITING BEHAVIORS AND EXPRESS THEIR IDEAS VERBALLY. START THIS PROCESS BY CREATING OPPORTUNITIES FOR PAIR-SHARE OR TURN-AND-TALK CONVERSATIONS WITH PEERS ABOUT TOPICS RELEVANT TO KINDERGARTNERS.

(Continued)

TABLE 12.10 (Continued)

Production and Distribution of Writing

4. (Begins in grade 3)

W.K.5. With guidance and support from adults, respond to questions and suggestions from peers and add details to strengthen writing as needed.

W.K.6. With guidance and support from adults, use a variety of digital tools to produce and publish writing, including in collaboration with peers.

ANNOTATION

STUDENTS ARE EXPECTED TO RESPOND TO QUESTIONS AND SUGGESTIONS ABOUT THEIR WRITING. THEY MUST LEARN HOW TO ADD DESCRIPTIVE WORDS AND KEY DETAILS TO THEIR WRITING AND HOW TO RECOGNIZE ERRORS IN SPELLING, GRAMMAR, AND SO ON. KINDERGARTNERS BEGIN DEVELOPING THE STRATEGIES AND SKILLS NEEDED TO USE TECHNOLOGY TO PUBLISH THEIR WRITING.

Research to Build and Present Knowledge

W.K.7. Participate in shared research and writing projects (e.g., explore a number of books by a favorite author and express opinions about them).

W.K.8. With guidance and support from adults, recall information from experience or gather information from provided sources to answer a question.

9. (Begins in grade 4)

ANNOTATION

THE CCSS REQUIRE KINDERGARTNERS TO PARTICIPATE IN SHARED RESEARCH PROJECTS. STUDENTS WILL NEED SUPPORT UNDERSTANDING THEIR JOB ON THE TEAM, AND THE WORK THEY WILL DO, FROM THE BEGINNING OF THE PROJECT TO THE END. TEACHERS SHOULD DEVELOP GRAPHIC ORGANIZERS, CHECK SHEETS, TASK CHARTS, AND/OR JOB LISTS TO SCAFFOLD THE STUDENTS AS THEY UNDERTAKE THIS WORK.

Range of Writing

10. (Begins in grade 3)

ANNOTATED

Kindergarten Speaking and Listening Standards

TABLE 12.11

Comprehension and Collaboration

SL.K.1. Participate in collaborative conversations with diverse partners about kindergarten topics and texts with peers and adults in small and larger groups.
    a. Follow agreed-upon rules for discussions (e.g., listening to others and taking turns speaking about the topics and texts under discussion)
    b. Continue a conversation through multiple exchanges.

SL.K.2. Confirm understanding of a text read aloud or information presented orally or through other media by asking and answering questions about key details and requesting clarification if something is not understood.
SL.K.3. Ask and answer questions in order to seek help, get information, or clarify something that is not understood.
ANNOTATION
TEACHERS NEED TO HELP STUDENTS NOTICE WHEN THE CLASS OR GROUP IS HAVING A GOOD DISCUSSION AND ELICIT THEIR THOUGHTS ABOUT THE KEY FEATURES OF A GOOD DISCUSSION. STUDENTS ENGAGE IN COLLABORATIVE CONVERSATIONS (BOOK GROUPS, BUDDY READING) AND DEVELOP SKILLS SUCH AS ACTIVE LISTENING, LOOKING AT THE SPEAKER, TAKING TURNS, LINKING IDEAS TO THE SPEAKER'S IDEAS, SHARING THE FLOOR, ETC. STUDENTS SHOULD BE ABLE TO LISTEN TO A SPEAKER AND ASK FOR CLARIFICATION IF NECESSARY. THEY NEED TO LEARN TO FORMULATE A QUESTION THAT IS ON TOPIC AND TO UNDERSTAND AND ANSWER QUESTIONS ASKED OF THEM.
Presentation of Knowledge and Ideas
SL.K.4. Describe familiar people, places, things, and events and, with prompting and support, provide additional detail.
SL.K.5. Add drawings or other visual displays to descriptions as desired to provide additional detail.
SL.K.6. Speak audibly and express thoughts, feelings, and ideas clearly.

(Continued)

TABLE 12.11 (Continued)

ANNOTATION
STUDENTS WILL LEARN HOW TO REPORT FACTS AND RELEVANT DETAILS ABOUT AN EXPERIENCE WITH CLARITY OF THOUGHT AND EMOTIONS. THEY NEED TO LEARN HOW TO CHOOSE VISUAL DISPLAYS THAT ADD TO AND SUPPORT THEIR THINKING ABOUT A TOPIC. THEY NEED TO ARTICULATE THEIR IDEAS IN A PURPOSEFUL WAY THAT IS APPROPRIATE FOR THEIR AUDIENCE.

ANNOTATED
Kindergarten Language Standards

TABLE 12.12

Conventions of Standard English
L.K.1. Demonstrate command of the conventions of standard English grammar and usage when writing or speaking.
(a) Print many upper- and lowercase letters.
(b) Use frequently occurring nouns and verbs.
(c) Form regular plural nouns orally by adding /s/ or /es/ (e.g., dog, *dogs*; wish, *wishes*).
L.K.2. Demonstrate command of the conventions of standard English capitalization, punctuation, and spelling when writing.
(a) Capitalize the first word in a sentence and the pronoun *I*.
(b) Recognize and name end punctuation.
(c) Write a letter or letters for most consonant and short-vowel sounds (phonemes).
(d) Spell simple words phonetically, drawing on knowledge of sound-letter relationships.
ANNOTATION
DEVELOP AGE-APPROPRIATE COMMAND OF THE GRAMMAR AND USAGE OF STANDARD SPOKEN AND WRITTEN ENGLISH. EMPHASIS IS ON USING COMPLETE SENTENCES, FORMING QUESTIONS, USING PLURALS AND ATTENDING TO CONVENTIONS OF ENDING PUNCTUATION, CAPITALIZING, AND SPELLING SIMPLE WORDS.
Knowledge of Language
3. (Begins in grade 2)

Vocabulary Acquisition and Use
L.K.4. Determine or clarify the meaning of unknown and multiple-meaning words and phrases based on *kindergarten reading and content.* (a) Identify new meanings for familiar words and apply them accurately (e.g., knowing *duck* is a bird and learning the verb *to duck*). (b) Use the most frequently occurring inflections and affixes (e.g.,*-ed,-s, re-, un-, pre-,-ful,-less*) as a clue to the meaning of an unknown word. L.K.5. With guidance and support from adults, explore word relationships and nuances in word meanings. (a) Sort common objects into categories (e.g., shapes, foods) to gain a sense of the concepts the categories represent. (b) Demonstrate understanding of frequently occurring verbs and adjectives by relating them to their opposites (antonyms). (c) Identify real-life connections between words and their use (e.g., note places at school that are *colorful*). (d) Distinguish shades of meaning among verbs describing the same general action (e.g., *walk, march, strut, prance*) by acting out the meanings. L.K.6. Use words and phrases acquired through conversations, reading and being read to, and responding to texts.
ANNOTATION
STUDENTS DEVELOP VOCABULARY IN ORDER TO MAKE PURPOSEFUL LANGUAGE CHOICES IN WRITING AND SPEAKING TO COMMUNICATE EFFECTIVELY IN PRINT AND DIGITAL TEXTS. THEY SHOULD USE REGISTERS APPROPRIATE TO THEIR AUDIENCE, CONTEXT, AND PURPOSE. STUDENTS WILL EXPLORE THE SHADES OF MEANING AMONG SYNONYMS FOR COMMON VERBS, WORKS WITH MULTIPLE MEANINGS, AND THE WAYS THAT WORDS ARE USED IN REAL-LIFE SETTINGS.

Three Tips for Teachers of the Cast of Kindergarten: The Musical

1. Reinforce Students' Mathematical Foundations: Provide Daily Free Play With Math Manipulatives

The CCSS–Math standards for kindergarten are age appropriate and can be taught effectively with the tried-and-true instructional strategies kindergarten teachers have been using for years. But kindergartners whose early learning experiences were in academically oriented settings may not have had experiences playing with pattern blocks, linking cubes, counting chips, tubs of little colored plastic bears, unit blocks, and counting beans or been given opportunities to explore, theorize, imagine, test, re-test, and internalize the mathematical knowledge that is built through play with mathematics materials. All children need space and time to get down on the floor and really get involved with these materials, and this is especially important for children who have not yet been able to explore mathematical concepts through free play.

Children who enter first grade without sufficient experience playing with and manipulating math learning materials are at a disadvantage: They lack the internal mathematical "sense" that enables students to grasp a concept quickly and move on. So, in addition to the mathematics instruction you provide to all your students, I suggest making at least one math manipulative available for free play on a daily basis.

2. Pair Read-Alouds With Think-Alouds

The CCSS-ELA has many standards in grades K–3 that require children to provide evidence from a text to support their opinions, to compare and contrast two books on the same topic, and to explain how a character felt, why he felt that way, and what information was provided by the text or illustration that helped you answer the question. In CCSS classrooms, children and teachers talk about text a lot.

One way to prepare your kindergartners for future success is an activity called "read-aloud/think aloud." You choose an interesting picture book or informational text and do a traditional real-aloud. After you finish the book, ask the students how the main character felt when her little brother broke her stool—you will get lots of answers!—and then ask the students how they knew how the main character felt—what information in the text (either words or pictures) helped them know that. Once you've piqued their curiosity, read the book again. Prompt the children to think about the setting, the plot, the characters, the problem. Or have them consider how the little brother felt: Do your students think he broke the stool on purpose? If so, what's their evidence—what can they point to in the text or illustration that supports their idea? Engaging in these kinds of conversations in kindergarten will enable your students and their reasoning to shine brightly through Grade 3 and beyond.

3. Share Your Knowledge of the Common Core State Standards With Your Students' Parents

Parents are mystified, confused, and concerned about the Common Core State Standards. You have probably already heard comments like these:

> "What are they and why do we need them?"
> "I don't want my five-year-old to have a rigorous curriculum!"
> "Isn't the Common Core too hard for kindergartners?"
> "Does the Common Core let kindergartners play?"

Hopefully, this book will provide you with some answers to the parents' questions.

However, I think what really makes parents very uncomfortable about the CCSS is how strange and unusual the instructional materials look—number bonds, ten frames, stacked boxes, bubbles linked by sticks—and how ineffectual they feel when they can't help their kindergartner with his homework. In Chapter Seven, I provide links to many different informational materials aimed at parents and families: Most of the materials are available in both English and Spanish; some of the materials are available in more than 10 languages. Talking with parents about the CCSS, letting them observe a lesson or work in the classroom during a lesson, and sharing printed information with them can really make a difference for parents.

I don't think any parent of a kindergartner imagined that one day she'd take her five-year-old child's homework out of his backpack and not be able to make any sense of it. That feeling of confusion can really leave parents rattled. Information and support will go a long way.

References

Common Core State Standards Initiative. (n.d.). *Standards-setting considerations.* Retrieved from http://www.corestandards.org/assets/Considerations.pdf

Copple, C., Bredekamp, S., Koralek, D., & Charner, K. (Eds.). (2013). *Developmentally appropriate practice: Focus on preschoolers.* Washington, DC: National Association for the Education of Young Children.

Goldstein, L. S. (2007a). Examining the unforgiving complexity of kindergarten teaching. *Early Childhood Research Quarterly, 22,* 39–54.

Goldstein, L. S. (2007b). Embracing multiplicity: Learning from two practitioners' pedagogical responses to the changing demands of kindergarten teaching in the United States. *Journal of Research in Childhood Education, 21* (4), 378–99.

Goldstein, L. S. (2008b). Kindergarten teachers making "street-level" education policy in the wake of No Child Left Behind. *Early Education and Development, 19* (3), 448–78.

National Governors Association Center for Best Practices, Council of Chief State School Officers. (2010). *Common Core State Standards in English language arts and literacy history/ social studies, science, and technical subjects.* Washington, DC: National Governors Association Center for Best Practices, Council of Chief State School Officers.

National Governors Association Center for Best Practices, Council of Chief State School Officers. (2010). *Common Core State Standards for mathematics.* Washington, DC: National Governors Association Center for Best Practices, Council of Chief State School Officers.

White, J., & Dauksas, L. (2012). CCSSM: Getting started in K–Grade 2. *Teaching Children Mathematics, 1* (7), 440–445.

13

USING DAP TO TEACH THE CCSS IN FIRST GRADE

Typical age range for first grade: 6–7 years old

Working metaphor for first graders: First graders are **marathon runners**.

Children spend approximately six years training and preparing for their first learning marathon: The intense, demanding, and achievement-filled experience commonly known as "first grade." This is the year when school truly kicks into high gear for young learners. Academic expectations are higher than ever before and there is very little time for play. Luckily, as child development expert Chip Wood states, "at six, the child is extremely open, receptive to all new learning. The eagerness, curiosity, imagination, drive, and enthusiasm of the six year old is perhaps never again matched in quantity or intensity during the life span" (Wood, 2007, p, 61). So, similar to the apparent ease with which Kenyan runners breeze through marathons, first graders' particular location on the continuum of child development makes them ideally suited to the challenges of learning to read, to write, and to spell; learning to count, to add, and to subtract; developing self-control, focus, and patience . . . all in a 9-month period. First graders' willingness to invest themselves fully in the daily work of learning brings great pleasure to their teachers and their parents alike.

Focus Topic: Emphasizing the Process, Rather Than the Product

Attending to and learning from the process of solving a problem is an important element of the CCSS. The standards have a strong, consistent focus on children developing and using mental strategies, explaining how an answer was calculated and why it worked, or learning how a classmate figured out what the main character of the story was thinking.

TABLE 13.1 Developmental Traits of First Graders Commonly Seen in Classrooms

Physical	Baby teeth are falling out and adult teeth are coming in; first graders may manage these uncomfortable physical sensations by chewing on pencils, fingernails, the drawstring on their hoodie, or the collar of their t-shirt. Fine motor skills continue to develop, more slowly for some children than for others.
Social-Emotional	Competitive and enthusiastic, first graders are industrious workers when they feel successful and easily discouraged when they are struggling. School becomes a significant influence on their behavior, and strong friendships begin to develop. First graders' capacity for engagement, learning, and productivity is remarkable.
Cognitive	Boisterous and noisy, first graders are typically more interested in the quantity of work they produce than the quality of that work. They are full of questions, explanations, and jokes. Play and hands-on experiences are still the most effective means through which they learn, but integrating lots of opportunity for creative self-expression into academic activities can help first graders integrate knowledge.

Regardless of whether or not the math problem was solved correctly or the accurate conclusion was reached, there is usually something for students to learn—something they should try to do, something they should try to avoid, something they should try to remember—from the process. This aspect of the CCSS—the value, attention, and consideration given to errors—is something that I particularly enjoy.

However, when I speak with friends who are long-time primary grade school-teachers, they often describe how difficult it is for them to emphasize the process rather than the product. Some find it painful to downplay a student's end product, to accept an incomplete or incorrect paper, to waste time talking about someone's careless mistake when they could be teaching the kids how to do the problem correctly and then moving on. One first grade teacher referred to the shift from focusing on the product to focusing on the process as "a radical change." Accustomed to being the sage on the stage, she has been finding it difficult to shift the locus of control from herself to a group of six-year-old children.

I understand my friends' discomfort and concerns about celebrating incorrect work. But I don't think it's the incorrect work that is being celebrated. Rather, I see an acknowledgement of the strong thinking that is taking place in the classroom community, and of all the strong thinkers who are willing to return to a math problem that gave them trouble, tease the problem apart, find the glitch, and rework the problem—multiple times, if necessary—in order to master the process. In addition to the satisfaction that comes with hard-won success, students with this persistent, never-give-up attitude toward learning—what psychologist Carol Dweck calls a growth mindset (2006)—are rewarded with a boost to their sense of competence and additional evidence that they really can accomplish great things just by deciding to try harder and keep trying.

In the remainder of this chapter you will find the following:

- Complete CCSS-Math Standards for Grade 1
- *Annotated* CCSS-Math Standards for Grade 1

  - All standards fully unpacked

- Complete CCSS-ELA Standards for Grade 1
- *Annotated* CCSS-ELA Standards for Grade 1

  - All standards fully unpacked

- Three tips for teachers working with students in Grade 1

The text for the Grade 1 standards for mathematical content and for English Language Arts is quoted verbatim from the CCSS-M and CCSS-ELA Standards documents. The annotations to the standards provided in each content area are my efforts to help get you started on unpacking the standards. The ideas and observations I present are nothing more than one person's interpretation of the knowledge and skills included in the standards—I wish it were possible for me to hear your interpretations!

Grade 1 Standards for Mathematical Content

In Grade 1, instructional time should focus on *four critical areas*:

(1) developing understanding of addition, subtraction, and strategies for addition and subtraction within 20;
(2) developing understanding of whole number relationships and place value, including grouping in tens and ones;
(3) developing understanding of linear measurement and measuring lengths as iterating length units;
(4) reasoning about attributes of, and composing and decomposing, geometric shapes.

Grade 1 Mathematics Standards by Domain

Operations and Algebraic Thinking (OA)

- **Represent and solve problems involving addition and subtraction.**

  1.OA.1 Use addition and subtraction within 20 to solve word problems involving situations of adding to, taking from, putting together, taking apart and comparing, with unknowns in all positions, e.g., by using objects, drawings, and equations with a symbol for the unknown number to represent the problem.

1.OA.2 Solve word problems that call for addition of three whole numbers whose sum is less than or equal to 20, e.g., by using objects, drawings, and equations with a symbol for the unknown number to represent the problem.

- **Understand and apply properties of operations and the relationship between addition and subtraction.**

1.OA.3 Apply properties of operations as strategies to add and subtract. *Examples: If 8 + 3 = 11 is known, then 3 + 8 = 11 is also known. (Commutative property of addition.) To add 2 + 6 + 4, the second two numbers can be added to make a ten, so 2 + 6 + 4 = 2 + 10 = 12. (Associative property of addition.)*

1.OA.4 Understand subtraction as an unknown addend problem. *For example, subtract 10 − 8 by finding the number that makes 10 when added to 8.*

- **Add and subtract within 20.**

1.OA.5 Relate counting to addition and subtraction (e.g., by counting on 2 to add 2).

1.OA.6 Add and subtract within 20, demonstrating fluency for addition and subtraction within 10. Use strategies such as counting on; making ten (e.g., $8 + 6 = 8 + 2 + 4 = 10 + 4 = 14$); decomposing a number leading to a ten (e.g., $13 − 4 = 13 − 3 − 1 = 10 − 1 = 9$); using the relationship between addition and subtraction (e.g., knowing that $8 + 4 = 12$, one knows $12 − 8 = 4$); and creating equivalent but easier known sums (e.g., adding 6 + 7 by creating the known equivalent $6 + 6 + 1 = 12 + 1 = 13$).

- **Work with addition and subtraction equations.**

1.OA.7 Understand the meaning of the equal sign, and determine if equations involving addition and subtraction are true or false. *For example, which of the following equations are true and which are false? 6 = 6, 7 = 8 − 1, 5 + 2 = 2 + 5, 4 + 1 = 5 + 2.*

1.OA.8 Determine the unknown whole number in an addition or subtraction equation relating three whole numbers. *For example, determine the unknown number that makes the equation true in each of the equations 8 + ? = 11, 5 = ? − 3, 6 = 6 = ?.*

Number and Operations in Base Ten (NBT)

- **Extend the counting sequence.**

1.NBT.1 Count to 120, starting at any number less than 120. In this range, read and write numerals and represent a number of objects with a written numeral.

- **Understand place value.**

  1.NBT.2 Understand that the two digits of a two-digit number represent amounts of tens and ones. Understand the following as special cases:
  - a. 10 can be thought of as a bundle of ten ones—called a "ten."
  - b. The numbers from 11–19 are composed of a ten and one, two, three, four, five, six, seven, eight, or nine ones.
  - c. The numbers 10, 20, 30, 40, 50, 60, 70, 80, 90 refer to one, two, three, four, five, six, seven, eight, or nine tens (and 0 ones).

  1.NBT.3 Compare two-digit numbers based on meanings of the tens and ones digits, recording the results of comparisons with the symbols >, =, <.

- **Use place value understanding and properties of operations to add and subtract.**

  1.NBT.4 Add within 100, including adding a two-digit number and a one-digit number, and adding a two-digit number and a multiple of 10, using concrete models or drawings and strategies based on place value, properties of operations, and/or the relationship between addition and subtraction; relate the strategy to a written method and explain the reasoning used. Understand that in adding two-digit numbers, one adds tens and tens, ones and ones; and sometimes it is necessary to compose a ten.

  1.NBT.5 Given a two-digit number, mentally find 10 more or 10 less than the number, without having to count; explain the reasoning used.

  1.NBT.6 Subtract multiples of 10 in the range of 10–90 from multiples of 10 in the range of 10–90 (positive or zero differences), using concrete models or drawings and strategies based on place value, properties of operations, and/or the relationship between addition and subtraction; relate the strategy to a written method and explain the reasoning used.

Measurement and Data (MD)

- **Measure lengths indirectly and by iterating length units.**

  1.MD.1 Order three objects by length; compare the lengths of two objects indirectly by using a third object.

  1.MD.2 Express the length of an object as a whole number of length units, by laying multiple copies of a shorter object (the length unit) end to end; understanding that the length measurement of an object is the number of same-size length units that span it with no gaps or overlaps.

- **Tell and write time.**

  1.MD.3 Tell and write time in hours and half-hours using analog and digital clocks.

- **Represent and interpret data.**

  1.MD.4 Organize, represent, and interpret data with up to three categories; ask and answer questions about the total number of data points, how many in each category, and how many more or less are in one category than in another.

Geometry (G)

- **Reason with shapes and their attributes.**

  1.G.1 Distinguish between defining attributes (e.g., triangles are closed and three-sided) versus non-defining attributes (e.g., color, orientation, overall size); build and draw shapes to possess defining attributes.

  1.G.2 Compose two-dimensional shapes (rectangles, squares, trapezoids, triangles, half-circles, and quarter-circles) or three-dimensional shapes (cubes, right rectangular prisms, right circular cones, and right circular cylinders) to create a composite shape, and compose new shapes from the composite shape.

  1.G.3 Partition circles and rectangles into two and four equal shares, describe the shares using the words *halves, fourths,* and *quarters,* and use the phrases *half of, fourth of, and quarter of.* Describe the whole as two of or four of the shares. Understand for these examples that decomposing into more equal shares create smaller shares.

Common Core State Standards for Mathematics Standards for Mathematical Practice (SMP)

TABLE 13.2 CCSS-M Standards for Mathematical Practice

CCSS STANDARDS FOR MATHEMATICAL PRACTICE (SMP)	SMP IN STUDENT-FRIENDLY LANGUAGE (White & Dauksas, 2012)
Make sense of problems and persevere in solving them.	I can try many times to understand and solve a math problem.
Reason abstractly and quantitatively.	I can think about the math problem in my head first.
Construct viable arguments and critique the reasoning of others.	I can make a plan, called a strategy, to solve the problem, and discuss other students' strategies too.
Model with mathematics.	I can use math symbols and numbers to solve the problem.

(Continued)

TABLE 13.2 (Continued)

CCSS STANDARDS FOR MATHEMATICAL PRACTICE (SMP)	SMP IN STUDENT-FRIENDLY LANGUAGE (White & Dauksas, 2012)
Use appropriate tools strategically.	I can use math tools, pictures, drawings, and objects to solve the problem.
Attend to precision.	I can check to see if my strategy and calculations are correct.
Look for and make use of structure.	I can use what I already know about math to solve the problem.
Look for and express regularity in repeated reasoning.	I can use a strategy that I used to solve another math problem.

ANNOTATED

Grade 1 Standards for Mathematical Content

In Grade 1, instructional time should focus on *four critical areas*:

(1) developing understanding of addition, subtraction, and strategies for addition and subtraction within 20;
(2) developing understanding of whole number relationships and place value, including grouping in tens and ones;
(3) developing understanding of linear measurement and measuring lengths as iterating length units;
(4) reasoning about attributes of, and composing and decomposing, geometric shapes.

MUCH OF THE LANGUAGE USED IN THE CCSS-MATHEMATICS DEPARTS FROM THE TYPICAL MATH TERMINOLOGY USED IN PAST STANDARDS. THE AUTHORS OF THE STANDARDS DELIBERATELY LIMIT THE USE OF GENERIC LANGUAGE IN ORDER TO INTRODUCE ACADEMIC LANGUAGE, E.G., THE LANGUAGE MATHEMATICIANS USE TO TALK ABOUT MATH.

Grade 1 Mathematics Standards by Domain

REMEMBER, THESE ARE THE EXPECTATIONS STUDENTS SHOULD BE ABLE TO MEET AT THE *END* OF GRADE 1.

Operations and Algebraic Thinking (OA)

• **Represent and solve problems involving addition and subtraction.**

1.OA.1 Use addition and subtraction within 20 to solve word problems involving situations of adding to, taking from, putting together, taking apart and comparing, with unknowns in all positions, e.g., by using objects, drawings, and equations with a symbol for the unknown number to represent the problem.

THIS STANDARD INTRODUCES A NEW TYPE OF ADDITION/ SUBTRACTION PROBLEM BEYOND THE FOUR LEARNED IN KINDERGARTEN: COMPARE. IN A COMPARE PROBLEM, TWO AMOUNTS ARE COMPARED TO FIND OUT HOW MANY MORE/ LESS. IN ORDER TO SOLVE COMPARE PROBLEMS, STUDENTS MUST THINK ABOUT A QUANTITY THAT IS NOT PHYSICALLY PRESENT AND CONCEPTUALIZE THE AMOUNT. FURTHER, THE QUESTION "HOW MANY MORE?" IS NEW AND UNFAMILIAR; MANY STUDENTS DEFAULT INTO HEARING "WHO HAS MORE?"

NOTE: STUDENTS IN FIRST GRADE LEARN TO USE THE ADDI- TION SYMBOL (+) TO REPRESENT JOINING SITUATIONS, THE SUBTRACTION SYMBOL (−) TO REPRESENT SEPARATING SITUATIONS, AND THE EQUAL SIGN (=) TO REPRESENT THE RELATIONSHIP BETWEEN ONE SIDE OF THE EQUATION AND THE OTHER.

1.OA.2 Solve word problems that call for addition of three whole numbers whose sum is less than or equal to 20, e.g., by using objects, drawings, and equations with a symbol for the unknown number to represent the problem.

STUDENTS SHOULD PRACTICE AND LEARN DIFFERENT STRAT- EGIES FOR SOLVING THESE PROBLEMS: USE A TEN FRAME, USE A NUMBER LINE, USE MENTAL MATHEMATICS, ETC.

• Understand and apply properties of operations and the relationship between addition and subtraction.

1.OA.3 Apply properties of operations as strategies to add and sub- tract. *Examples: If 8 + 3 = 11 is known, then 3 + 8 = 11 is also known. (Commutative property of addition.) To add 2 + 6 + 4, the second two numbers can be added to make a ten, so 2 + 6 + 4 = 2 + 10 = 12. (Associative property of addition.)*

FIRST GRADE STUDENTS' UNDERSTANDING OF THE COM- MUTATIVE AND ASSOCIATIVE PROPERTIES OF ADDITION IS CENTRAL TO THEIR RECOGNITION OF THE RELATION- SHIPS BETWEEN AND AMONG NUMBERS. THEY SHOULD USE MATHEMATICAL TOOLS AND REPRESENTATIONS (LINKING CUBES, COUNTING BEARS, COUNTERS, 100 CHART, ETC.) TO

INTERNALIZE THE WAY THE PROPERTIES WORK. THEN THEY CAN USE THE PROPERTIES OF OPERATIONS AS A STRATEGY FOR SOLVING ADDITION AND SUBTRACTION PROBLEMS.

1.OA.4 Understand subtraction as an unknown addend problem. *For example, subtract 10 – 8 by finding the number that makes 10 when added to 8.*

A SOLID UNDERSTANDING OF ADDITION FACTS CAN HELP FIRST GRADERS SOLVE SUBTRACTION PROBLEMS. FOR EXAMPLE, 10 – 4 = ☐ CAN BE SOLVED BY THINKING "WHAT PLUS 4 EQUALS 10?"

• **Add and subtract within 20.**

1.OA.5 Relate counting to addition and subtraction (e.g., by counting on 2 to add 2).

MASTERY OF THE COUNTING ALL, COUNTING ON, AND COUNTING BACK STRATEGIES IS A FOUNDATION FOR USING TEN AS A BENCHMARK NUMBER.

1.OA.6 Add and subtract within 20, demonstrating fluency for addition and subtraction within 10. Use strategies such as counting on; making ten (e.g., 8 + 6 = 8 + 2 + 4 = 10 + 4 = 14); decomposing a number leading to a ten (e.g., 13 – 4 = 13 – 3 – 1 = 10 – 1 = 9); using the relationship between addition and subtraction (e.g., knowing that 8 + 4 = 12, one knows 12 – 8 = 4); and creating equivalent but easier known sums (e.g., adding 6 + 7 by creating the known equivalent 6 + 6 + 1 = 12 + 1 = 13).

A STUDENT'S MATHEMATICAL PROFICIENCY DEPENDS ON THE EFFICIENT USE OF STRATEGIES THAT SIMPLIFY COMPLEX PROBLEMS AND MAKE THEM EASIER TO SOLVE, E.G., DECOMPOSING AND RECOMPOSING NUMBERS TO MAKE 10 AND/OR TO MAKE AN EASIER PROBLEM WITH KNOWN SUMS, COUNTING ON, MAKING 10, DOUBLES PLUS 1 AND SO ON. IT'S CRITICALLY IMPORTANT FOR FIRST GRADERS TO MASTER THESE VARIOUS STRATEGIES BEFORE MOVING ON TO SECOND GRADE.

• **Work with addition and subtraction equations.**

1.OA.7 Understand the meaning of the equal sign, and determine if equations involving addition and subtraction are true or false. *For example, which of the following equations are true and which are false? 6 = 6, 7 = 8 – 1, 5 + 2 = 2 + 5, 4 + 1 = 5 + 2.*

THE EQUAL SIGN SHOULD NOT BE AN INDICATION THAT THE ANSWER COMES NEXT (AS IN 3 + 4 = ☐) BUT RATHER AS AN INDICATION THAT BOTH SIDES OF THE EQUATION NEED TO BE EQUAL SO THE EQUATION WILL BE BALANCED. IN OTHER WORDS, THE LEFT SIDE OF THE EQUATION MUST EXPRESS A QUANTITY THAT IS EQUAL TO THE QUANTITY ON THE RIGHT SIDE OF THE EQUATION. AN EFFECTIVE WAY TO REINFORCE THIS IS BY FRAMING PROBLEMS (OR DISCUSSIONS ABOUT PROBLEMS) BY ASKING STUDENTS TO "DETERMINE THE UNKNOWN NUMBER THAT MAKES THE EQUATION TRUE."

1.OA.8 Determine the unknown whole number in an addition or subtraction equation relating three whole numbers. *For example, determine the unknown number that makes the equation true in each of the equations 8 + ? = 11, 5 = ? – 3, 6 = 6 = ?.*

STUDENTS USE THEIR UNDERSTANDING OF AND STRATEGIES RELATED TO ADDITION AND SUBTRACTION TO SOLVE EQUATIONS WITH AN UNKNOWN. REMEMBER, THEIR GOAL IS TO FIND THE NUMBER THAT MAKES THE EQUATION TRUE.

Number and Operations in Base Ten (NBT)

• Extend the counting sequence.

1.NBT.1 Count to 120, starting at any number less than 120. In this range, read and write numerals and represent a number of objects with a written numeral.

FIRST GRADERS COUNT BY ROTE TO 120 BEGINNING FROM ANY NUMBER LESS THAN 120. THEY ALSO LEARN TO READ AND WRITE THE NUMERALS THAT REPRESENT A GIVEN AMOUNT.

• Understand place value.

1.NBT.2 Understand that the two digits of a two-digit number represent amounts of tens and ones. Understand the following as special cases:

    a.   10 can be thought of as a bundle of ten ones—called a "ten."

THINKING ABOUT TEN INDIVIDUAL OBJECTS JOINING TOGETHER AND TURNING INTO SOMETHING CALLED A "TEN"—IN OTHER WORDS, "UNITIZING"—CAN BE DIFFICULT FOR FIRST GRADERS. STUDENTS MAY NEED A LOT OF TIME,

PRACTICE, AND A RANGE OF EXPERIENCES TO FULLY GRASP THIS CONCEPT. IN THEIR EARLY WORK WITH TENS AND ONES, IT IS VERY IMPORTANT THAT STUDENTS WORK WITH INDIVIDUAL ITEMS THAT CAN BE LOOSELY GROUPED INTO TENS (BEANS, BLOCKS, CUBES, BEADS, COUNTERS, TEN FRAMES) AND EASILY SEPARATED BACK OUT INTO ONES, RATHER THAN USING PRE-GROUPED MATERIALS LIKE BASE TEN BLOCKS OR BEAN STICKS THAT REQUIRE "TRADING."

b. The numbers from 11–19 are composed of a ten and one, two, three, four, five, six, seven, eight, or nine ones.

FIRST GRADERS WORK WITH QUANTITIES BETWEEN 11 AND 19 TO BUILD AN UNDERSTANDING THAT THE TEEN NUMBERS ARE BUILT WITH ONE "TEN" AND LOOSE ONES.

ALSO, STUDENTS LEARN THAT A NUMERAL (E.G., 9) CAN REPRESENT MANY DIFFERENT AMOUNTS DEPENDING ON ITS POSITION OR PLACE IN A NUMBER. IN 19, THE 9 REPRESENTS 9 ONES; IN 91, THE 9 REPRESENTS 9 TENS. THIS CAN BE CONFUSING AND REQUIRES PRACTICE.

c. The numbers 10, 20, 30, 40, 50, 60, 70, 80, 90 refer to one, two, three, four, five, six, seven, eight, or nine tens (and 0 ones).

STUDENTS APPLY THEIR KNOWLEDGE OF "TENS" TO THE DECADE NUMBERS AND REALIZE THAT EACH DECADE NUMBER IS COMPRISED OF A CERTAIN AMOUNT OF GROUPS OF TEN WITH NO LEFTOVERS.

1.NBT.3 Compare two–digit numbers based on meanings of the tens and ones digits, recording the results of comparisons with the symbols >, =, <.

FIRST GRADERS USE THEIR KNOWLEDGE OF GROUPS OF TEN AND THE ORDER OF DIGITS TO DISCUSS TWO NUMBERS USING COMPARISON VOCABULARY. AFTER REPEATED OPPORTUNITIES TO PRACTICE THIS, STUDENTS WILL SHIFT TO USING THE WRITTEN SYMBOLS FOR GREATER THAN, LESS THAN, AND EQUAL TO.

• Use place value understanding and properties of operations to add and subtract.

1.NBT.4 Add within 100, including adding a two-digit number and a one-digit number, and adding a two-digit number and a multiple of 10, using concrete models or drawings and strategies based on place value, properties of operations, and/or the relationship between addition and subtraction; relate the strategy to a written method and explain the reasoning used. Understand that in adding two-digit numbers, one adds tens and tens, ones and ones; and sometimes it is necessary to compose a ten.

STUDENTS MUST BE FLEXIBLE WITH NUMBERS AS THEY SOLVE PROBLEMS WITHIN THE BASE-TEN SYSTEM USING THEIR ADDITION AND SUBTRACTION STRATEGIES.

NOTE: CARRYING AND BORROWING ARE NOT AN EXPECTATION IN GRADE 1.

1.NBT.5 Given a two-digit number, mentally find 10 more or 10 less than the number, without having to count; explain the reasoning used.

FIRST GRADERS BUILD ON THEIR COUNTING BY TENS WORK BY ADDING TEN MORE AND TEN LESS THAN ANY NUMBER LESS THAN 100. THEY ARE NOT EXPECTED TO COMPUTE DIFFERENCES OF TWO-DIGIT NUMBERS OTHER THAN MULTIPLES OF TEN.

1.NBT.6 Subtract multiples of 10 in the range of 10–90 from multiples of 10 in the range of 10–90 (positive or zero differences), using concrete models or drawings and strategies based on place value, properties of operations, and/or the relationship between addition and subtraction; relate the strategy to a written method and explain the reasoning used.

STUDENTS USE CONCRETE MODELS, DRAWINGS, AND PLACE VALUE STRATEGIES TO SUBTRACT MULTIPLES OF 10 FROM DECADE NUMBERS, USING STRATEGIES SIMILAR TO THOSE DISCUSSED IN 1.OA.4. STUDENTS ARE EXPECTED TO EXPLAIN THE REASONING THEY USED TO ARRIVE AT THEIR SOLUTION.

Measurement and Data (MD)

• Measure lengths indirectly and by iterating length units.

1.MD.1 Order three objects by length; compare the lengths of two objects indirectly by using a third object.

FIRST GRADERS USE DIRECT COMPARISON TO COMPARE LENGTHS. DIRECT COMPARISON MEANS THAT STUDENTS COMPARE THE AMOUNT OF AN ATTRIBUTE IN TWO OBJECTS WITHOUT MEASUREMENT. INDIRECT COMPARISON, USING THE TRANSITIVITY PROPERTY, IS ALSO AN OPTION: IF THE GIRL IS TALLER THAN THE BOY AND THE BOY IS TALLER THAN THE TEACHER, WE KNOW THAT THE GIRL IS TALLER THAN THE TEACHER.

1.MD.2 Express the length of an object as a whole number of length units, by laying multiple copies of a shorter object (the length unit) end to end; understanding that the length measurement of an object is the number of same-size length units that span it with no gaps or overlaps.

FIRST GRADERS NEED TO LEARN THE IMPORTANCE OF PRE-CISE AND ACCURATE MEASUREMENT—NO GAPS AND NO OVERLAPS—IN ORDER TO BE SUCCESSFUL WITH COMPUTING AREA IN GRADE 3.

* **Tell and write time.**

1.MD.3 Tell and write time in hours and half-hours using analog and digital clocks.

FIRST GRADERS LEARN TO TELL TIME BY BEGINNING WITH A CLOCK THAT HAS NO MINUTE HAND TO FOCUS THEIR ATTEN-TION ON THE IMPORTANT ROLE PLAYED BY THE MOVEMENT AND PLACEMENT OF THE HOUR HAND.

* **Represent and interpret data.**

1.MD.4 Organize, represent, and interpret data with up to three categories; ask and answer questions about the total number of data points, how many in each category, and how many more or less are in one category than in another.

FIRST GRADERS GATHER DATA BY WRITING A QUESTION (PRE-FERRED ICE CREAM FLAVORS, FAVORITE MOVIE), SPECIFYING THREE POSSIBLE OPTIONS, AND POLLING THEIR CLASSMATES. WHEN THE DATA ARE COLLECTED, THE STUDENTS INTERPRET THE RESULTS, INCLUDING THE TOTAL NUMBER OF RESPONSES COLLECTED, THE TOTAL EARNED BY EACH OPTION, ETC., AND SHARE THEIR FINDINGS.

NOTE: INTEGRATE ELA INTO THIS ACTIVITY BY REQUIRING STUDENTS TO WRITE UP THEIR FINDINGS AND MAKE THEM PUBLIC.

Geometry (G)

- Reason with shapes and their attributes.

1.G.1 Distinguish between defining attributes (e.g., triangles are closed and three-sided) versus non-defining attributes (e.g., color, orientation, overall size); build and draw shapes to possess defining attributes.

1.G.2 Compose two-dimensional shapes (rectangles, squares, trapezoids, triangles, half-circles, and quarter-circles) or three-dimensional shapes (cubes, right rectangular prisms, right circular cones, and right circular cylinders) to create a composite shape, and compose new shapes from the composite shape.

FIRST GRADERS USE ONE TYPE OF SHAPE (E.G., TRIANGLES) TO COMPOSE A DIFFERENT SHAPE (E.G., RECTANGLES) AND THEN TALK ABOUT THEIR SHAPE USING DESCRIPTIONS OF THEIR GEOMETRIC ATTRIBUTES AND PROPERTIES.

1.G.3 Partition circles and rectangles into two and four equal shares, describe the shares using the words *halves, fourths,* and *quarters,* and use the phrases *half of, fourth of, and quarter of.* Describe the whole as two of or four of the shares. Understand for these examples that decomposing into more equal shares create smaller shares.

PARTITIONING WHOLES INTO EQUAL SHARES BUILDS A FOUNDATION FOR FUTURE WORK WITH FRACTIONS. USING MATHEMATICAL LANGUAGE TO DISCUSS THE WORK—HALVES, FOURTHS, QUARTERS, WHOLE—FURTHER STRENGTHENS THIS ACTIVITY.

Grade 1 Reading Standards

TABLE 13.3

Reading Standards: Literature	Reading Standards: Informational Text
Key Ideas and Details	
RL.1.1. Ask and answer questions about key details in a text.	RI.1.1. Ask and answer questions about key details in a text.
RL.1.2. Retell familiar stories, including key details, and demonstrate understanding of their central message or lesson.	RI.1.2. Identify the main topics and retell key details of a text.

(Continued)

TABLE 13.3 (Continued)

RL.1.3. Describe characters, settings, and major events in a story, using key details	RI.1.3. Describe the connection between two individuals, events, ideas, or pieces of information in a text.
Craft and Structure	
RL.1.4. Identify words and phrases in stories or poems that suggest feelings or appeal to the senses.	RI.1.4. Ask and answer questions to help determine or clarify the meaning of words and phrases in a text.
RL.1.5. Explain major differences between books that tell stories and books that give information, drawing on a wide reading of a range of text types.	RI.1.5. Know and use various text features (e.g., headings, tables of contents, glossaries, electronic menus, icons) to locate key facts or information in a text.
RL.1.6. Identify who is telling the story at various points in a text.	RI.1.6. Distinguish between information provided by pictures or other illustrations and information provided by the words in a text.
Integration of Knowledge and Ideas	
RL.1.7. Use illustrations and details in a story to describe its characters, setting, or events. 8. (Not applicable to literature) RL.1.9. Compare and contrast the adventures and experiences of characters in stories.	RI.1.7. Use the illustrations and details in a text to describe its key ideas. RI.1.8. Identify the reasons an author gives to support points in a text. RI.1.9. Identify basic similarities and differences between two texts on the same topic (e.g., illustrations, descriptions, or procedures).
Range of Reading and Level of Text Complexity	
RL.1.10. With prompting and support, read prose and poetry of appropriate complexity for grade 1.	RI.1.10. With prompting and support, read information texts appropriately complex for grade 1.

TABLE 13.4

Reading Standards: Foundational Skills

Print Concepts

RF.1.1. Demonstrate understanding of the organization and basic features of print.

    a. Recognize the distinguishing features of a sentence (e.g., first word, capitalization, ending punctuation).

Phonological Awareness

RF.1.2. Demonstrate understanding of spoken words, syllables, and sounds (phonemes).

    a. Distinguish long from short vowel sounds in spoken single-syllable words.

    b. Orally produce single-syllable words by blending sounds (phonemes), including consonant blends.

    c. Isolate and pronounce the initial, medial vowel, and final sounds (phonemes) in spoken single-syllable words.

    d. Segment spoken single-syllable words into their complete sequence of individual sounds (phonemes).

Phonics and Word Recognition

RF.1.3. Know and apply grade-level phonics and word analysis skills in decoding words.

    a. Know the spelling-sound correspondences for common consonant digraphs.

    b. Decode regularly spelled one-syllable words.

    c. Know final -e and common vowel team conventions for representing long vowel sounds

    d. Use knowledge that every syllable must have a vowel sound to determine the number of syllables in a printed word.

    e. Decode two-syllable words following basic patterns by breaking the words into syllables.

    f. Read words with inflectional endings.

    g. Recognize and read grade-appropriate irregularly spelled words.

Fluency

RF.1.4. Read with sufficient accuracy and fluency to support comprehension.

    a. Read on-level text with purpose and understanding.

    b. Read on-level text orally with accuracy, appropriate rate, and expression on successive readings.

    c. Use context to confirm or self-correct word recognition and understanding, rereading as necessary.

Grade 1 Writing Standards

TABLE 13.5

Text Types and Purposes
W.1.1. Write opinion pieces in which they introduce the topic or name of the book they are writing about, state an opinion, supply a reason for the opinion, and provide some sense of closure.
W.1.2. Write informative/explanatory texts in which they name a topic, supply some facts about the topic, and provide some sense of closure.
W.1.3. Write narratives in which they recount two or more appropriately sequenced events, include some details regarding what happened, use temporal words to signal event order, and provide some sense of closure.
Production and Distribution of Writing
4. (Begins in grade 3)
W.1.5. With guidance and support from adults, focus on a topic, respond to questions and suggestions from peers, and add details to strengthen writing as needed.
W.1.6. With guidance and support from adults, use a variety of digital tools to produce and publish writing, including in collaboration with peers.
Research to Build and Present Knowledge
W.1.7. Participate in shared research and writing projects (e.g., explore a number of "how-to" books on a given topic and use them to write a sequence of instructions).
W.1.8. With guidance and support from adults, recall information from experience or gather information from provided sources to answer a question.
W.1.9. (Begins in grade 4)
Range of Writing
10. (Begins in grade 3)

Grade 1 Speaking and Listening Standards

TABLE 13.6

Comprehension and Collaboration
SL.1.1. Participate in collaborative conversations with diverse partners about grade 1 topics and texts with peers and adults in small and larger groups.   (a) Follow agreed-upon rules for discussions (e.g., listening to others with care, speaking one at a time about the topics and texts under discussion).   (b) Build on others' talk in conversations by responding to the comments of others through multiple exchanges.   (c) Ask questions to clear up any confusion about the topics and texts under discussion.
SL.1.2. Ask and answer questions about key details in a text read aloud or information presented orally or through other media.
SL.1.3. Ask and answer questions about what a speaker says in order to gather additional information or clarify something that is not understood.
Presentation of Knowledge and Ideas
SL.1.4. Describe people, places, things, and events with relevant details, expressing ideas and feelings clearly.
SL.1.5. Add drawings or other visual displays to descriptions when appropriate to clarify ideas, thoughts, and feelings.
SL.1.6. Produce complete sentences when appropriate to task and situation.

Grade 1 Language Standards

TABLE 13.7

Conventions of Standard English
L.1.1. Demonstrate command of the conventions of standard English grammar and usage when writing or speaking.

    (a)   Print all upper- and lowercase letters.

    (b)   Use common, proper, and possessive nouns.

    (c)   Use singular and plural nouns with matching verbs in basic sentences (e.g., *He hops; We hop*).

    (d)   Use personal possessive and indefinite pronouns (e.g., *I, me, my; they, them, their; anyone, everything*).

    (e)   Use verbs to convey a sense of past, present, and future (e.g., *Yesterday I walked home; Today I walk home; Tomorrow I will walk home*).

    (f)   Use frequently occurring adjectives.

    (g)   Use frequently occurring conjunctions (e.g., *and, but, or, because*).

    (h)   Use determiners (e.g., articles, demonstratives).

    (i)   Use frequently occurring prepositions (e.g., *during, beyond, toward*).

    (j)   Produce/expand complete simple and compound declarative, interrogative, imperative, and exclamatory sentences in response to prompts.

L.1.2. Demonstrate command of the conventions of standard English capitalization, punctuation, and spelling when writing.

    (a)   Capitalize dates and names of people.

    (b)   Use end punctuation for sentences.

    (c)   Use commas in dates and to separate single words in a series.

    (d)   Use conventional spelling for words with common spelling patterns and for frequently occurring irregular words.

    (e)   Spell untaught words phonetically, drawing on phonemic awareness and spelling conventions.

Knowledge of Language
3. (Begins in grade 2)

Vocabulary Acquisition and Use

L.1.4. Determine or clarify the meaning of unknown and multiple-meaning words and phrases based on *grade 1 reading and content,* choosing flexibly from an array of strategies.

    (a) Use sentence-level context as a clue to the meaning of a word or phrase.

    (b) Use frequently occurring affixes as a clue to the meaning of a word.

    (c) Identify frequently occurring root words (e.g., *look*) and their inflectional forms (e.g., *looks, looked, looking*).

L.1.5. With guidance and support from adults, demonstrate understanding of word relationships and nuances in word meanings.

    (a) Sort words into categories (e.g., colors, clothing) to gain a sense of the concepts the categories represent.

    (b) Define words by category and by one or more key attributes (e.g., a *duck* is a bird that swims; a *tiger* is a large cat with stripes).

    (c) Identify real life connections between words and their use (e.g., note places at home that are *cozy*).

    (d) Distinguish shades of meaning among verbs differing in manner (e.g., *look, peek, glance, stare, glare, scowl*) and adjectives differing in intensity (e.g., *large, gigantic*) by defining or choosing them or by acting out the meanings.

L.1.6. Use words and phrases acquired through conversations, reading and being read to, and responding to texts, including using frequently occurring conjunctions to signal simple relationships (e.g., *because*).

ANNOTATED
Grade 1 Reading Standards

TABLE 13.8

Reading Standards: Literature	Reading Standards: Informational Text
Key Ideas and Details	
RL.1.1. Ask and answer questions about key details in a text.	RI.1.1. Ask and answer questions about key details in a text.
RL.1.2. Retell familiar stories, including key details, and demonstrate understanding of their central message or lesson.	RI.1.2. Identify the main topics and retell key details of a text.

(Continued)

TABLE 13.8 (Continued)

RL.1.3. Describe characters, settings, and major events in a story, using key details.	RI.1.3. Describe the connection between two individuals, events, ideas, or pieces of information in a text.
ANNOTATION	ANNOTATION
STUDENTS NEED TO KNOW WHAT MAKES SOMETHING A "KEY DETAIL" AND WHAT KINDS OF QUESTIONS COULD BE ASKED AND ANSWERED ABOUT A KEY DETAIL. THEY NEED TO PUT KEY DETAILS IN SEQUENTIAL ORDER TO RETELL A FAMILIAR STORY. THEY ALSO HAVE TO RECOGNIZE AND NAME ELEMENTS IN A STORY: CHARACTERS, PROBLEM, SETTING, ETC.	STUDENTS NEED TO BE ABLE TO THINK ABOUT WHAT THEY READ AND CREATE THEIR OWN QUESTIONS ABOUT KEY DETAILS IN A TEXT.
Craft and Structure	
RL.1.4. Identify words and phrases in stories or poems that suggest feelings or appeal to the senses.	RI.1.4. Ask and answer questions to help determine or clarify the meaning of words and phrases in a text.
RL.1.5. Explain major differences between books that tell stories and books that give information, drawing on a wide reading of a range of text types.	RI.1.5. Know and use various text features (e.g., headings, tables of contents, glossaries, electronic menus, icons) to locate key facts or information in a text.
RL.1.6. Identify who is telling the story at various points in a text.	RI.1.6. Distinguish between information provided by pictures or other illustrations and information provided by the words in a text.

ANNOTATION	ANNOTATION
DRAWING ATTENTION TO EVOCATIVE WORDS AND PHRASES ENRICHES STUDENTS' VOCABULARIES, WHICH, IN TURN, ENRICHES THEIR WRITING AND THEIR THINKING.	TEACHING STUDENTS TO ASK CLARIFYING QUESTIONS ABOUT UNFAMILIAR WORDS IS A GREAT WAY TO BOOST THEIR VOCABULARY DEVELOPMENT AND THEIR INTEREST IN WORDS. KNOWLEDGE OF VARIOUS TEXT FEATURES WILL BE HELPFUL, BUT IT'S MORE IMPORTANT FOR STUDENTS TO LEARN THAT HUMANS HAVE ALWAYS LOOKED FOR ANSWERS AND INFORMATION, AND THE PLACES WE LOOK AND HOW WE FIND OUR ANSWERS CHANGES CONTINUALLY OVER TIME.

Integration of Knowledge and Ideas

RL.1.7. Use illustrations and details in a story to describe its characters, setting, or events.	RI.1.7. Use the illustrations and details in a text to describe its key ideas.
8. (Not applicable to literature)	RI.1.8. Identify the reasons an author gives to support points in a text.
RL.1.9. Compare and contrast the adventures and experiences of characters in stories.	RI.1.9. Identify basic similarities and differences between two texts on the same topic (e.g., illustrations, descriptions, or procedures).
ANNOTATION	ANNOTATION
STUDENTS MUST LEARN TO "READ" PICTURES AND CONSIDER THEM SOURCES OF INFORMATION ABOUT THE SETTING, CHARACTERS, AND EVENTS.	IDENTIFYING THE BASIC SIMILARITIES AND DIFFERENCES IS NOT AS PRODUCTIVE AS EVALUATING THE SIMILARITIES AND DIFFERENCES AND DRAWING CONCLUSIONS ABOUT THE AUTHOR'S INTENT OR PURPOSE.

(Continued)

TABLE 13.8 (Continued)

Range of Reading and Level of Text Complexity	
RL.1.10. With prompting and support, read prose and poetry of appropriate complexity for grade 1.	RI.1.10. With prompting and support, read information texts appropriately complex for grade 1.
ANNOTATION	ANNOTATION
THIS STANDARD IS SELF-EXPLANATORY.	THIS STANDARD IS SELF-EXPLANATORY.

TABLE 13.9

Reading Standards: Foundational Skills
Print Concepts
RF.1.1. Demonstrate understanding of the organization and basic features of print. (a) Recognize the distinguishing features of a sentence (e.g., first word, capitalization, ending punctuation).
ANNOTATION
MANY FIRST GRADERS MAY FIND THIS STANDARD TOO SIMPLE. EMPHASIZE CONCEPTS OF PRINT ONLY WITH THE STUDENTS WHO NEED REINFORCEMENT IN THIS AREA.
Phonological Awareness
RF.1.2. Demonstrate understanding of spoken words, syllables, and sounds (phonemes). a. Distinguish long from short vowel sounds in spoken single-syllable words. b. Orally produce single-syllable words by blending sounds (phonemes), including consonant blends. c. Isolate and pronounce the initial, medial vowel, and final sounds (phonemes) in spoken single-syllable words. d. Segment spoken single-syllable words into their complete sequence of individual sounds (phonemes).
ANNOTATION
CUSTOMIZE QUESTIONS/PROMPTS TO BE APPROPRIATELY CHALLENGING FOR THE VARIOUS STUDENTS IN YOUR CLASS. ASK MORE CAPABLE STUDENTS HARDER QUESTIONS THAN YOU WOULD ASK THE STRUGGLING STUDENTS.

Phonics and Word Recognition

RF.1.3. Know and apply grade-level phonics and word analysis skills in decoding words.

    a. Know the spelling-sound correspondences for common consonant digraphs.

    b. Decode regularly spelled one-syllable words.

    c. Know final -e and common vowel team conventions for representing long vowel sounds.

    d. Use knowledge that every syllable must have a vowel sound to determine the number of syllables in a printed word.

    e. Decode two-syllable words following basic patterns by breaking the words into syllables.

    f. Read words with inflectional endings.

    g. Recognize and read grade-appropriate irregularly spelled words.

ANNOTATION

THE RANGE OF ACADEMIC ABILITY ACROSS THE STUDENTS IN A FIRST GRADE CLASS CAN BE ENORMOUS. IT MAKES SENSE TO ASK QUESTIONS THAT ARE SPECIFICALLY TARGETED TO CHALLENGE STUDENTS IN AN APPROPRIATE WAY. NO STUDENT WANTS TO ANSWER A QUESTION THAT IS WAY TOO DIFFICULT OR WAY TOO EASY.

Fluency

RF.1.4. Read with sufficient accuracy and fluency to support comprehension.

    a. Read on-level text with purpose and understanding.

    b. Read on-level text orally with accuracy, appropriate rate, and expression on successive readings.

    c. Use context to confirm or self-correct word recognition and understanding, rereading as necessary.

ANNOTATION

STUDENTS NEED GUIDANCE IN MAKING THEIR READING ALOUD SOUND NATURAL. TEACHERS CAN USE PROMPTS AND SUGGESTIONS SUCH AS: MAKE YOUR READING SOUND LIKE THE CHARACTERS ARE TALKING; MAKE YOUR VOICE SOUND LIKE THE WORDS ARE SMOOTH AND FIT TOGETHER; MAKE YOUR VOICE GO UP WHEN YOU SEE THE QUESTION MARK AT THE END OF THE SENTENCE; MAKE YOUR VOICE GO DOWN WHEN YOU SEE THE PERIOD AT THE END OF THE SENTENCE; GO BACK AND REREAD WHEN IT DOESN'T SOUND OR LOOK LIKE YOU THINK IT SHOULD.

ANNOTATED

Grade 1 Writing Standards

TABLE 13.10

Text Types and Purposes
W.1.1. Write opinion pieces in which they introduce the topic or name of the book they are writing about, state an opinion, supply a reason for the opinion, and provide some sense of closure.
W.1.2. Write informative/explanatory texts in which they name a topic, supply some facts about the topic, and provide some sense of closure.
W.1.3. Write narratives in which they recount two or more appropriately sequenced events, include some details regarding what happened, use temporal words to signal event order, and provide some sense of closure.
ANNOTATION
FIRST GRADERS SHOULD BE ABLE TO WRITE OPINION PIECES THAT CLEARLY STATE THEIR PREFERENCES AND PROVIDE A REASON FOR THEIR PREFERENCE. STUDENTS ARE EXPECTED TO INCLUDE BOTH AN INTRODUCTION AND A CLOSING STATEMENT IN THEIR WRITING. STUDENTS WILL NEED TO LEARN STRATEGIES FOR INTRODUCING CONCEPTS AND CONCLUDING THEIR THOUGHTS (WRITING A SUMMARY STATEMENT) AND TO USE APPROPRIATE TEMPORAL WORDS (NOW, WHEN, THEN) TO SHOW ORDER OF EVENTS.
Production and Distribution of Writing
4. (Begins in grade 3)
W.1.5. With guidance and support from adults, focus on a topic, respond to questions and suggestions from peers, and add details to strengthen writing as needed.
W.1.6. With guidance and support from adults, use a variety of digital tools to produce and publish writing, including in collaboration with peers.
ANNOTATION
STUDENTS ARE EXPECTED TO RESPOND TO QUESTIONS AND SUGGESTIONS ABOUT THEIR WRITING. THEY MUST LEARN HOW TO ADD DESCRIPTIVE WORDS AND KEY DETAILS TO THEIR WRITING AND HOW TO RECOGNIZE ERRORS IN SPELLING, GRAMMAR, AND SO ON. STUDENTS SHOULD BEGIN DEVELOPING THE STRATEGIES AND SKILLS NEEDED TO USE TECHNOLOGY TO PUBLISH THEIR WRITING.

Research to Build and Present Knowledge
W.1.7. Participate in shared research and writing projects (e.g., explore a number of "how-to" books on a given topic and use them to write a sequence of instructions).
W.1.8. With guidance and support from adults, recall information from experience or gather information from provided sources to answer a question.
9. (Begins in grade 4)
ANNOTATION
THE CCSS REQUIRE FIRST GRADERS TO PARTICIPATE IN SHARED RESEARCH PROJECTS. STUDENTS WILL NEED SUPPORT UNDERSTANDING THEIR JOB ON THE TEAM AND THE WORK THEY WILL DO, FROM THE BEGINNING OF THE PROJECT TO THE END. TEACHERS SHOULD DEVELOP GRAPHIC ORGANIZERS, CHECK SHEETS, TASK CHARTS, AND/OR JOB LISTS TO SCAFFOLD THE STUDENTS AS THEY UNDERTAKE THIS WORK.
Range of Writing
10. (Begins in grade 3)

ANNOTATED
Grade 1 Speaking and Listening Standards

TABLE 13.11

Comprehension and Collaboration
SL.1.1. Participate in collaborative conversations with diverse partners about grade 1 topics and texts with peers and adults in small and larger groups.
(a) Follow agreed-upon rules for discussions (e.g., listening to others with care, speaking one at a time about the topics and texts under discussion).
(b) Build on others' talk in conversations by responding to the comments of others through multiple exchanges.
(c) Ask questions to clear up any confusion about the topics and texts under discussion.
SL.1.2. Ask and answer questions about key details in a text read aloud or information presented orally or through other media.
SL.1.3. Ask and answer questions about what a speaker says in order to gather additional information or clarify something that is not understood.

(Continued)

TABLE 13.11 (Continued)

ANNOTATION
TEACHERS NEED TO HELP STUDENTS NOTICE WHEN THE CLASS OR GROUP IS HAVING A GOOD DISCUSSION AND ELICIT THEIR THOUGHTS ABOUT THE FEATURES OF A GOOD DISCUSSION. STUDENTS ENGAGE IN COLLABORATIVE CONVERSATIONS (BOOK GROUPS, BUDDY READING) AND DEVELOP SKILLS SUCH AS ACTIVE LISTENING, LOOKING AT THE SPEAKER, TAKING TURNS, LINKING IDEAS TO THE SPEAKER'S IDEAS, SHARING THE FLOOR, ETC. STUDENTS SHOULD BE ABLE TO LISTEN TO A SPEAKER AND ASK FOR CLARIFICATION IF NECESSARY. THEY NEED TO LEARN TO FORMULATE A QUESTION THAT IS ON TOPIC AND TO UNDERSTAND AND ANSWER QUESTIONS ASKED OF THEM.

Presentation of Knowledge and Ideas

SL.1.4. Describe people, places, things, and events with relevant details, expressing ideas and feelings clearly.

SL.1.5. Add drawings or other visual displays to descriptions when appropriate to clarify ideas, thoughts, and feelings.

SL.1.6. Produce complete sentences when appropriate to task and situation.

ANNOTATION
FIRST GRADERS LEARN HOW TO REPORT FACTS AND RELEVANT DETAILS ABOUT AN EXPERIENCE WITH CLARITY OF THOUGHT AND EMOTIONS. THEY LEARN HOW TO CHOOSE VISUAL DISPLAYS THAT ADD TO AND SUPPORT THEIR THINKING ABOUT A TOPIC. THEY LEARN TO ARTICULATE THEIR IDEAS IN A PURPOSEFUL WAY THAT IS APPROPRIATE FOR THEIR AUDIENCE.

ANNOTATED
Grade 1 Language Standards

TABLE 13.12

Conventions of Standard English

L.1.1. Demonstrate command of the conventions of standard English grammar and usage when writing or speaking.

    (a)   Print all upper- and lowercase letters.

    (b)   Use common, proper, and possessive nouns.

    (c)   Use singular and plural nouns with matching verbs in basic sentences (e.g., *He hops; We hop*).

    (d)   Use personal possessive and indefinite pronouns (e.g., *I, me, my; they, them, their; anyone, everything*).

(e) Use verbs to convey a sense of past, present, and future (e.g., *Yesterday I walked home; Today I walk home; Tomorrow I will walk home*).

(f) Use frequently occurring adjectives.

(g) Use frequently occurring conjunctions (e.g., *and, but, or, because*).

(h) Use determiners (e.g., *articles, demonstratives*).

(i) Use frequently occurring prepositions (e.g., *during, beyond, toward*).

(j) Produce/expand complete simple and compound declarative, interrogative, imperative, and exclamatory sentences in response to prompts.

L.1.2. Demonstrate command of the conventions of standard English capitalization, punctuation, and spelling when writing.

(a) Capitalize dates and names of people.

(b) Use end punctuation for sentences.

(c) Use commas in dates and to separate single words in a series.

(d) Use conventional spelling for words with common spelling patterns and for frequently occurring irregular words.

(e) Spell untaught words phonetically, drawing on phonemic awareness and spelling conventions.

ANNOTATION

STUDENTS DEVELOP AGE-APPROPRIATE COMMAND OF THE GRAMMAR AND USAGE OF STANDARD SPOKEN AND WRITTEN ENGLISH. EMPHASIS IS ON USING COMPLETE SENTENCES, FORMING QUESTIONS, USING PLURALS, AND ATTENDING TO CONVENTIONS OF ENDING PUNCTUATION, CAPITALIZING, AND SPELLING SIMPLE WORDS.

Knowledge of Language

3. (Begins in grade 2)

Vocabulary Acquisition and Use

L.1.4. Determine or clarify the meaning of unknown and multiple-meaning words and phrases based on *grade 1 reading and content*, choosing flexibly from an array of strategies.

(a) Use sentence-level context as a clue to the meaning of a word or phrase.

(b) Use frequently occurring affixes as a clue to the meaning of a word.

(c) Identify frequently occurring root words (e.g., *look*) and their inflectional forms (e.g., *looks, looked, looking*).

L.1.5. With guidance and support from adults, demonstrate understanding of word relationships and nuances in word meanings.

(a) Sort words into categories (e.g., *colors, clothing*) to gain a sense of the concepts the categories represent.

(b) Define words by category and by one or more key attributes (e.g., a *duck* is a bird that swims; a *tiger* is a large cat with stripes).

(Continued)

TABLE 13.12 (Continued)

(c) Identify real life connections between words and their use (e.g., note places at home that are cozy).   (d) Distinguish shades of meaning among verbs differing in manner (e.g., *look, peek, glance, stare, glare, scowl*) and adjectives differing in intensity (e.g., *large, gigantic*) by defining or choosing them or by acting out the meanings. L.1.6. Use words and phrases acquired through conversations, reading and being read to, and responding to texts, including using frequently occurring to signal simple relationships (e.g., *because*).
ANNOTATION
FIRST GRADERS DEVELOP VOCABULARY IN ORDER TO MAKE PURPOSEFUL LANGUAGE CHOICES IN WRITING AND SPEAKING TO COMMUNICATE EFFECTIVELY IN PRINT AND DIGITAL TEXTS. THEY SHOULD USE REGISTERS APPROPRIATE TO THEIR AUDIENCE, CONTEXT, AND PURPOSE. FIRST GRADERS WILL DISTINGUISH THE SHADES OF MEANING IN VERBS DESCRIBING THE SAME ACTION AND USE WORDS ACQUIRED BY READING AND BEING READ TO, IN CONVERSATIONS, AND IN SOCIAL SETTINGS.

Three Tips for Teachers Working With First Grade Marathon Runners

1. If You Don't Love Change, Don't Become a Teacher

Do you want to hear my favorite teacher joke?

Q: Teachers only hate two things. What are they?
A: The way things are now, and change.

At some point in the past, teaching preschool, kindergarten, and the primary grades was framed by a ritualized, never-ending cycle of seasons and holidays: apples in September, pumpkins in October, turkeys and Pilgrims in November, and so on. People became early childhood teachers either because they loved this kind of cozy routine or because they entered the profession for some good reason but were accidentally sucked into the vortex of traditional practices and cute crafts and couldn't find their way out. Although there are still a few visible remnants of this holiday-and-harvest type practice floating in the chilly November wind, teaching is a very different profession now than it was back in the sepia-toned day. Today, many features of teaching are changing continually: We have new curricula, new standards, new technology, new federal and state policies, new trends in instructional practice, new data dashboards, new report cards, new spirit t-shirts, new fundraisers, new portable classrooms, new computer teachers, a new

Mandarin Immersion program, a new assistant principal, and much more. As an early childhood educator, the only things you can count on are (a) head lice and (b) change.

2. Don't Let Confusing Instructional Materials Ruin Your Day

The implementation of the CCSS has been accompanied by the arrival of new and unfamiliar instructional materials. You might find some of these materials confusing, unclear, or inappropriate for your students. Don't worry—they aren't likely to be around forever. It takes a fairly long time to develop a textbook series; even though the big-deal publishers have been working on their textbooks since 2010, they're not ready yet. The instructional materials that are being used by the school districts in my area—EngageNY (New York State Education Department, n.d.) and Envision (Pearson Instructional Resources, 2012)—appear to be among the only options available at this time. These curricula were developed fairly quickly, and they might fade just as quickly when the big publishing houses introduce their textbooks and supplemental materials.

3. Trust Your Experience and Trust Your Students

When students are struggling to learn a new concept, teachers will support their learning by any means necessary. But, at a certain point, even the most resourceful teacher runs out of tricks. This is the point at which you should definitely not give up. Dig deep into your memory, and find another time when you tried every instructional possibility you could imagine. What finally worked? If that technique got your students unstuck, try it again now. Just because a technique or practice is old, or out of fashion, or offbeat doesn't mean it won't work for you and your students. And, if all else fails, ask your students what they need and how you can help them. Sometimes they have a clear sense of what would work for them—match the steps of the process to the tune of a familiar song or nursery rhyme, make hand motions that are linked to the structure of the essay, invent a game that involves tossing a ball and yelling the names of the state capitals. You and your students are the only people who need to know how all of you, working together, got things to click.

References

Dweck, C. S. (2006). *Mindset: The new psychology of success.* New York: Ballantine Books.

National Governors Association Center for Best Practices, Council of Chief State School Officers. (2010). *Common Core State Standards in English language arts and literacy in history/social studies, science and technical subjects.* Washington, DC: National Governors Association Center for Best Practices, Council of Chief State School Officers.

National Governors Association Center for Best Practices, Council of Chief State School Officers. (2010). *Common Core State Standards for mathematics.* Washington, DC: National Governors Association Center for Best Practices, Council of Chief State School Officers.

New York State Education Department. (n.d.). EngageNY Mathematics. New York: NYSED.

Pearson Instructional Resources. (2012). *enVisionMATH Common Core © 2012*. Upper Saddle River, NJ: Pearson Education.

White, J., & Dauksas, L. (2012). CCSSM: Getting started in K–grade 2. *Teaching Children Mathematics, 1* (7), 440–445.

Wood, C. (2007). *Yardsticks: Children in the classroom ages 4–14*. Greenfield, MA: Northeast Foundation for Children.

14

USING DAP TO TEACH THE CCSS IN SECOND GRADE

Typical age range for second graders: 7–8 years old

Overarching metaphor for second graders: Second graders are **hobbits** (a fictional humanoid race that plays a prominent role in J.R.R. Tolkien's books *The Hobbit* and *The Lord of the Rings* trilogy).

Hobbits live nestled amidst bucolic, rolling hills dotted with vegetable gardens and beautiful flowers. They are clear thinkers, hard workers, and resourceful problem solvers with strong opinions about good and bad. Practical and sensible, hobbits are blissfully unaware of the harsh realities of life beyond the borders of their homeland, The Shire. Generally speaking, hobbits like things to remain as they are right now: cozy homes, warm hearths, good food, comfortable beds, friends and family, and more of the same tomorrow. Like hobbits, second graders are often unaware of the nuances and complexities of life. This gives them a great deal of clarity about issues that perplex everyone else: If it's against the law to buy illegal drugs, why would anyone do it? If smoking cigarettes can give you cancer, why does anyone smoke? If using gasoline to drive our cars is destroying the earth, why are we still driving our gasoline-powered cars? Second graders are at the apex of their capabilities as young learners: They have faced and mastered most of the developmental and academic challenges of early childhood and are coasting along happily toward Grade 3. Whenever there's a complex task that needs to be completed quickly and effectively, I recommend finding two second graders, giving each of them a clipboard, and letting them do what they do best: think clearly, ask insightful questions, make good decisions, consult with others when making difficult decisions, and get things done properly.

TABLE 14.1 Developmental Traits of Second Graders Typically Seen in Classrooms

Physical	Second graders' physical capabilities are consolidating, although fine motor skills might still be difficult for some students. Challenges coordinating the hand and the eye make copying from the board difficult for some second graders.
Social-Emotional	Occasionally moody or withdrawn, second graders can be very sensitive to personal insults, social injustice, and unfairness. Friendships can be fraught with emotion and appear to shift frequently. A warm, consistent relationship with their teacher helps them feel grounded and secure.
Cognitive	Second graders are curious and analytical—they like to take things apart and rebuild them, to create and crack codes, to memorize facts and information, learn new words and their meanings—and are beginning to reorganize their mental structures to accommodate their new capabilities and interests. They typically have a strong work ethic, but are often stymied by perfectionism: Second-grade work is frequently submitted with a hole or two made by harsh or repeated erasures. Second graders enjoy working alone or with a single partner rather than in a group, and they tend to work slowly. Their language is precise and specific.

Focus Topic: Academics Versus Play?

Because standardized testing begins in Grade 3, second grade is typically the last grade in which children's need to play and to learn through play is acknowledged and accommodated. Unfortunately, second grade teachers often feel caught between external pressure to focus on teaching young children academic knowledge and skills and their own professional understanding of young students' need to play in order to learn. But this is a false dilemma. In reality, there is no tension between academics and play if teachers choose not to frame these two types of experiences as "competing" impulses.

First, in most developmentally appropriate classrooms, children typically don't recognize a distinction between learning and play. Play is how children learn best, so play and learning are always intertwined. Creating a classroom post office, for example, and "staffing" it with young learners can motivate many reluctant readers and writers to embrace literacy-driven play in order to participate in the complex and challenging "work" that is done at the post office. Integrating new vocabulary into the post office organizational system could create further opportunities for emergent readers and writers to develop academic skills to achieve goals they set for themselves. And all this literacy and mathematics learning is scaffolded by the support that play provides.

Second, teaching academic content to young children can be considered an aspect of culturally appropriate practice. As mentioned in Chapter 1, culturally appropriate practice includes two distinct areas of focus: socioculturally appropriate practice and sociopolitically appropriate practice. Today, young children in the United States are immersed in a social and cultural context—especially in states that have adopted the CCSS—in which student mastery of rigorous academic standards has been prioritized by local, state, and federal policy. In other words, providing young children with dense, academic learning experiences is deemed "appropriate practice" within the sociopolitical context of the United States. The DAP guidelines, explicitly acknowledging "the powerful influence of context on all development and learning" (Bredekamp, 1997, p. 41), points us toward accommodating adults' desire to see more academics in primary settings. In order to be developmentally appropriate, then, teachers' practical decisions must be informed by thoughtful consideration of the demands and expectations of their community in conjunction with the familiar, well-established dimensions of DAP.

Early childhood teachers encounter contradictions within DAP as a result— mastery of certain academic skills may be sociopolitically appropriate but not age appropriate, for example—but resolving contradictions is already an established feature of developmentally appropriate teaching (Bredekamp, 1997, p. 45). Teachers' familiarity with the complexities of working within the DAP framework and their facility as professional decision makers will help them determine how to resolve those tensions effectively in relation to the demands of their specific professional contexts.

In the remainder of this chapter you will find the following:

* Complete CCSS-Math Standards for Grade 2
* *Annotated* CCSS-Math Standards for Grade 2

  * All standards fully unpacked

* Complete CCSS-ELA Standards for Grade 2
* *Annotated* CCSS-ELA Standards for Grade 2

  * All standards fully unpacked

* Three tips for teachers working with second graders

The text for the Grade 2 standards for mathematical content and for English Language Arts is quoted verbatim from the CCSS-M and CCSS-ELA Standards documents. The annotations to the standards provided in each content area are my efforts to help get you started on unpacking the standards. The ideas and observations I present are nothing more than one person's interpretation of the knowledge and skills included in the standards—I wish it were possible for me to hear your interpretations!

Grade 2 Standards for Mathematical Content

In Grade 2, instructional time should focus on *four critical areas*:

(1) extending understanding of base-ten notation;

(2) building fluency with addition and subtraction;
(3) using standard units of measure;
(4) describing and analyzing shapes.

Grade 2 Mathematics Standards by Domain

Operations and Algebraic Thinking (OA)

•   **Represent and solve problems involving addition and subtraction.**

2.OA.1 Use addition and subtraction within 100 to solve one-and two-step word problems involving situations of adding to, taking from, putting together, taking apart, and comparing, with unknowns in all positions, e.g., by using drawings and equations with a symbol for the unknown number to represent the problem.

•   **Add and subtract within 20.**

2.OA.2 Fluently add and subtract within 20 using mental strategies. By the end of Grade 2, know from memory all sums of two one-digit numbers.

•   **Work with equal groups of objects to gain foundations for multiplication.**

2.OA.3 Determine whether a group of objects (up to 20) has an odd or even number of members, e.g., by pairing objects or counting them by 2s; write an equation to express an even number as a sum of two equal addends.
2.OA.4 Use addition to find the total number of objects arranged in rectangular arrays with up to 5 rows and 5 columns; write an equation to express the total as a sum of equal addends.

Number and Operations in Base Ten (NBT)

•   **Understand place value.**

2.NBT.1 Understand that the three digits of a three-digit number represent amounts of hundred, tens, and ones; e.g., 706 equals 7 hundreds, 0 tens, and 6 ones. Understand the following as special cases:

a.   100 can be thought of as a bundle of ten tens—called a "hundred."
b.   The numbers 100, 200, 300, 400, 500, 600, 700, 800, 900 refer to one, two, three four, five, six, seven, eight, or nine hundreds (and 0 tens and 0 ones).

2.NBT.2 Count within 1000; skip-count by 5s, 10s, and 100s.
2.NBT.3 Read and write numbers from 1000 using base-ten numerals, number names, and expanded form.

2.NBT.4 Compare two three-digit numbers based on meanings of the hundreds, tens, and ones digits, using >, =, and < symbols to record the result of the comparisons.

- **Use place value understanding and properties of operations to add and subtract.**

2.NBT.5 Fluently add and subtract within 100 using strategies based on place value, properties of operations, and/or the relationship between addition and subtraction.

2.NBT.6 Add up to four two-digit numbers using strategies based on place value and properties of operations.

2.NBT.7 Add and subtract within 1000, using concrete models or drawings and strategies based on place value, properties of operations, and/or the relationship between addition and subtraction; relate the strategy to a written method. Understand that in adding or subtracting three-digit numbers, one adds or subtracts hundreds and hundreds, tens and tens, ones and ones; and sometimes it is necessary to compose or decompose tens and hundreds.

2.NBT.8 Mentally add 10 or 100 to a given number 100–900 and mentally subtract 10 or 100 from a given number 100–900.

2.NBT.9 Explain why addition and subtraction strategies work, using place value and the properties of operations.

Measurement and Data (MD)

- **Measure and estimate lengths in standard units.**

2.MD.1 Measure the length of an object by selecting and using appropriate tools such as rulers, yardsticks, meter sticks, or measuring tapes.

2.MD.2 Measure the length of objects twice, using length units of different lengths for the two measurements; describe how the two measurements relate to the size of the unit chosen.

2.MD.3 Estimate lengths using units of inches, feet, centimeters, and meters.

2.MD.4 Measure to determine how much longer one object is that another, expressing the length difference in terms of a standard length unit.

- **Relate addition and subtraction to length.**

2.MD.5 Use addition and subtraction within 100 to solve word problems involving lengths that are given in the same units, e.g., by using drawings (such as drawings of rulers) and equations with a symbol for the unknown number to represent the problem.

2.MD.6 Represent whole numbers as lengths from 0 on a number line diagram with equally spaced points corresponding to the numbers 0, 1, 2, . . . and represent whole number sums and differences within 100 on a number line diagram.

- **Work with time and money.**

    2.MD.7 Tell and write time from analog and digital clocks to the nearest five minutes, using a.m. and p.m.

    2.MD.8 Solve word problems involving dollar bills, quarters, dimes, nickels, and pennies, using $ and ¢ symbols appropriately. Example: *If you have 2 dimes and 3 pennies, how many cents do you have?*

- **Represent and interpret data.**

    2.MD.9 Generate measurement data by measuring lengths of several objects to the nearest whole unit, or by making repeated measurements of the same object. Show the measurement by making a line plot, where the horizontal scale is marked off in whole-number units.

    2.MD.10 Draw a picture graph and a bar graph (with single unit scale) to represent a data set with up to four categories. Solve simple put-together, take-apart, and compare problems using information presented in a bar graph.

Geometry (G)

- **Reason with shapes and their attributes**

    2.G.1 Recognize and draw shapes having specific attributes, such as a given number of angles or a given number of equal faces. Identify triangles, quadrilaterals, pentagons, hexagons, and cubes.

    2.G.2 Partition a rectangle into rows and columns of same-size squares and count to find the total number of them.

    2.G.3 Partition circles and rectangles into two, three, or four equal shares, describe the shares using the words *halves, thirds, half of, a third of,* etc., and describe the whole as two halves, three thirds, four fourths. Recognize that equal shares of identical wholes need not have the same shape.

TABLE 14.2 CCSS-M Standards for Mathematical Practice

CCSS STANDARDS FOR MATHEMATICAL PRACTICE (SMP)	SMP IN STUDENT-FRIENDLY LANGUAGE (White & Dauksas, 2012)
Make sense of problems and persevere in solving them.	I can try many times to understand and solve a math problem.
Reason abstractly and quantitatively.	I can think about the math problem in my head first.
Construct viable arguments and critique the reasoning of others.	I can make a plan, called a strategy, to solve the problem, and discuss other students' strategies too.
Model with mathematics.	I can use math symbols and numbers to solve the problem.

CCSS STANDARDS FOR MATHEMATICAL PRACTICE (SMP)	SMP IN STUDENT-FRIENDLY LANGUAGE (White & Dauksas, 2012)
Use appropriate tools strategically.	I can use math tools, pictures, drawings, and objects to solve the problem.
Attend to precision.	I can check to see if my strategy and calculations are correct.
Look for and make use of structure.	I can use what I already know about math to solve the problem.
Look for and express regularity in repeated reasoning.	I can use a strategy that I used to solve another math problem.

ANNOTATED

Grade 2 Standards for Mathematical Content

In Grade 2, instructional time should focus on *four critical areas*:

(1) extending understanding of base-ten notation;
(2) building fluency with addition and subtraction;
(3) using standard units of measure;
(4) describing and analyzing shapes.

MUCH OF THE LANGUAGE USED IN THE CCSS-MATHEMATICS DEPARTS FROM THE TYPICAL MATH TERMINOLOGY USED IN PAST STANDARDS. THE AUTHORS OF THE STANDARDS DELIBERATELY LIMIT THE USE OF GENERIC LANGUAGE IN ORDER TO INTRODUCE ACADEMIC LANGUAGE, E.G., THE LANGUAGE MATHEMATICIANS USE TO TALK ABOUT MATH.

Grade 2 Mathematics Standards by Domain

REMEMBER, THESE ARE THE EXPECTATIONS STUDENTS SHOULD BE ABLE TO MEET AT THE *END* OF GRADE 2.

Operations and Algebraic Thinking (OA)

*   Represent and solve problems involving addition and subtraction.

    2.OA.1 Use addition and subtraction with in 100 to solve one-and two-step word problems involving situations of adding to, taking from, putting together, taking apart, and comparing, with unknowns in all positions, e.g., by using drawings and equations with a symbol for the unknown number to represent the problem.

STUDENTS REPRESENT AND SOLVE THREE KINDS OF WORD PROBLEMS—RESULT UNKNOWN, CHANGE UNKNOWN, AND START UNKNOWN. THE ONE-STEP PROBLEMS SHOULD HAVE A SIMPLER STRUCTURE AND A HIGHER LEVEL OF MATH-EMATICAL CHALLENGE (E.G., PERFORMING TWO DIFFERENT OPERATIONS); THE TWO-STEP PROBLEMS, BECAUSE THEY HAVE A MORE COMPLEX STRUCTURE, SHOULD INVOLVE A SINGLE OPERATION AND SINGLE DIGIT NUMBERS.

- Add and subtract within 20.

2.OA.2 Fluently add and subtract within 20 using mental strategies. By the end of Grade 2, know from memory all sums of two one-digit numbers.

STUDENTS DEVELOP FLUENCY AND INTERNALIZE MATH FACTS BY USING EFFICIENT STRATEGIES THAT MAKE SENSE TO THEM. WHEN THIS STANDARD IS MASTERED, STUDENTS' ADDITION AND SUBTRACTION ARE FLEXIBLE, EFFICIENT, AND ACCURATE. STUDENTS SHOULD NOT MEMORIZE DISCON-NECTED MATH FACTS AND COMPLETE TIMED TESTS. THE STANDARD REQUIRES THAT STUDENTS KNOW MATH FACTS FROM MEMORY; THIS KNOWLEDGE IS GAINED BY REPEATED PRACTICE WITH MENTAL STRATEGIES SUCH AS COUNTING ON, MAKING TEN, DOUBLES AND DOUBLES PLUS ONE, AND SO ON.

- Work with equal groups of objects to gain foundations for multipli-cation.

2.OA.3 Determine whether a group of objects (up to 20) has an odd or even number of members, e.g., by pairing objects or counting them by 2s; write an equation to express an even number as a sum of two equal addends.

MORE EVIDENCE OF THE POWER OF MENTAL MATH STRATE-GIES: STUDENTS DRAW ON THEIR UNDERSTANDING OF THE CONCEPT OF "DOUBLES" TO DETERMINE WHETHER A NUM-BER IS EVEN OR ODD. THEY SHOULD BEGIN THEIR WORK WITH CONCRETE OBJECTS, THEN MOVE TO DRAWINGS, AND THEN TO MEMORY.

2.OA.4 Use addition to find the total number of objects arranged in rectangular arrays with up to 5 rows and 5 columns; write an equation to express the total as a sum of equal addends.

WORK WITH RECTANGULAR ARRAYS AND REPEATED ADDITION BUILDS THE FOUNDATION FOR MULTIPLICATION. REMIND STUDENTS THAT, THANKS TO THE COMMUTATIVE PROPERTY, THEY CAN ADD EITHER THE COLUMNS OR THE ROWS AND ARRIVE AT THE SAME SOLUTION.

Number and Operations in Base Ten (NBT)

- Understand place value.

  2.NBT.1 Understand that the three digits of a three-digit number represent amounts of hundred, tens, and ones; e.g., 706 equals 7 hundreds, 0 tens, and 6 ones.

  STUDENTS EXTEND THEIR BASE TEN KNOWLEDGE TO RECOGNIZE TEN "TENS" AS A UNIT CALLED A "HUNDRED" AND MAKE A CONNECTION BETWEEN WRITTEN 3-DIGIT NUMBERS AND HUNDREDS, TENS, AND ONES. NOTE THAT STUDENTS' UNDERSTANDING THE VALUE OF THE DIGITS IS MORE IMPORTANT THAN THEIR ABILITY TO STATE THE NUMBER OF HUNDREDS, TENS, OR ONES. TO BE SURE THAT STUDENTS UNDERSTAND, ASK THEM TO MODEL THE NUMBER WITH SOME KIND OF VISUAL REPRESENTATION.

  Understand the following as special cases:

  a. 100 can be thought of as a bundle of ten tens—called a "hundred."
  b. The numbers 100, 200, 300, 400, 500, 600, 700, 800, 900 refer to one, two, three, four, five, six, seven, eight, or nine hundreds (and 0 tens and 0 ones).

  STUDENTS CAN REPRESENT THESE NUMBERS WITH GROUPABLE OR PREGROUPED MANIPULATIVES.

  2.NBT.2 Count within 1000; skip-count by 5s, 10s, and 100s.

  STUDENTS SHOULD BE ABLE TO COUNT TO ANY NUMBER WITHIN 1000 AND TO SAY THE FEW NUMBERS THAT COME AFTER THE TARGET NUMBER.

  2.NBT.3 Read and write numbers from 1000 using base-ten numerals, number names, and expanded form.

  WHEN NAMING NUMBERS, BE SURE TO AVOID THE USE OF "AND" (E.G., TWO HUNDRED AND FORTY THREE). THE

CORRECT NAME FOR THAT NUMBER IS "TWO HUNDRED FORTY THREE."

2.NBT.4 Compare two three-digit numbers based on meanings of the hundreds, tens, and ones digits, using >, =, and < symbols to record the result of the comparisons.

STUDENTS LOOK AT HUNDREDS, TENS, AND ONES TO COMPARE THREE-DIGIT NUMBERS. HOWEVER, WHEN THEY TRULY UNDERSTAND PLACE VALUE, THEY WILL BE ABLE TO EXPLAIN WHY YOU WOULD BEGIN COMPARING NUMBERS BY LOOKING AT THE HUNDREDS PLACE FIRST.

- **Use place value understanding and properties of operations to add and subtract.**

2.NBT.5 Fluently add and subtract within 100 using strategies based on place value, properties of operations, and/or the relationship between addition and subtraction.

STUDENTS IN SECOND GRADE ARE NOT EXPECTED TO USE CARRYING AND BORROWING TO SOLVE MULTIPLE-DIGIT ADDITION AND SUBTRACTION PROBLEMS. RATHER, THEY SHOULD USE THE STRATEGIES SUCH AS PLACE VALUE, DECOMPOSING INTO TENS, AND THE COMMUTATIVE PROPERTY.

2.NBT.6 Add up to four two-digit numbers using strategies based on place value and properties of operations.

STUDENTS IN SECOND GRADE ARE NOT EXPECTED TO USE CARRYING AND BORROWING TO SOLVE MULTIPLE-DIGIT ADDITION AND SUBTRACTION PROBLEMS. RATHER, THEY SHOULD USE THE STRATEGIES SUCH AS PLACE VALUE, DECOMPOSING INTO TENS, AND THE COMMUTATIVE PROPERTY.

2.NBT.7 Add and subtract within 1000, using concrete models or drawings and strategies based on place value, properties of operations, and/or the relationship between addition and subtraction; relate the strategy to a written method. Understand that in adding or subtracting three-digit numbers, one adds or subtracts hundreds and hundreds, tens and tens, ones and ones; and sometimes it is necessary to compose or decompose tens and hundreds.

STUDENTS SHOULD USE A NUMBER LINE, BASE TEN BLOCKS, AND MENTAL STRATEGIES TO SOLVE THESE PROBLEMS. DO NOT USE REGROUPING.

2.NBT.8 Mentally add 10 or 100 to a given number 100–900 and mentally subtract 10 or 100 from a given number 100–900.

PROVIDE STUDENTS WITH PREGROUPED OBJECTS, FACILITATED DISCUSSION, AND ENOUGH HANDS-ON EXPERIENCES FOR THEM TO REALIZE THAT SUBTRACTING TEN ONLY IMPACTS THE TENS PLACE AND SUBTRACTING ONE HUNDRED ONLY IMPACTS THE HUNDREDS PLACE. ONCE STUDENTS ARE COMFORTABLE ADDING AND SUBTRACTING WITHIN THE SAME HUNDRED, MOVE ON TO OPPORTUNITIES TO ADD AND SUBTRACT ACROSS HUNDREDS.

2.NBT.9 Explain why addition and subtraction strategies work, using place value and the properties of operations.

STUDENTS MAY USE DRAWINGS OR OBJECTS TO SUPPORT THEIR EXPLANATIONS. THEY SHOULD ALSO DISCUSS THEIR EXPLANATIONS AND STRATEGIES WITH PEERS.

Measurement and Data (MD)

• Measure and estimate lengths in standard units.

2.MD.1 Measure the length or an object by selecting and using appropriate tools such as rulers, yardsticks, meter sticks, or measuring tapes.

PROVIDE STUDENTS WITH MEASUREMENT OPPORTUNITIES THAT INCLUDE PARTITION (A LARGE UNIT CAN BE SUBDIVIDED INTO EQUIVALENT SMALLER UNITS), ITERATION (AN OBJECT OR A SERIES OF IDENTICAL OBJECTS CAN BE USED REPEATEDLY TO DETERMINE THE LENGTH OF AN OBJECT), AND THE COMPENSATORY PRINCIPLE (THE RELATIONSHIP BETWEEN THE SIZE OF A UNIT TO THE NUMBER OF UNITS NEEDED, E.G., THE SMALLER THE UNIT OF MEASURE THE MORE UNITS WILL BE NEEDED).

2.MD.2 Measure the length of objects twice, using length units of different lengths for the two measurements; describe how the two measurements relate to the size of the unit chosen.

ANOTHER EXAMPLE OF THE COMPENSATORY PRINCIPLE.

2.MD.3 Estimate lengths using units of inches, feet, centimeters, and meters.

NOTE THAT MAKING AN ESTIMATION CREATES A PROBLEM TO BE SOLVED BY THE STUDENT RATHER THAN JUST A TASK TO BE COMPLETED. BE SURE TO FOCUS STUDENTS' ATTENTION ON THE RELATIONSHIP OF THEIR ESTIMATES TO THE ACTUAL MEASUREMENTS OF THE OBJECT.

2.MD.4 Measure to determine how much longer one object is that another, expressing the length difference in terms of a standard length unit.

STUDENTS CHOOSE TWO OBJECTS TO MEASURE, SELECT AN APPROPRIATE MEASUREMENT TOOL AND UNIT, MEASURE BOTH OBJECTS, AND DETERMINE THE DIFFERENCE IN LENGTH.

•   Relate addition and subtraction to length.

2.MD.5 Use addition and subtraction within 100 to solve word problems involving lengths that are given in the same units, e.g., by using drawings (such as drawings of rulers) and equations with a symbol for the unknown number to represent the problem.

2.MD.6 Represent whole numbers as lengths from 0 on a number line diagram with equally spaced points corresponding to the numbers 0, 1, 2, . . . and represent whole number sums and differences within 100 on a number line diagram.

STUDENTS SHOULD REALIZE THAT A NUMBER LINE IS LIKE A RULER. THIS WILL ONLY HAPPEN IF THE PROBLEMS WE PRESENT TO STUDENTS FOCUS EXCLUSIVELY ON LENGTH.

•   Work with time and money.

2.MD.7 Tell and write time from analog and digital clocks to the nearest five minutes, using a.m. and p.m.

STUDENTS NEED TO UNDERSTAND HOW TO READ A DIAL-TYPE INSTRUMENT TO BEGIN TO UNDERSTAND AN ANALOG CLOCK. ALSO, MAKING CONNECTIONS TO SKIP-COUNTING BY FIVES AND TELLING TIME ON AN ANALOG CLOCK CAN HELP STUDENTS MAKE SENSE OF THE NUMERALS (1–12) AROUND THE CLOCK FACE.

2.MD.8 Solve word problems involving dollar bills, quarters, dimes, nickels, and pennies, using $ and ¢ symbols appropriately. Example: *If you have 2 dimes and 3 pennies, how many cents do you have?*

DON'T ASSUME STUDENTS HAVE NO EXPERIENCE USING AND COUNTING MONEY; ACTIVATE THEIR PRIOR KNOWL-EDGE AND ASK FOR INPUT FROM STUDENTS WHO HAVE USED MONEY ON THEIR OWN. SINCE STUDENTS HAVE NOT YET BEEN INTRODUCED TO DECIMALS, THE WORK ON THIS STANDARD SHOULD BE CARRIED OUT IN TERMS OF $ AND ¢.

- Represent and interpret data.

2.MD.9 Generate measurement data by measuring lengths of several objects to the nearest whole unit, or by making repeated measurements of the same object. Show the measurement by making a line plot, where the horizontal scale is marked off in whole-number units.

THE INTENT OF THIS STANDARD IS FOR STUDENTS TO POSE A QUESTION, GATHER DATA, ANALYZE DATA, CREATE REPRESENTATIONS, AND INTERPRET RESULTS; MEASUREMENT IS THE SOURCE OF THE DATA, BUT IT IS NOT THE FOCUS OF THE STANDARD.

2.MD.10 Draw a picture graph and a bar graph (with single unit scale) to represent a data set with up to four categories. Solve simple put-together, take-apart, and compare problems using information presented in a bar graph.

AS WITH 2.MD.9, THE INTENT OF THIS STANDARD IS FOR STUDENTS TO POSE A QUESTION, GATHER AND ANALYZE DATA, CREATE REPRESENTATIONS, AND INTERPRET RESULTS. SOLVING SIMPLE ADDITION AND SUBTRACTION PROBLEMS IS JUST AN ADD-ON THAT ENRICHES THE EXPERIENCE.

Geometry (G)

- Reason with shapes and their attributes

2.G.1 Recognize and draw shapes having specific attributes, such as a given number of angles or a given number of equal faces. Identify triangles, quadrilaterals, pentagons, hexagons, and cubes.

STUDENTS ARE GIVEN KEY ATTRIBUTES OF A SHAPE—NUMBER OF ANGLES, ETC.—AND ARE EXPECTED TO RECOGNIZE, NAME, AND DRAW THE SHAPES. THE STANDARD INCLUDES TWO- AND THREE-DIMENSIONAL SHAPES.

2.G.2 Partition a rectangle into rows and columns of same-size squares and count to find the total number of them.

THIS STANDARD CONNECTS TO MAKING ARRAYS OF OBJECTS (PREPARATION FOR MULTIPLICATION).

2.G.3 Partition circles and rectangles into two, three, or four equal shares, describe the shares using the words *halves, thirds, half of, a third of*, etc., and describe the whole as two halves, three thirds, four fourths. Recognize that equal shares of identical wholes need not have the same shape.

STUDENTS BENEFIT FROM LOTS OF HANDS-ON EXPERIENCE EXPLORING THE CONCEPT OF PARTS AND WHOLES. STUDENTS SHOULD BE ENCOURAGED TO USE MATHEMATICAL TERMINOL-OGY (HALVES, THIRDS, FOURTHS, QUARTERS, WHOLES) AND TO THINK OF THE "WHOLE" SHAPE AS BEING COMPOSED OF THREE THIRDS OR FOUR FOURTHS.

Grade 2 Reading Standards

TABLE 14.3

Reading Standards for Literature	Reading Standards for Informational Text
Key Ideas and Details	
RL.2.1. Ask and answer such questions as *who, what, where, when, why,* and *how* to demonstrate understanding of key details in a text.	RI.2.1. Ask and answer such questions as *who, what, where, when, why,* and *how* to demonstrate understanding of key details in a text.
RL.2.2. Recount stories, including fables and folktales from diverse cultures, and determine their central message, lesson, or moral.	RI.2.2. Identify the main topic of a multiparagraph text as well as the focus of specific paragraphs within the text.
RL.2.3. Describe how characters in a story respond to major events and challenges.	RI.2.3. Describe the connection between a series of historical events, scientific ideas, or concepts, or steps in technical procedures in a text.

Craft and Structure

RL.2.4. Describe how words and phrases (i.e., regular beats, alliteration, rhymes, repeated lines) supply rhythm and meaning in a story, poem, or song.	RI.2.4. Determine the meaning of words and phrases in a text relevant to a *grade 2 topic or subject area.*
RL.2.5. Describe the overall structure of a story, including describing how the beginning introduces the story and the ending concludes the action.	RI.2.5. Know and use various text features (e.g., captions, bold print, subheadings, glossaries, indexes, electronic menus, icons) to locate key facts or information in a text efficiently.
RL.2.6. Acknowledge differences in the points of view of characters, including by speaking in a different voice for each character when reading a dialogue aloud.	RI.2.6. Identify the main purpose of a text including what the author wants to answer, explain, or describe.

Integration of Knowledge and Ideas

RL.2.7. Use information gained from the illustrations and words in a print or digital text to demonstrate understanding of its characters setting or plot.	RI.2.7. Explain how specific images (e.g., a diagram showing how a machine works) contribute to and clarify a text.
8. (Not applicable to literature)	RI.2.8. Describe how reasons support specific points the author makes in a text.
RL.2.9. Compare and contrast two or more versions of the same story (e.g., Cinderella stories) by different authors or from different cultures.	RI.2.9. Compare and contrast the most important points presented by two texts on the same topic.

(Continued)

TABLE 14.3 (Continued)

Range of Reading and Level of Text Complexity	
RL.2.10. By the end of the year, read and comprehend literature, including stories and poetry, in the grades 2–3 text complexity band proficiently, with scaffolding as needed at the high end of the range.	RI.2.10. By the end of the year, read and comprehend literature, including history/social studies, sciences, and technical texts, in the grades 2–3 text complexity band proficiently, with scaffolding as needed at the high end of the range.

TABLE 14.4

Reading Standards: Foundational Skills
Print Concepts
1. (Only in kindergarten and grade 1)
Phonological Awareness
2. (Only in kindergarten and grade 1)
Phonics and Word Recognition

RF.2.3. Know and apply grade-level phonics and word analysis skills in decoding words.
   a. Distinguish long and short vowels when reading regularly spelled one-syllable words.
   b. Know spelling-sound correspondences for additional common vowel teams.
   c. Decode regularly spelled two-syllable words with long vowels.
   d. Decode words with common prefixes and suffixes.
   e. Identify words with inconsistent but common spelling-sound correspondences.
   f. Recognize and read grade-appropriate irregularly spelled words.

Fluency

RF.2.4. Read with sufficient accuracy and fluency to support comprehension.
   a. Read on-level text with purpose and understanding.
   b. Read on-level text orally with accuracy, appropriate rate, and expression on successive readings.
   c. Use context to confirm or self-correct word recognition and understanding, rereading as necessary.

Grade 2 Writing Standards

TABLE 14.5

Text Types and Purposes
W.2.1. Write opinion pieces in which they introduce the topic or name of the book they are writing about, state an opinion, supply reasons that support the opinion, use linking words (e.g., *because, and, also*) to connect opinion and reasons, and provide a concluding statement or section.
W.2.2. Write informative/explanatory texts in which they name a topic, use facts and definitions to develop points, and provide a concluding statement or section.
W.2.3. Write narratives in which they recount a well-elaborated event or short sequence of events, include detail to describe actions, thoughts, and feelings, use temporal words to signal event order, and provide a sense of closure.
Production and Distribution of Writing
4. (Begins in grade 3)
W.2.5. With guidance and support from adults and peers, focus on a topic, and strengthen writing as needed by revising and editing.
W.2.6. With guidance and support from adults, use a variety of digital tools to produce and publish writing, including in collaboration with peers.
Research to Build and Present Knowledge
W.2.7. Participate in shared research and writing projects (e.g., read a number of books on a single topic to produce a report, record science observations).
W.2.8. Recall information from experience or gather information from provided sources to answer a question.
9. (Begins in grade 4)
Range of Writing
10. (Begins in grade 3)

Grade 2 Speaking And Listening Standards

TABLE 14.6

Comprehension and Collaboration
SL.2.1. Participate in collaborative conversations with diverse partners about *grade 2 topics and texts* with peers and adults in small and larger groups. (a) Follow agreed-upon rules for discussions (e.g., gaining the floor in respectful ways, listening to others with care, speaking one at a time about the topics and texts under discussion). (b) Build on others' talk in conversations by linking their comments to the remarks of others. (c) Ask for clarification and further explanation as needed about the topics and texts under discussion. SL.2.2. Recount or describe key ideas or details from a text read aloud or information presented orally or through other media. SL.2.3. Ask and answer questions about what a speaker says in order to clarify comprehension, gather additional information, or deepen understanding of a topic or issue.
Presentation of Knowledge and Ideas
SL.2.4. Tell a story or recount an experience with appropriate facts and relevant descriptive details, speaking audibly in coherent sentences. SL.2.5. Create audio recordings of stories or poems; add drawings or other visual displays to stories or recounts of experiences when appropriate to clarify ideas, thoughts, and feelings. SL.2.6. Produce complete sentences when appropriate to task and situation in order to provide requested detail or clarification.

Grade 2 Language Standards

TABLE 14.7

Conventions of Standard English
L.2.1. Demonstrate command of the conventions of standard English grammar when writing or speaking.

    (a) Use collective nouns (e.g., *group*).

    (b) Form and use frequently occurring irregular plural nouns (e.g., *feet, children, teeth, mice, fish*).

    (c) Use reflexive pronouns (e.g., *myself, ourselves*).

    (d) Form and use the past tense of frequently occurring irregular verbs (e.g., *sat, hid, told*).

    (e) Use adjectives and adverbs, and choose between them depending on what is to be modified.

    (f) Produce, expand, and rearrange complete simple and compound sentences (e.g., *The boy watched the movie; The little boy watched the movie; The action movie was watched by the little boy*).

L.2.2. Demonstrate command of the conventions of standard English capitalization, punctuation, and spelling when writing.

    (a) Capitalize holidays, product names, and geographic names.

    (b) Use commas in greetings and closings of letters.

    (c) Use an apostrophe to form contractions and frequently occurring possessives.

    (d) Generalize learned spelling patterns when writing words (e.g., cage→badge; boy→boil).

    (e) Consult reference materials, including beginning dictionaries, as needed to check and correct spellings.

Knowledge of Language
L.2.3. Use knowledge of language and its conventions when writing, speaking, reading, or listening.

    (a) Compare formal and informal uses of English.

(Continued)

TABLE 14.7 (Continued)

Vocabulary Acquisition and Use

L.2.4. Determine or clarify the meaning of unknown and multiple-meaning words and phrases based on grade 2 reading and content, choosing flexibly from an array of strategies.

    (a) Use sentence-level context as a clue to the meaning of a word or phrase.

    (b) Determine the meaning of the new word formed when a known prefix is added to a known word (e.g., *happy/unhappy, tell/retell*).

    (c) Use a known root word as a clue to the meaning of an unknown word with the same root (e.g., *addition, additional*).

    (d) Use knowledge of the meaning of individual words to predict the meaning of compound words (e.g., *birdhouse, lighthouse, housefly; bookshelf, notebook, bookmark*).

    (e) Use glossaries and beginning dictionaries, both print and digital, to determine or clarify the meaning of words and phrases.

L.2.5. With guidance and support from adults, demonstrate understanding of word relationships and nuances in word meanings.

    (a) Identify real-life connections between words and their use (e.g., describe foods that are *spicy* or *juicy*).

    (b) Distinguish shades of meaning among closely related verbs (e.g., *toss, throw, hurl*) and closely related adjectives (e.g., *thin, slender, skinny, scrawny*).

L.2.6. Use words and phrases acquired through conversations, reading and being read to, and responding to texts, including using adjectives and adverbs to describe (e.g., *When other kids are happy that makes me happy*).

ANNOTATED

Grade 2 Reading Standards

TABLE 14.8

Reading Standards for Literature	Reading Standards for Informational Text
Key Ideas and Details	
RL.2.1. Ask and answer such questions as *who, what, where, when, why,* and *how* to demonstrate understanding of key details in a text.	RI.2.1. Ask and answer such questions as *who, what, where, when, why,* and *how* to demonstrate understanding of key details in a text.
RI.2.2. Identify the main topic of a multiparagraph text as well as the focus of specific paragraphs within the text.	RL.2.2. Recount stories, including fables and folktales from diverse cultures, and determine their central message, lesson, or moral.
RI.2.3. Describe the connection between a series of historical events, scientific ideas, or concepts, or steps in technical procedures in a text.	RL.2.3. Describe how characters in a story respond to major events and challenges.
ANNOTATION	ANNOTATION
STUDENTS CONTINUE TO USE TEXTUAL EVIDENCE TO SUPPORT THEIR THINKING AS THEY ASK AND ANSWER GENERAL QUESTIONS. DETERMINING THE CENTRAL MESSAGE OF A STORY CAN BE DIFFICULT; TEACHERS MIGHT WANT TO START WITH AESOP'S FABLES (SINCE THE MORAL IS EXPLICITLY STATED AT THE END) TO PROVIDE EXAMPLES OF A CENTRAL MESSAGE. STUDENTS FOCUS ON CHARACTER DEVELOPMENT, USING CHARACTERS' REACTIONS TO EVENTS IN THE STORY AS A SPRINGBOARD.	IN GRADE 2 STUDENTS ARE EXPECTED TO BE ABLE NOT ONLY TO IDENTIFY THE MAIN TOPIC IN A PARAGRAPH, BUT TO SYNTHESIZE MULTIPLE PARAGRAPHS AND PROVIDE A STATEMENT OF THE OVERALL FOCUS/PURPOSE OF THOSE PARAGRAPHS. ALSO, STUDENTS NEED EXPOSURE TO TEXTS THAT DESCRIBE THE CONNECTION BETWEEN A SERIES OF HISTORICAL EVENTS, SCIENTIFIC PROCEDURES OR CONCEPTS, OR STEPS IN TECHNICAL PROCEDURES. BE SURE TO CHOOSE INFORMATIONAL TEXTS THAT PROVIDE OPPORTUNITIES FOR STUDENTS TO PRACTICE THESE SKILLS.

(Continued)

TABLE 14.8 (Continued)

Craft and Structure	
RL.2.4. Describe how words and phrases (i.e., regular beats, alliteration, rhymes, repeated lines) supply rhythm and meaning in a story, poem, or song.	RI.2.4. Determine the meaning of words and phrases in a text relevant to a *grade 2 topic or subject area.*
RL.2.5. Describe the overall structure of a story, including describing how the beginning introduces the story and the ending concludes the action.	RI.2.5. Know and use various text features (e.g., captions, bold print, subheadings, glossaries, indexes, electronic menus, icons) to locate key facts or information in a text efficiently.
RL.2.6. Acknowledge differences in the points of view of characters, including by speaking in a different voice for each character when reading a dialogue aloud.	RI.2.6. Identify the main purpose of a text including what the author wants to answer, explain, or describe.
ANNOTATION	ANNOTATION
STUDENTS CAN IDENTIFY RHYME, REPETITION, AND RHYTHM BUT MAY NEED ASSISTANCE WITH "ALLITERATION"—IT'S NOT DIFFICULT FOR STUDENTS TO IDENTIFY ONCE THEY KNOW WHAT IT IS. STUDENTS BEGIN TO UNDERSTAND THAT CHARACTERS IN A STORY OFTEN HAVE A DIFFERENT POINT OF VIEW; TO SUPPORT THIS DEVELOPMENT, ASK STUDENTS TO USE DIFFERENT VOICES FOR DIFFERENT CHARACTERS.	STUDENTS NEED TO LEARN STRATEGIES FOR DETERMINING THE MEANING OF UNFAMILIAR WORDS, INCLUDING USING A DICTIONARY, GLOSSARY, OR OTHER TEXTUAL ELEMENTS. STUDENTS UNDERSTAND THE GOALS OF AN AUTHOR OF AN INFORMATIONAL TEXT ARE TO ANSWER A QUESTION AND EXPLAIN OR DESCRIBE SOMETHING, AND THEY LEARN HOW TO IDENTIFY THE MAIN PURPOSE OF AN INFORMATIONAL TEXT.

Integration of Knowledge and Ideas

RL.2.7. Use information gained from the illustrations and words in a print or digital text to demonstrate understanding of its characters setting or plot.	RI.2.7. Explain how specific images (e.g., a diagram showing how a machine works) contribute to and clarify a text.
8. (Not applicable to literature)	RI.2.8. Describe how reasons support specific points the author makes in a text.
RL.2.9. Compare and contrast two or more versions of the same story (e.g., Cinderella stories) by different authors or from different cultures.	RI.2.9. Compare and contrast the most important points presented by two texts on the same topic.
ANNOTATION	ANNOTATION
STUDENTS LEARN TO CONSIDER PICTURES AND ILLUSTRATIONS AS WAYS TO GAIN ADDITIONAL INFORMATION ABOUT A STORY'S CHARACTERS, SETTING, OR PLOT. READING MULTIPLE VERSIONS OF THE SAME STORY IS A GREAT OPPORTUNITY TO DISCUSS THE ROLE OF AN AUTHOR'S AND ILLUSTRATOR'S DECISIONS ABOUT HOW A STORY WILL BE TOLD.	LINK THE IDEA THAT THE AUTHOR OF AN INFORMATIONAL TEXT IS TRYING TO ANSWER, EXPLAIN, OR DESCRIBE SOMETHING (2.RI.6) WITH THE COMPARE/CONTRAST STANDARD (2.RI.9): THE DIFFERENCES IN TWO TEXTS ON THE SAME TOPIC ARE REFLECTIONS OF THE SPECIFIC GOALS OF EACH AUTHOR.

Range of Reading and Level of Text Complexity

RL.2.10. By the end of the year, read and comprehend literature, including stories and poetry, in the grades 2–3 text complexity band proficiently, with scaffolding as needed at the high end of the range.	RI.2.10. By the end of the year, read and comprehend literature, including history/ social studies, sciences, and technical texts, in the grades 2–3 text complexity band proficiently, with scaffolding as needed at the high end of the range.

(Continued)

TABLE 14.8 (Continued)

ANNOTATION	ANNOTATION
THE CCSS USE "GRADE BANDS" RATHER THAN GRADE LEVELS TO DISCUSS TEXT COMPLEXITY.	THE CCSS USE "GRADE BANDS" RATHER THAN GRADE LEVELS TO DISCUSS TEXT COMPLEXITY.

TABLE 14.9

Reading Standards: Foundational Skills
Print Concepts
1. (Only in kindergarten and grade 1)
Phonological Awareness
2. (Only in kindergarten and grade 1)
Phonics and Word Recognition

RF.2.3. Know and apply grade-level phonics and word analysis skills in decoding words.
    a. Distinguish long and short vowels when reading regularly spelled one-syllable words.
    b. Know spelling-sound correspondences for additional common vowel teams.
    c. Decode regularly spelled two-syllable words with long vowels.
    d. Decode words with common prefixes and suffixes.
    e. Identify words with inconsistent but common spelling-sound correspondences.
    f. Recognize and read grade-appropriate irregularly spelled words.

ANNOTATION
STUDENTS CONTINUE TO DEVELOP STRATEGIES FOR DECODING WORDS IN TEXTS, INCLUDING ATTENDING TO AFFIXES AND VOWEL PATTERNS. THIS KNOWLEDGE STRENGTHENS THEIR VOCABULARY, SPELLING ABILITY, AND DECODING SKILLS.
Fluency

RF.2.4. Read with sufficient accuracy and fluency to support comprehension.
    a. Read on-level text with purpose and understanding.
    b. Read on-level text orally with accuracy, appropriate rate, and expression on successive readings.
    c. Use context to confirm or self-correct word recognition and understanding, rereading as necessary.

ANNOTATION
MOST SECOND GRADE STUDENTS ARE ABLE TO READ SILENTLY TO THEMSELVES, WHICH MAKES IT MORE DIFFICULT FOR TEACHERS TO ASSESS THEIR FLUENCY AND THEIR COMPREHENSION OF WHAT THEY READ. TRY TO BALANCE SILENT READING WITH READING ALOUD TO ENSURE THAT ALL STUDENTS ARE MAKING APPROPRIATE PROGRESS.

ANNOTATED
Grade 2 Writing Standards

TABLE 14.10

Text Types and Purposes
W.2.1. Write opinion pieces in which they introduce the topic or name of the book they are writing about, state an opinion, supply reasons that support the opinion, use linking words (e.g., because, and also) to connect opinion and reasons, and provide a concluding statement or section.
W.2.2. Write informative/explanatory texts in which they name a topic, use facts and definitions to develop points, and provide a concluding statement or section.
W.2.3. Write narratives in which they recount a well-elaborated event or short sequence of events, include detail to describe actions, thoughts, and feelings, use temporal words to signal event order, and provide a sense of closure.
ANNOTATION
SECOND GRADERS NEED FREQUENT OPPORTUNITIES TO EXPRESS OPINIONS—VERBALLY AND IN WRITING—AND TO SHARE THEIR REASONING WITH OTHERS. STATING AN OPINION IS EASY, BUT STUDENTS WILL REQUIRE EXPLICIT INSTRUCTION IN HOW TO BUILD AN ARGUMENT OR EXPLAIN THEIR THINKING IN WRITING. SECOND GRADERS SHOULD WRITE NARRATIVES IN WHICH THEY FOCUS ON MAKING SPECIFIC, INTENTIONAL CHOICES ABOUT THE WORDS THEY USE TO COMMUNICATE THEIR IDEAS. SECOND GRADERS SHOULD WRITE ACROSS GENRES, INCLUDING OPINION PIECES, INFORMATIVE/EXPLANATORY, AND NARRATIVE TEXTS. TO DO THIS, STUDENTS MUST LEARN STRATEGIES FOR GATHERING FACTS BY RESEARCHING A TOPIC, IDENTIFYING THE MOST RELEVANT FACTS, SELECTING THE RIGHT FORMAT, AND COMPOSING THE REPORT. SECOND GRADERS USE TRANSITIONAL WORDS, WRITE COMPLEX SENTENCES, AND FOCUS ON LINKING THE PARTS OF THEIR WRITING TOGETHER .

(Continued)

TABLE 14.10 (Continued)

Production and Distribution of Writing

4. (Begins in grade 3)

W.2.5. With guidance and support from adults and peers, focus on a topic, and strengthen writing as needed by revising and editing.

W.2.6. With guidance and support from adults, use a variety of digital tools to produce and publish writing, including in collaboration with peers.

ANNOTATION

WITH ASSISTANCE FROM ADULTS AND PEERS, SECOND GRADERS WILL FOCUS THEIR WRITING ON A TOPIC AND WORK ON DEVELOPING THEIR REVISING AND EDITING SKILLS, INCLUDING UNDERSTANDING HOW TO IMPROVE WORD CHOICES, LEARNING STRATEGIES FOR CHANGING SENTENCE STRUCTURE, AND PROOFREADING TO CATCH AND CORRECT ERRORS IN SPELLING, PUNCTUATION, AND GRAMMAR. TEACHER-DEVELOPED CHECKLISTS, PEER EDITING, AND SMALL GROUP DISCUSSIONS ARE HELPFUL WAYS TO BUILD MASTERY OF THESE SKILLS. DIGITAL PUBLICATION OF WRITING CONTINUES TO BE A FOCUS, PARTICULARLY SINCE IT WIDENS THE AUDIENCE OF POTENTIAL READERS.

Research to Build and Present Knowledge

W.2.7. Participate in shared research and writing projects (e.g., read a number of books on a single topic to produce a report, record science observations).

W.2.8. Recall information from experience or gather information from provided sources to answer a question.

9. (Begins in grade 4)

ANNOTATION

THE CCSS REQUIRE SECOND GRADERS TO PARTICIPATE IN SHARED RESEARCH PROJECTS. STUDENTS WILL NEED SUPPORT IN UNDERSTANDING THEIR JOBS ON THE TEAM AND THE WORK THEY ARE EXPECTED TO DO, FROM THE BEGINNING OF THE PROJECT TO THE END. TEACHERS SHOULD DEVELOP GRAPHIC ORGANIZERS, CHECK SHEETS, TASK CHARTS, AND/OR JOB LISTS TO SCAFFOLD THE STUDENTS AS THEY UNDERTAKE THIS WORK.

Range of Writing

10. (Begins in grade 3)

ANNOTATED

Grade 2 Speaking and Listening Standards

TABLE 14.11

Comprehension and Collaboration
SL.2.1. Participate in collaborative conversations with diverse partners about *grade 2 topics and texts* with peers and adults in small and larger groups. (a) Follow agreed-upon rules for discussions (e.g., gaining the floor in respectful ways, listening to others with care, speaking one at a time about the topics and texts under discussion). (b) Build on others' talk in conversations by linking their comments to the remarks of others. (c) Ask for clarification and further explanation as needed about the topics and texts under discussion. SL.2.2. Recount or describe key ideas or details from a text read aloud or information presented orally or through other media. SL.2.3. Ask and answer questions about what a speaker says in order to clarify comprehension, gather additional information, or deepen understanding of a topic or issue.
ANNOTATION
TEACHERS NEED TO HELP STUDENTS NOTICE WHEN THE CLASS OR GROUP IS HAVING A GOOD DISCUSSION AND ELICIT THEIR THOUGHTS ABOUT THE FEATURES OF A GOOD DISCUSSION. STUDENTS ENGAGE IN COLLABORATIVE CONVERSATIONS (BOOK GROUPS, BUDDY READING) AND DEVELOP SKILLS SUCH AS ACTIVE LISTENING, LOOKING AT THE SPEAKER, TAKING TURNS, LINKING IDEAS TO THE SPEAKER'S IDEAS, SHARING THE FLOOR, ETC. STUDENTS SHOULD BE ABLE TO LISTEN TO A SPEAKER AND ASK FOR CLARIFICATION IF NECESSARY. THEY NEED TO LEARN TO FORMULATE A QUESTION THAT IS ON TOPIC AND TO UNDERSTAND AND ANSWER QUESTIONS ASKED OF THEM.
Presentation of Knowledge and Ideas
SL.2.4. Tell a story or recount an experience with appropriate facts and relevant descriptive details, speaking audibly in coherent sentences. SL.2.5. Create audio recordings of stories or poems, add drawings or other visual displays to stories or recounts of experiences when appropriate to clarify ideas, thoughts, and feelings. SL.2.6. Produce complete sentences when appropriate to task and situation in order to provide requested detail or clarification.

(Continued)

TABLE 14.11 (Continued)

ANNOTATION
SECOND GRADERS USE AN AUDIBLE VOICE AND COHERENT, CONNECTED SENTENCES TO TELL STORIES OR DESCRIBE EXPERIENCES. THEY INCLUDE CAREFULLY CHOSEN WORDS, DESCRIPTIVE DETAILS, AND RELEVANT FACTS, AND ARE ABLE TO PROVIDE ADDITIONAL DETAIL OR CLARIFICATION AS NEEDED. THEY USE DIGITAL MEDIA TO CREATE AUDIO RECORDINGS OF STORIES OR POEMS AND CREATE VISUAL DISPLAYS THAT ENHANCE THE STORY/POEM BY CLARIFYING THE IDEAS, THOUGHTS, AND FEELINGS OF THE AUTHOR.

ANNOTATED

Grade 2 Language Standards

TABLE 14.12

Conventions of Standard English
L.2.1. Demonstrate command of the conventions of standard English grammar when writing or speaking.
(a) Use collective nouns (e.g., *group*).
(b) Form and use frequently occurring irregular plural nouns (e.g., *feet, children, teeth, mice, fish*).
(c) Use reflexive pronouns (e.g., *myself, ourselves*).
(d) Form and use the past tense of frequently occurring irregular verbs (e.g., *sat, hid, told*).
(e) Use adjectives and adverbs, and choose between them depending on what is to be modified.
(f) Produce, expand, and rearrange complete simple and compound sentences (e.g., *The boy watched the movie; The little boy watched the movie; The action movie was watched by the little boy*).
L.2.2. Demonstrate command of the conventions of standard English capitalization, punctuation, and spelling when writing.
(a) Capitalize holidays, product names, and geographic names.
(b) Use commas in greetings and closings of letters.
(c) Use an apostrophe to form contractions and frequently occurring possessives.
(d) Generalize learned spelling patterns when writing words (e.g., cage→badge; boy→boil).
(e) Consult reference materials, including beginning dictionaries, as needed to check and correct spellings.

ANNOTATION
SECOND GRADERS LOVE TO COMMUNICATE AND TO BE HEARD. SO, WHEN WORKING WITH SECOND GRADERS ON LANGUAGE CONVENTIONS, FOCUS ON THE WAYS IN WHICH ADHERING TO THESE CONVENTIONS MAKES IT EASIER FOR A READER OR LISTENER TO UNDERSTAND THE POINTS THEY ARE MAKING. TEACH STUDENTS HOW TO LOOK UP WORDS IN A PAPER OR ELECTRONIC DICTIONARY AND HOW TO USE A THESAURUS TO SHARPEN THE PRECISION OF THEIR WORD CHOICES.

Knowledge of Language

L.2.3. Use knowledge of language and its conventions when writing, speaking, reading, or listening.

   (a)   Compare formal and informal uses of English.

ANNOTATION
STUDENTS IN GRADE 2 CAN UNDERSTAND THAT FORMAL AND INFORMAL ENGLISH ARE THE SAME LANGUAGE BUT EACH USES DIFFERENT RULES, VOCABULARY, SENTENCE STRUCTURE, AND GRAMMAR, AND EACH IS APPROPRIATE FOR USE IN DIFFERENT SETTINGS. BEING AWARE OF BOTH REGISTERS AND KNOWING WHEN TO USE EACH ONE HELPS SPEAKERS TO BE UNDERSTOOD BY OTHERS AND TO COMMUNICATE WITH MORE TYPES OF PEOPLE.

Vocabulary Acquisition and Use

L.2.4. Determine or clarify the meaning of unknown and multiple-meaning words and phrases based on *grade 2 reading and content,* choosing flexibly from an array of strategies.

   (a)   Use sentence-level context as a clue to the meaning of a word or phrase.

   (b)   Determine the meaning of the new word formed when a known prefix is added to a known word (e.g., *happy/unhappy, tell/retell).*

   (c)   Use a known root word as a clue to the meaning of an unknown word with the same root (e.g., *addition, additional).*

   (d)   Use knowledge of the meaning of individual words to predict the meaning of compound words (e.g., *birdhouse, lighthouse, housefly; bookshelf, notebook, bookmark).*

   (e)   Use glossaries and beginning dictionaries, both print and digital, to determine or clarify the meaning of words and phrases.

(Continued)

TABLE 14.12 (Continued)

L.2.5. With guidance and support from adults, demonstrate understanding of word relationships and nuances in word meanings.
   (a) Identify real-life connections between words and their use (e.g., describe foods that are *spicy* or *juicy*).
   (b) Distinguish shades of meaning among closely related verbs (e.g., *toss, throw, hurl*) and closely related adjectives (e.g., *thin, slender, skinny, scrawny*).
L.2.6. Use words and phrases acquired through conversations, reading and being read to, and responding to texts, including using adjectives and adverbs to describe (e.g., *When other kids are happy that makes me happy*).

ANNOTATION
SECOND GRADERS DEVELOP VOCABULARY IN ORDER TO MAKE PURPOSEFUL LANGUAGE CHOICES IN WRITING AND SPEAKING TO COMMUNICATE EFFECTIVELY IN PRINT AND DIGITAL TEXTS. THEY SHOULD USE REGISTERS APPROPRIATE TO THEIR AUDIENCE, CONTEXT, AND PURPOSE. SECOND GRADERS WILL DISTINGUISH THE SHADES OF MEANING IN VERBS DESCRIBING THE SAME ACTION AND USE WORDS ACQUIRED BY READING AND BEING READ TO, IN CONVERSATIONS, AND IN SOCIAL SETTINGS.

Three Tips for Teachers of Second Grade Hobbits

1. Find Richness and Depth in the Curriculum

Second grade is often considered the easiest grade to teach. Most students have a handle on the basics of reading, writing, and mathematics, an understanding of the expectations for behavior (and the ability to meet those expectations much of the time), and a level of social skill that enables them to work in pairs and groups successfully. The second grade curriculum contains no content that poses major intellectual challenges for the students (unlike the curricula for first grade and third grade). Second grade seems to be a year in which students are focused on the consolidation and integration of everything they learned and experienced in prekindergarten, kindergarten, and first grade.

Quite frankly, although you are blessed with students who are truly delightful and very interested in learning, teaching second grade can get boring. To be a successful and effective teacher, you must dig deep into the second grade curriculum and find—or create—things to love.

If your social studies curriculum focuses on "People Who Make a Difference," and the exclusive curricular focus on the accomplishments of heroic, exceptional individuals feels unbalanced and counterproductive, you might design and implement a supplemental curricular strand focused on solidarity and the accomplishments of people working in groups. If you have a personal interest in sustainability and environmental responsibility, you could turn that commitment into an interdisciplinary theme that threads throughout the curriculum over the course of the year. Your excitement about the content and the learning experiences you have planned will heighten your students' engagement and interest.

2. Put Your Students' Clarity, Capabilities, and Sense of Mastery to Work

Second graders are amazing. At the apex of early childhood, these children's capabilities as young learners are fully developed. And they know it: You can almost smell their powerful sense of mastery. They feel themselves to be mature, intelligent, and able. And they are ready and willing to tackle any challenge you put before them. Take advantage of this golden moment and put your second graders to work for the good of the school, the community, or the world.

Talk with your students about their areas of interest and the ways in which they would most like to make a difference (Bam! See that connection to the social studies curriculum?). Would they like to partner with a class of younger students with special needs? Do they want to learn Spanish to look after the children of recent immigrants while they are taking an ESL class? Do they want to record oral histories of the elderly population living in the school community? Can they volunteer at an animal shelter? Or a soup kitchen? Service learning projects benefit the individuals receiving the services provided by the children, but they also provide powerful learning opportunities for the students.

3. Don't Rush Your Students

Although second graders are levelheaded, sensible, and industrious, it is important for second grade teachers to remember that their students are still little kids. They love to be silly, to play dress up, to pretend they're horses, or superheroes, or superhorses. They like crude humor, singing together, and playing cooperative games as a class. Board games, blocks, ramps and balls, marble towers, action figures and plastic animals, doing floor-sized jigsaw puzzles, and laughing until their sides hurt. Although they can be remarkably capable and responsible, second graders' days as young children are numbered. Make sure to create opportunities for your students to have unadulterated fun while they can.

References

Bredekamp, S. (1997). Developmentally appropriate practice: The early childhood teacher as decision maker. In S. Bredekamp & C. Copple (Eds.), *Developmentally appropriate practice in early childhood programs. Revised edition* (pp. 33–52). Washington, DC: National Association for the Education of Young Children.

National Governors Association Center for Best Practices, Council of Chief State School Officers. (2010). *Common Core State Standards in English language arts and literacy in history/social studies, science, and technical subjects.* Washington, DC: National Governors Association Center for Best Practices, Council of Chief State School Officers.

National Governors Association Center for Best Practices, Council of Chief State School Officers. (2010). *Common Core State Standards for mathematics.* Washington, DC: National Governors Association Center for Best Practices, Council of Chief State School Officers.

White, J., & Dauksas, L. (2012). CCSSM: Getting started in K–grade 2. *Teaching Children Mathematics, 1* (7), 440–445.

15

USING DAP TO TEACH THE CCSS IN THIRD GRADE

Typical age range for third graders: 8–9 years old

    Working metaphor for third graders: Third graders are **hipsters**.

    Hipsters—the cool, arty, urban types you've seen standing around nonchalantly wearing thrift shop sweaters, odd scarves, and ironic eyeglasses—have been there and done that so many times that they're already over it. Often the behavior of third graders suggests a similar kind of ennui. They know their multiplication tables and can write in cursive . . . sigh . . . whatever. However, beneath their jaded façades, hipsters—and third graders—are often very uncertain about who they are and unsure of what their futures hold. At this moment, are they perched at the summit of coolness? Or are they on the lowest rung of a ladder that extends into a more exclusive arena of cool? Their world changes quickly, and it can be difficult for them to maintain their equilibrium. Teachers who understand this disaffected, "too cool for school" stance as a strategy third graders use to mask their vulnerability can create opportunities for their students to feel successful, competent, connected, and engaged.

Focus Topic: Standardized Testing

The CCSS are part of the standards-based education systems in 44 states, the District of Columbia, and seven U.S. territories. Standards-based education involves three elements:

1. Content standards are established at each grade level in selected content areas
2. Curricula and instructional materials to teach the content to students are developed and distributed to teachers

TABLE 15.1 Developmental Traits of Third Graders Typically Seen in Classrooms

Physical	Third graders are highly energetic and need regular opportunities to get outdoors and burn off some energy. As their coordination improves, they can push themselves too hard and become fatigued.
Social-Emotional	As friendship groups expand, third graders enjoy working cooperatively with others; many are able to focus on the task at hand while also chatting and socializing with friends. Although they are unsure of their own competence, third graders are also resilient and bounce back quickly from mistakes or setbacks. At times, they can also be sullen and moody.
Cognitive	Industrious and hard-working, third graders are beginning to experience the benefits that come with mastery of academic skills. They have a tendency to begin huge tasks without any plan for how they will complete the process; teachers should help third graders break their work into smaller, more manageable segments that can be tackled and completed successfully (Wood, 2007).

3. Students' mastery of all standards for their grade level is assessed using standardized tests

In states that have implemented the CCSS,

1. CCSS-ELA and CCSS-Math are the content standards
2. Most commercially published curricula and instructional materials are still in development
3. Standardized assessments for Grades 3–11 have been developed in one of three ways:

    a. by the Smarter Balanced Assessment Consortium (SBAC), which includes 17 states
    b. by the Partnership for Assessment of Readiness for College and Careers (PARCC), which includes 9 states and the District of Columbia
    c. by individual states

The assessments developed by SBAC and the assessments developed by PARCC are similar in many ways:

*   Assessments are administered on computers to students in Grades 3–11 to test mastery of English-Language Arts and Mathematics.

- Items are written to align to the subject-specific knowledge and skills described in the CCSS.
- Assessments contain different kinds of questions. Some are familiar formats, such as selected response (multiple choice) and constructed response (essay). Novel item formats, such as performance-based tasks and technology-enhanced items, have been crafted to better assess not just what students know but also what they can do.
- Combined components will assess not only where students are at any one point in time, but also how much they have grown, and the extent to which they are becoming prepared to start college or a career upon graduation from high school.
- In addition to end-of-year assessments, the full assessment system will include formative and interim test materials intended to help teachers and parents better understand the strengths and weaknesses of students throughout the school year, enabling them to take action through targeted interventions before the year is over.
- There will be two required components completed by students in the final weeks of the school year.
- By using machine and human scoring, results will be available within two weeks.
- The cost for all summative components is about $20 per student per year.

These assessments are also different from each other (Assessment 101, 2014; Keany, 2013):

- The PARCC assessment uses a fixed-form delivery model: All students receive test questions that are deemed appropriate for their grade level.
- The SBAC assessment includes test questions that are computer-adapted, meaning that a student's test questions are adjusted automatically based on her/his responses to previous questions on the exam. This feature is intended to enable administrators to more quickly identify students' ability levels.
- PARCC contains one optional diagnostic and one optional mid-year assessment.
- SBAC contains optional interim assessments for Grades 3–12.

The individual test questions—both in ELA and math—that will appear in both the PARCC and the SBAC assessments present much higher cognitive demand than the questions on summative standardized assessments previously used in the United States. The image below (adapted from Smarter Balanced Assessment Consortium, n.d.) compares the mathematics problem on the left, which reflects the typical complexity level of questions included in the standardized achievement tests taken by third graders in the past, to the mathematics problem on the right, which reflects the heightened complexity today's third graders can expect to encounter on their Smarter Balanced standardized tests.

A DIFFERENT APPROACH TO TEST ITEMS

This item, from the Smarter Balanced Assessment Consortium, illustrates one of many examples of how two state testing consortia are trying to guide vendors as they design tests for the common standards.

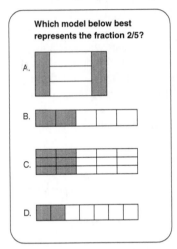

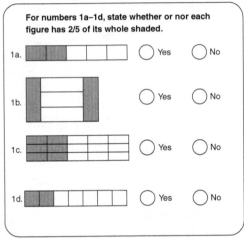

Even if students don't truly have a deep understanding of what two-fifths means, they are likely to choose Option B over the others because it looks like a more traditional way of representing fractrions. Restructuring this problem into a multipart item offers a clearer sense of how deeply a student understands the concept of two-fifths.

This item is more complex because students now have to look at each part separately and decide whether two-fifths can take different forms. The total number of ways to respond to this item is 16. "Guessing" the correct combination of responses is much less likely than for a traditional four-option selected-response item.

FIGURE 15.1 Comparison of a typical standardized test question of the past (left) to an SBAC standardized test question (right) for third grade

Both consortia developing new standardized achievement tests aligned with the Common Core—Smarter Balanced Assessment Consortium (called SBAC or Smarter Balanced) and the Partnership for Assessment of Readiness for College and Careers (PARCC)—have released sample questions to the public. These questions suggest the new tests will present more complexity and challenge than the tests faced by third grade students in the past.

This two-part question, "The Field," is from the PARCC sample question bank for Grade 3 (PARCC-Math, 2013):

Grade 3 – The Field

Part A

A farmer plants 3/4 of the field with soybeans.
Drag the soybean to the field as many times as needed to show the fraction of the field that is planted with soybeans.

Farmer's Fields

Soybean

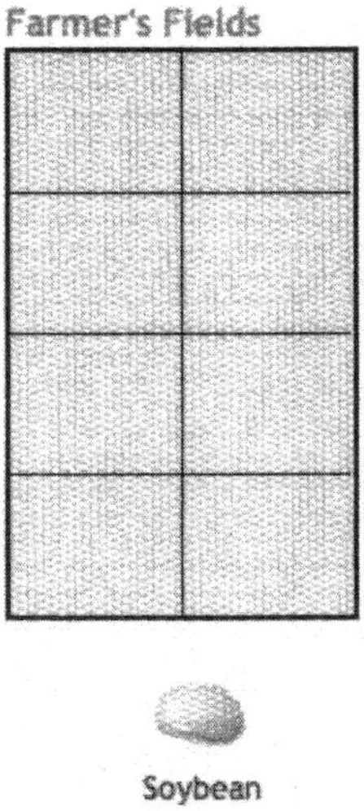

FIGURE 15.2 PARCC

Part B

Type a fraction different than 3/4 in the boxes that also represents the fractional part of the farmer's field that is planted with soybeans.

Farmer's Fields

$$\frac{3}{4} = \frac{\boxed{}}{\boxed{}}$$

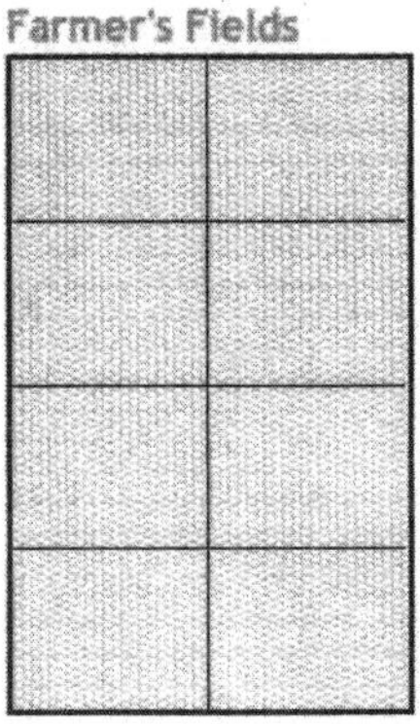

Reset

Explain why the two fractions above are equal.

FIGURE 15.3 PARCC sample mathematics question, third grade (part b)

This question from the SBAC sample question bank (SBAC-Math, 2013) assesses similar skills to the PARCC question.

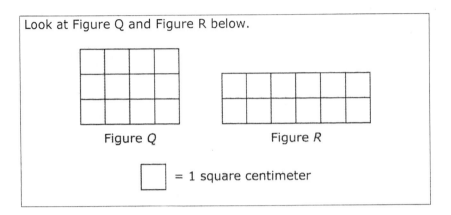

Look at Figure Q and Figure R below.

Figure *Q*   Figure *R*

☐ = 1 square centimeter

FIGURE 15.4 SBAC sample mathematics question, third grade (part 1)

Grade 3 Mathematics Sample ER Item Claim 3

Mia said Figure Q and Figure R have equal areas and equal perimeters. She supported her thinking by saying that any two figures made of an equal number of unit squares always have equal areas and equal perimeters.

Is Mia correct? In the space below, use pictures, numbers, and words to explain why or why not.

FIGURE 15.5 SBAC sample mathematics question, third grade (part 2)

The ELA questions developed by the two consortia are also very complex, particularly in their expectation that students will (A) express an opinion; (B) identify specific passages from the text that provide evidence to support their opinion; and (C) explain how the passages they identified support their opinion. First, an example from SBAC (SBAC-ELA, 2013) in which third grade students must write a convincing argument:

Stimulus Text:

Read the paragraph and complete the task that follows it.

Children should choose their own bedtime. There are things to do, and most have homework. Some people need more sleep, but children like talking to friends. The time to go to bed should be children's decision when they are tired they go to bed earlier. There are activities to go to, so children learn to be responsible.

Item Prompt:

Rewrite the paragraph by organizing it correctly and adding ideas that support the opinion that is given.

FIGURE 15.6 SBAC sample writing prompt, third grade

The PARCC sample question presented here requires third grade students to read a passage from an age-appropriate informational text and complete a performance task (PARCC-ELA, 2013).

Sample Item 3: Questions and Standards

Question:
You have read two texts about famous people in American history who solved a problem by working to make a change.

Write an article for your school newspaper describing how Eliza and Carver faced challenges to change something in America.

- In your article, be sure to describe in detail why some solutions they tried worked and others did not work.
- Tell how the challenges each one faced were the same and how they were different.

FIGURE 15.7 PARCC sample writing prompt, third grade

The PARCC and SBAC assessments were piloted in the 2013–14 academic year in order to identify and resolve any glitches or problem areas. The assessments' first "high stakes" administration will occur in 2015.

All teachers, but especially those whose students are in Grade 3 or higher, would benefit from spending time examining and discussing the sample test questions for their grade level with colleagues. The difference between these questions and the questions asked on the standardized summative assessments of the past is dramatic, and perhaps even a little bit terrifying. But isn't it better to be forewarned (so you and your students can be forearmed) than ambushed?

For a map showing the member states in the PARCC consortium and the member states in the Smarter Balanced consortium, see http://www.governing. com/blogs/view/two-paths-toward-common-core-standards-assessments.html. If your state is developing its own standardized assessments or using some other means for assessing students' mastery of the CCSS, you can contact your state's department of education, your county's office of education, your local school district, or your building administrator for assistance.

Both SBAC and PARCC have made sample test questions and examples of graded student writing samples available online.

- To access PARCC test items: www.parcconline.org/samples/item-task-prototypes
- To access SBAC test items: www.smarterbalanced.org/sample-items-and-performance-tasks

In the remainder of this chapter you will find the following:

- Complete CCSS-Math Standards for Grade 3
- Annotated CCSS-Math Standards for Grade 3

  - All standards fully unpacked

- Complete CCSS-ELA Standard for Grade 3
- Annotated CCSS-ELA Standards for Grade 3

  - All standards fully unpacked

- Three tips for teachers working with Grade 3 hipsters

The text for the Grade 3 standards for mathematical content and for English Language Arts is quoted verbatim from the CCSS-M and CCSS-ELA Standards documents. The annotations to the standards provided in each content area are my efforts to help get you started on unpacking the standards. The ideas and observations I present are nothing more than one person's interpretation of the knowledge and skills included in the standards—I wish it were possible for me to hear your interpretations!

Grade 3 Standards for Mathematical Content

In Grade 3, instructional time should focus on *four critical areas:*

(1) developing understanding of multiplication and division and strategies for multiplication and division within 100;
(2) developing understanding of fractions, especially unit fractions (fractions with numerator 1);
(3) developing understanding of the structure of rectangular arrays and of area;
(4) describing and analyzing two-dimensional shapes.

Grade 3 Mathematics Standards by Domain

Operations and Algebraic Thinking (OA)

• **Represent and solve problems involving multiplication and division**

3.OA.1 Interpret products of whole numbers, e.g., interpret 5×7 as the total number of objects in five groups of 7 objects each. *For example, describe a context in which a total number of objects can be expressed as 5×7.*

3.OA.2 Interpret whole-number quotients of whole numbers, e.g., interpret $56 \div 8$ as the number of objects in each share when 56 objects are partitioned into equal shares of 8 objects each. *For example, describe a context in which a number of shares or a number of groups can be expressed as $56 \div 8$.*

3.OA.3 Use multiplication and division within 100 to solve word problems in situations involving equal groups, arrays, and measurement quantities, e.g., by using drawings and equations with a symbol for the unknown number to represent the problem.

3.0A.4 Determine the unknown whole number in a multiplication or division equation relating three whole numbers. For example, determine the unknown number that makes the equation true in each of the equations $8 \times ? = 48$, $5 = ? + 3$, $6 \times 6 = ?$

- **Understand the properties of multiplication and the relationship between multiplication and division.**

    3.OA.5 Apply properties of operations as strategies to multiply and divide. Examples: If $6 \times 4 = 24$ is known, then $4 \times 6 = 24$ is also known (commutative property of multiplication). $3 \times 5 \times 2$ can be found by $3 \times 5 = 15$, then $15 \times 2 = 30$ or by $5 \times 2 = 10$, then $3 \times 10 = 30$ (associative property of multiplication). Knowing that $8 \times 5 = 40$ and $8 \times 2 = 16$, one can find 8×7 as $8 \times (5 + 2) = (8 \times 5) + (8 \times 2) = 40 + 16 = 56$ (distributive property).

    3.OA.6 Understand division as an unknown factor problem. *For example, find 32 ÷ 8 by finding the number that makes 32 when multiplied by 8.*

- **Multiply and divide within 100.**

    3.OA.7 Fluently multiply and divide within 100 using strategies such as the relationship between multiplication and division (e.g., knowing that $8 \times 5 = 40$, one knows $40 \div 5 = 8$) or properties of operations. By the end of Grade 3, know from memory all products of two one-digit numbers.

- **Solve problems involving the four operations, and identify and explain patterns in arithmetic.**

    3.OA.8 Solve two-step word problems using the four operations. Represent these problems using equations with a letter standing for the unknown quantity. Assess the reasonableness of answers using mental computation and estimation strategies including rounding.

    3.OA.9 Identify arithmetic patterns (including patterns in the addition table or multiplication table), and explain them using properties of operations. *For example, observe that 4 times a number is always even, and explain why 4 times a number can be decomposed into two equal addends.*

Number and Operations in Base Ten (NBT)

- **Use place value understanding and properties of operations to perform multi-digit arithmetic.**

    3.NBT.1 Use place value understanding to round whole numbers to the nearest 10 or 100.

    3.NBT.2 Fluently add and subtract within 1000 using strategies and algorithms based on place value, properties of operations, and/or the relationship between addition and subtraction.

    3.NBT.3 Multiply one-digit whole numbers by multiples of 10 in the range 10–90 (e.g., 9×80, 5×60) using strategies based on place value and properties of operations.

Number and Operations—Fractions (NF)

- **Develop understanding of fractions as numbers.**

3.NF.1 Understand a fraction 1/b as the quantity formed by 1 part when a whole is partitioned into b equal parts; understand a fraction a/b as the quantity formed by a parts of size 1/b.

3.NF.2 Understand a fraction as a number on the number line; represent fractions on a number line diagram.

    a. Represent a fraction 1/b on a number line diagram by defining the interval from 0 to 1 as the whole and partitioning it into b equal parts. Recognize that each part has size 1/b and that the endpoint of the part based at 0 locates the number 1/b on the number line.

    b. Represent fraction a/b on a number line diagram by marking off a lengths 1/b from 0. Recognize the resulting interval has size a/b and that its endpoint locates the number a/b on the number line.

3.NF.3 Explain equivalence of fractions in special cases, and compare fractions by reasoning about their size.

    a. Understand two fractions as equivalent (equal) if they are the same size or at the same point on a number line.

    b. Recognize and generate simple equivalent fractions, e.g., 1/2 = 2/4, 4/6 = 2/3. Explain why the fractions are equivalent, e.g., by using a visual fraction model.

    c. Express whole numbers as fractions, and recognize fractions that are equivalent to whole numbers. Examples: Express 3 in the form 3 = 3/1; recognize that 6/1 = 6; locate 4/4 and 1 at the same point of a number line diagram.

    d. Compare two fractions with the same numerator or the same denominator by reasoning about their size. Recognize that comparisons are valid only when the two fractions refer to the same whole. Record the results of comparisons with the symbols >, =, <, and justify the conclusions, e.g., by using a visual fraction model.

Measurement and Data (MD)

- **Solve problems involving measurement and estimation of intervals of time, liquid volumes, and masses of objects.**

3.MD.1 Tell and write time to the nearest minute and measure time intervals in minutes. Solve word problems involving addition and subtraction of time intervals in minutes, e.g., by representing the problem on a number line diagram.

3.MD.2 Measure and estimate liquid volumes and masses of objects using standard units of grams (g), kilograms (kg), and liters (l). Add, subtract, multiply, or divide to solve one-step word problems involving masses or volumes that are given in the same units, e.g., by using drawings (such as a beaker with a measurement scale) to represent the problem.

• **Represent and interpret data.**

3.MD.3 Draw a scaled picture graph and a scaled bar graph to represent a data set with several categories. Solve one- and two-step "how many more" and "how many less" problems using information presented in the scaled bar graphs. For example: *draw a bar graph in which each square of the bar graph might represent 5 pets.*

3.MD.4 Generate measurement data by measuring lengths using rules marked with halves and fourths of an inch. Show the data by making a line plot, where the horizontal scale is marked off in appropriate units—whole numbers, halves, or quarters.

• **Geometric measurement: understand concepts of area and relate area to multiplication and to addition.**

3.MD.5 Recognize area as an attribute of plane figures and understand concepts of area measurement.

   a. A square with side length 1 unit, called a unit square, is said to have "one square unit" of area, and can be used to measure area.
   b. A plane figure which can be covered without gaps or overlaps by *n* unit squares is said to have an area of *n* square units.

3.MD.6 Measure areas by counting unit squares (square cm, square m, square in, square ft and improvised units).

3.MD.7 Relate area to the operations of multiplication and division.

   a. Find the area of a rectangle with whole-number side lengths by tiling it, and show that the area is the same as would be found by multiplying the side lengths.
   b. Multiply side lengths to find areas of rectangles with whole-number side lengths in the context of solving real world and mathematical problems, and represent whole-number products as rectangular areas in mathematical reasoning.
   c. Use tiling to show in a concrete case that the area of a rectangle with whole-number side lengths a and b + c is the sum of a × b and a × c. Use area models to represent the distributive property in mathematical reasoning.
   d. Recognize area as additive. Find areas of rectilinear figures by decomposing them into non-overlapping rectangles and adding the areas of the non-overlapping parts, applying this technique to solve real world problems.

- **Geometric measurement: recognize perimeter as an attribute of plane figures and distinguish between linear and area measures.**

    3.MD.8 Solve real world and mathematical problems involving perimeters of polygons, including finding the perimeter given the side lengths, finding an unknown side length, and exhibiting rectangles with the same perimeter and different areas or with the same area and different perimeters.

Geometry (G)

- **Reason with shapes and their attributes.**

    3.G.1 Understand that shapes in different categories (e.g., rhombuses, rectangles, and others) may share attributes (e.g., having four sides), and that the shared attributes can define a larger category (e.g., quadrilaterals). Recognize rhombuses, rectangles, and squares as examples of quadrilaterals, and draw examples of quadrilaterals that do not belong to any of these subcategories.
    3.G.2 Partition shapes into parts with equal areas. Express the area of each part as a unit fraction of the whole. For example: *partition a shape into 4 parts with equal area, and describe the area of each part as 1/4 of the area of the shape.*

TABLE 15.2 CCSS-M Standards for Mathematical Practice

CCSS STANDARDS FOR MATHEMATICAL PRACTICE (SMP)	SMP IN STUDENT-FRIENDLY LANGUAGE (White & Dauksas, 2012)
Make sense of problems and persevere in solving them.	I can try many times to understand and solve a math problem.
Reason abstractly and quantitatively.	I can think about the math problem in my head first.
Construct viable arguments and critique the reasoning of others.	I can make a plan, called a strategy, to solve the problem, and discuss other students' strategies too.
Model with mathematics.	I can use math symbols and numbers to solve the problem.
Use appropriate tools strategically.	I can use math tools, pictures, drawings, and objects to solve the problem.
Attend to precision.	I can check to see if my strategy and calculations are correct.

(Continued)

TABLE 15.2 (Continued)

CCSS STANDARDS FOR MATHEMATICAL PRACTICE (SMP)	SMP IN STUDENT-FRIENDLY LANGUAGE (White & Dauksas, 2012)
Look for and make use of structure.	I can use what I already know about math to solve the problem.
Look for and express regularity in repeated reasoning.	I can use a strategy that I used to solve another math problem.

ANNOTATED
Grade 3 Standards for Mathematical Content

In Grade 3, instructional time should focus on *four critical areas*:

(1) developing understanding of multiplication and division and strategies for multiplication and division within 100;
(2) developing understanding of fractions, especially unit fractions (fractions with numerator 1);
(3) developing understanding of the structure of rectangular arrays and of area;
(4) describing and analyzing two-dimensional shapes.

MUCH OF THE LANGUAGE USED IN THE CCSS-MATHEMATICS DEPARTS FROM THE TYPICAL MATH TERMINOLOGY USED IN PAST STANDARDS. THE AUTHORS OF THE STANDARDS DELIBERATELY LIMIT THE USE OF GENERIC LANGUAGE IN ORDER TO INTRODUCE ACADEMIC LANGUAGE, E.G., THE LANGUAGE MATHEMATICIANS USE TO TALK ABOUT MATH.

Grade 3 Mathematics Standards by Domain

REMEMBER, THESE ARE THE EXPECTATIONS STUDENTS SHOULD BE ABLE TO MEET AT THE *END* OF GRADE 3.

Operations and Algebraic Thinking (OA)

• **Represent and solve problems involving multiplication and division**

MULTIPLICATION REQUIRES STUDENTS TO THINK IN TERMS OF GROUPS OF THINGS RATHER THAN INDIVIDUAL THINGS. STUDENTS SHOULD BE TAUGHT THAT THE "x" IN A MULTIPLICATION PROBLEM MEANS "GROUPS OF," SO 5 × 7 CAN BE INTERPRETED AS "5 GROUPS OF 7."

3.OA.1 Interpret products of whole numbers, e.g., interpret 5 × 7 as the total number of objects in five groups of 7 objects each. *For* *example, describe a context in which a total number of objects can be expressed as 5 × 7.*

BE SURE TO DISCUSS AND CLARIFY THE MATHEMATICAL USE AND MEANING OF THE WORD "PRODUCT." IT DOES NOT REFER TO STUFF YOU PUT IN YOUR HAIR OR TO SOMETHING PRODUCED IN A FACTORY.

3.OA.2 Interpret whole-number quotients of whole numbers, e.g., interpret 56 ÷ 8 as the number of objects in each share when 56 objects are partitioned into equal shares of 8 objects each. *For example, describe a context in which a number of shares or a number of groups can be expressed as 56 ÷ 8.*

THIS STANDARD FOCUSES ON TWO MODELS OF DIVISION: PARTITION AND MEASUREMENT (REPEATED SUBTRACTION). PARTITION MODELS PROVIDE THE TOTAL NUMBER AND THE NUMBER OF GROUPS, STUDENTS ARE ASKED "HOW MANY OBJECTS ARE IN EACH GROUP SO THAT THE GROUPS ARE EQUAL?" MEASUREMENT MODELS PROVIDE THE TOTAL NUMBER AND THE NUMBER OF OBJECTS IN EACH GROUP, STUDENTS ARE ASKED "HOW MANY EQUAL GROUPS CAN YOU MAKE?"

3.OA.3 Use multiplication and division within 100 to solve word problems in situations involving equal groups, arrays, and measurement quantities, e.g., by using drawings and equations with a symbol for the unknown number to represent the problem.

TEACHERS SHOULD MAKE AN EFFORT TO WRITE ALL DIFFERENT KINDS OF MULTIPLICATION AND DIVISION PROBLEMS FOR THEIR STUDENTS:

EQUAL GROUPS/PRODUCT UNKNOWN
EQUAL GROUPS/GROUP SIZE UNKNOWN
EQUAL GROUPS/NUMBER OF GROUPS UNKNOWN

ARRAY AREA/ PRODUCT UNKNOWN
ARRAY AREA/GROUP SIZE UNKNOWN

ARRAY AREA/NUMBER OF GROUPS UNKNOWN
COMPARE/PRODUCT UNKNOWN
COMPARE/GROUP SIZE UNKNOWN
COMPARE/NUMBER OF GROUPS UNKNOWN

3.0A.4 Determine the unknown whole number in a multiplication or division equation relating three whole numbers. For example, determine the unknown number that makes the equation true in each of the equations 8 × ? = 48, 5 = ? + 3, 6 × 6 = ?

THE FOCUS OF THIS STANDARD EXTENDS BEYOND THE TRADITIONAL NOTION OF FACT FAMILIES BY HAVING STUDENTS

EXPLORE THE INVERSE RELATIONSHIP OF MULTIPLICATION AND DIVISION.

- Understand the properties of multiplication and the relationship between multiplication and division.

USE AND TEACH THE STUDENTS TO USE APPROPRIATE MATHEMATICAL LANGUAGE SUCH AS OPERATION, MULTIPLY, DIVIDE, FACTOR, QUOTIENT, STRATEGIES, PROPERTIES, ETC.

3.OA.5 Apply properties of operations as strategies to multiply and divide. Examples: if $6 \times 4 = 24$ is known, then $4 \times 6 = 24$ is also known (commutative property of multiplication). $3 \times 5 \times 2$ can be found by $3 \times 5 = 15$, then $15 \times 2 = 30$ or by $5 \times 2 = 10$, then $3 \times 10 = 30$ (associative property of multiplication). Knowing that $8 \times 5 = 40$ and $8 \times 2 = 16$, one can find 8×7 as $8 \times (5 + 2) = (8 \times 5) + (8 \times 2) = 40 + 16 = 56$ (distributive property).

THIS STANDARD FOCUSES ON USING PROPERTIES OF OPERATIONS AS STRATEGIES—SPECIFICALLY, THE COMMUTATIVE PROPERTY, THE ASSOCIATIVE PROPERTY, AND THE DISTRIBUTIVE PROPERTY. STUDENTS SHOULD UNDERSTAND THESE OPERATIONS AS EXPRESSING SOMETHING TRUE ABOUT HOW NUMBERS WORK.

3.OA.6 Understand division as an unknown factor problem. *For example, find $32 \div 8$ by finding the number that makes 32 when multiplied by 8.*

SINCE MULTIPLICATION AND DIVISION ARE INVERSE OPERATIONS, STUDENTS CAN USE THEIR KNOWLEDGE OF MULTIPLICATION TO SOLVE CERTAIN KINDS OF DIVISION PROBLEMS.

- Multiply and divide within 100.

3.OA.7 Fluently multiply and divide within 100 using strategies such as the relationship between multiplication and division (e.g., knowing that $8 \times 5 = 40$, one knows $40 \div 5 = 8$) or properties of operations. By the end of Grade 3, know from memory all products of two one-digit numbers.

STUDENTS SHOULD DEMONSTRATE FLUENCY WITH DIVISION AND MULTIPLICATION, WHICH INCLUDES ACCURACY, EFFICIENCY, AND FLEXIBILITY. KNOWING FROM MEMORY IMPLIES UNDERSTANDING OF THE OPERATIONS AND HOW THEY WORK, NOT JUST MEMORIZING FACTS.

- Solve problems involving the four operations, and identify and explain patterns in arithmetic.

3.OA.8 Solve two-step word problems using the four operations. Represent these problems using equations with a letter standing for the unknown quantity. Assess the reasonableness of answers using mental computation and estimation strategies including rounding.

STUDENTS SOLVE TWO-STEP WORD PROBLEMS USING ALL FOUR OPERATIONS AND REPRESENTING THE UNKNOWN QUANTITY WITH A LETTER, THE STANDARD PRACTICE IN ALGEBRA. THE STANDARD ALSO REQUIRES STUDENTS TO ASSESS THE REASONABLENESS OF THEIR ANSWERS USING MENTAL COMPUTATION AND ROUNDING NUMBERS. THIS REQUIRES PRIOR STUDY OF AND EXPERIENCE WITH ESTIMATION, ROUNDING, AND REASONABLENESS.

3.OA.9 Identify arithmetic patterns (including patterns in the addition table or multiplication table), and explain them using properties of operations. *For example, observe that 4 times a number is always even, and explain why 4 times a number can be decomposed into two equal addends.*

STUDENTS USE ADDITION TABLES, MULTIPLICATION TABLES, A 100 CHART, AND OBSERVATION TO IDENTIFY AND EXPLAIN MATHEMATICAL PATTERNS USING THE PROPERTIES OF OPERATIONS.

Number and Operations in Base Ten (NBT)

- Use place value understanding and properties of operations to perform multi-digit arithmetic.

3.NBT.1 Use place value understanding to round whole numbers to the nearest 10 or 100.

THE PRIMARY EMPHASIS IN THIS STANDARD IS THE STUDENTS' UNDERSTANDING OF PLACE VALUE, RATHER THAN THEIR ABILITY TO ROUND WHOLE NUMBERS.

3.NBT.2 Fluently add and subtract within 1000 using strategies and algorithms based on place value, properties of operations, and/or the relationship between addition and subtraction.

THIS STANDARD INTEGRATES AND SYNTHESIZES ALL THE PLACE VALUE WORK STUDENTS HAVE DONE IN THE PRIMARY GRADES. IN THE CCSS-MATH, FLUENTLY MEANS WITH ACCURACY, FLEXIBILITY, AND EFFICIENCY. AN ALGORITHM IS A PROCEDURE OR A SERIES OF STEPS THAT LEADS TO THE SAME RESULT EACH TIME IT IS USED.

3.NBT.3 Multiple one-digit whole numbers by multiples of 10 in the range 10–90 (e.g., 9 × 80, 5 × 60) using strategies based on place value and properties of operations.

THE INTENT OF THIS STANDARD IS FOR STUDENTS TO USE THEIR UNDERSTANDING OF MULTIPLICATION, PLACE VALUE, AND THE PROPERTIES OF OPERATIONS TO SOLVE THESE PROBLEMS—DO NOT USE TRICKS LIKE "ADDING ZEROES" TO MAKE THINGS EASIER; THOSE TRICKS MAKE THINGS MORE DIFFICULT BECAUSE THEY DISRUPT THE DEVELOPMENT OF STUDENTS' MATHEMATICAL UNDERSTANDING.

Number and Operations—Fractions (NF)

• Develop understanding of fractions as numbers.

FRACTIONS IN GRADE 3 INCLUDE ONLY WORK WITH AREA (PARTS OF A WHOLE), MODELS (CIRCLES, RECTANGLES, SQUARES), OR THE NUMBER LINE. SET MODELS (PARTS OF A GROUP) ARE NOT CONSIDERED IN GRADE 3.

3.NF.1 Understand a fraction 1/b as the quantity formed by 1 part when a whole is partitioned in to b equal parts; understand a fraction a/b as the quantity formed by a parts of size 1/b.

STUDENTS START WITH UNIT FRACTIONS (FRACTIONS WITH "1" AS THE NUMERATOR) TO SOLIDIFY THE UNDERSTANDING THAT COMBINING EACH PORTION TOGETHER CREATES ONE WHOLE. STUDENTS SHOULD THINK OF FRACTIONS AS A "FAIR SHARE." SHIFT STUDENTS' LANGUAGE FROM CALLING THE FRACTIONAL PIECES "THE SAME SIZE AND SHAPE" TO CALLING THEM "EQUAL PARTS" OR "EQUAL MEASUREMENTS."

3.NF.2 Understand a fraction as a number on the number line; represent fractions on a number line diagram.

PREPARE STUDENTS TO POSITION FRACTIONS ON A NUMBER LINE BY POINTING OUT THAT FRACTIONS AREN'T WHOLE NUMBERS—THEY ARE PARTS OF A WHOLE. PROVIDE LOTS OF HANDS-ON PRACTICE WITH STRING AND SENTENCE STRIPS SO STUDENTS WILL KNOW—FROM THEIR OWN EXPERIENCE— THAT 1/2 IS EXACTLY BETWEEN 0 AND 1 ON THE NUMBER LINE.

a.   Represent a fraction 1/b on a number line diagram by defining the interval from 0 to 1 as the whole and partitioning it into b equal parts. Recognize that each part has size 1/b and that the endpoint of the part based at 0 locates the number 1/b on the number line.

b. Represent fraction a/b on a number line diagram by marking off a lengths 1/b from 0. Recognize the resulting interval has size a/b and that its endpoint locates the number a/b on the number line.

3.NF.3 Explain equivalence of fractions in special cases, and compare fractions by reasoning about their size.

WHEN COMPARING FRACTIONS, IT IS IMPORTANT TO LOOK AT THE SIZE OF THE PARTS AND THE NUMBER OF THE PARTS. 1/8 IS SMALLER THAN 1/2 BECAUSE CUTTING A WHOLE INTO 8 PIECES RESULTS IN SMALLER PIECES THAN CUTTING A WHOLE IN HALF.

a. Understand two fractions as equivalent (equal) if they are the same size or at the same point on a number line.

b. Recognize and generate simple equivalent fractions, e.g., 1/2 = 2/4, 4/6 = 2/3. Explain why the fractions are equivalent, e.g., by using a visual fraction model.

STUDENTS SHOULD ONLY EXPLORE THE IDEA OF FRACTIONS USING MODELS—DO NOT USE ALGORITHMS OR PROCEDURES.

c. Express whole numbers as fractions, and recognize fractions that are equivalent to whole numbers. Examples: Express 3 in the form 3 = 3/1; recognize that 6/1 = 6; locate 4/4 and 1 at the same point of a number line diagram.

d. Compare two fractions with the same numerator or the same denominator by reasoning about their size. Recognize that comparisons are valid only when the two fractions refer to the same whole. Record the results of comparisons with the symbols >, =, <, and justify the conclusions, e.g., by using a visual fraction model.

ENCOURAGE STUDENTS TO MAKE CONNECTIONS TO THE WAY FRACTIONS ARE USED IN THEIR LIVES—FAIR SHARE OF PIZZA OR CAKE, FOR EXAMPLE. ALSO, STUDENTS MUST KNOW THAT COMPARISONS ARE ONLY VALID IF THE WHOLES ARE IDENTICAL: RECEIVING HALF OF A PIZZA WITH A DIAMETER OF 6 INCHES GIVES YOU MUCH LESS PIZZA THAN RECEIVING HALF OF A PIZZA WITH A DIAMETER OF 16 INCHES.

Measurement and Data (MD)

- Solve problems involving measurement and estimation of intervals of time, liquid volumes, and masses of objects.

3.MD.1 Tell and write time to the nearest minute and measure time intervals in minutes. Solve word problems involving addition and subtraction of time intervals in minutes, e.g., by representing the problem on a number line diagram.

IF STUDENTS HAVE USED NUMBER LINES FOR VARIOUS PURPOSES BEFORE, IT WILL BE EASY FOR THEM TO TRANSFER THE SKILL TO THE CONTEXT OF TELLING TIME. IF THEY HAVEN'T CONSIDERED USING A NUMBER LINE FOR ANYTHING OTHER THAN ADDITION AND SUBTRACTION, IT MIGHT REQUIRE SOME ADDITIONAL EXPLANATION.

3.MD.2 Measure and estimate liquid volumes and masses of objects using standard units of grams (g), kilograms (kg), and liters (l). Add, subtract, multiply, or divide to solve one-step word problems involving masses or volumes that are given in the same units, e.g., by using drawings (such as a beaker with a measurement scale) to represent the problem.

THIS IS THE FIRST TIME THAT STUDENTS HAVE MEASURED MASS AND VOLUME AND, FOR SOME, THIS WILL BE THEIR INTRODUCTION TO THE METRIC MEASUREMENT SYSTEM. PREVIEW THE METRIC MEASUREMENT SYSTEM A WEEK OR TWO BEFORE YOU ATTEMPT TO WORK WITH THIS STANDARD; FIND OUT WHAT STUDENTS KNOW OR THINK ABOUT THIS CONTENT.

• Represent and interpret data.

3.MD.3 Draw a scaled picture graph and a scaled bar graph to represent a data set with several categories. Solve one- and two-step "how many more" and "how many less" problems using information presented in the scaled bar graphs. For example: *draw a bar graph in which each square of the bar graph might represent 5 pets.*

SCALED PICTOGRAPHS INCLUDE PICTURES THAT REPRESENT MULTIPLE UNITS (EACH STAR REPRESENTS FIVE PEOPLE, FOR EXAMPLE, SO FIVE STARS EQUALS 25 PEOPLE). STUDENTS SHOULD HAVE OPPORTUNITIES TO READ AND SOLVE PROBLEMS USING SCALED PICTURE GRAPHS BEFORE BEGINNING TO WORK ON THIS STANDARD.

3.MD.4 Generate measurement data by measuring lengths using rulers marked with halves and fourths of an inch. Show the data by making a line plot, where the horizontal scale is marked off in appropriate units—whole numbers, halves, or quarters.

THIS STANDARD DOES DOUBLE DUTY—IT'S A LESSON ABOUT MEASUREMENT AND ALSO A LESSON THAT REVIEWS STUDENTS' KNOWLEDGE OF FRACTIONS.

- Geometric measurement: understand concepts of area and relate area to multiplication and to addition.

  3.MD.5 Recognize area as an attribute of plane figures and understand concepts of area measurement.

  STUDENTS EXPLORE THE IDEA OF COVERING A REGION WITH "UNIT SQUARES." STUDENTS MIGHT NEED A GREAT DEAL OF PRACTICE WITH HANDS-ON EXPERIENCES TO UNDERSTAND AREA.

  a. A square with side length 1 unit, called a unit square, is said to have "one square unit" of area, and can be used to measure area.
  b. A plane figure that can be covered without gaps or overlaps by n unit squares is said to have an area of n square units.

  3.MD.6 Measure areas by counting unit squares (square cm, square m, square in, square ft, and improvised units).

  USING UNIT SQUARES OF VARYING SIZES (SQUARE CM, SQUARE M, SQUARE IN, SQUARE FT, ETC.) MAY HELP STUDENTS INTERNALIZE THE DIFFERENCES BETWEEN THE MEASUREMENT UNITS OF THE METRIC SYSTEM AND THE MEASUREMENT UNITS TYPICALLY USED IN THE U.S.

  3.MD.7 Relate area to the operations of multiplication and division.

  ANOTHER STANDARD THAT INTEGRATES TWO DIFFERENT MATHEMATICAL DOMAINS.

  a. Find the area of a rectangle with whole-number side lengths by tiling it, and show that the area is the same as would be found by multiplying the side lengths.

  POINT OUT TO STUDENTS THAT THE TILED AREA LOOKS LIKE AN ARRAY; THAT MIGHT NUDGE THEM TO THINK ABOUT USING MULTIPLICATION TO COUNT THE SQUARE UNITS.

  b. Multiply side lengths to find areas of rectangles with whole-number side lengths in the context of solving real world and mathematical problems, and represent whole-number products as rectangular areas in mathematical reasoning.
  c. Use tiling to show in a concrete case that the area of a rectangle with whole-number side lengths a and b + c is the sum of a × b and a × c. Use area models to represent the distributive property in mathematical reasoning.

  STUDENTS USE CONCRETE OBJECTS OR DRAWINGS TO PRACTICE COMPOSING AND DECOMPOSING SHAPES AND MANAGING SPATIAL STRUCTURE BEFORE MOVING ON TO SHOW THESE CONCEPTS USING AREA MODELS AND MATHEMATICAL REASONING.

d. Recognize area as additive. Find areas of rectilinear figures by decomposing them into non-overlapping rectangles and adding the areas of the non-overlapping parts, applying this technique to solve real world problems.

PREPARATION FOR MEETING THIS STANDARD WILL INVOLVE PRACTICE WITH HANDS-ON OBJECTS THAT CAN BE MANIP-ULATED TO ALLOW STUDENTS TO TEST AND RE-TEST THEIR THEORIES ABOUT HOW AREA WORKS.

- Geometric measurement: recognize perimeter as an attribute of plane figures and distinguish between linear and area measures.

3.MD.8 Solve real world and mathematical problems involving perimeters of polygons, including finding the perimeter given the side lengths, finding an unknown side length, and exhibiting rectangles with the same perimeter and different areas or with the same area and different perimeters.

BEGIN THE INVESTIGATION OF PERIMETER WITH PHYSICAL ACTIVITY: WALKING THE PERIMETER OF THE SCHOOL YARD, THE GYM, THE CAFETERIA; OUTLINING SHAPES WITH RUBBER BANDS ON A GEOBOARD, ETC. WHEN THE PHYSICAL EXPERI-ENCE OF PERIMETER IS CONTRASTED TO THE TILING WORK DONE WITH AREA, THE DIFFERENCE BETWEEN THESE TWO MEASURES WILL BE VERY CLEAR.

Geometry (G)

- Reason with shapes and their attributes.

3.G.1 Understand that shapes in different categories (e.g., rhombuses, rectangles, and others) may share attributes (e.g., having four sides), and that the shared attributes can define a larger category (e.g., quadrilaterals). Recognize rhombuses, rectangles, and squares as examples of quadrilaterals, and draw examples of quadrilaterals that do not belong to any of these subcategories.

WORKING WITH PATTERN BLOCKS AND TANGRAM PIECES CAN HELP STUDENTS INTERNALIZE THE DISTINCTION BETWEEN THE DIFFERENT SHAPE CATEGORIES.

3.G.2 Partition shapes into parts with equal areas. Express the area of each part as a unit fraction of the whole. For example: *partition a shape into 4 parts with equal area, and describe the area of each part as 1/4 of the area of the shape.*

REVISITING AND REINFORCING A CONCEPT FROM ANOTHER DOMAIN.

Grade 3 Reading Standards

TABLE 15.3

Reading Standards: Literature	Reading Standards: Informational Text
Key Ideas and Details	
RL.3.1. Ask and answer such questions to demonstrate understanding of a text, referring explicitly to the text as the basis for the answers.	RI.3.1. Ask and answer questions to demonstrate understanding of a text, referring explicitly to the text as the basis for the answers.
RL.3.2. Recount stories, including fables and folktales from diverse cultures, determine their central message, lesson, or moral and explain how it is conveyed through key details in the text.	RI.3.2. Determine the main idea of a text; recount the key details and explain how they support the main idea.
RL.3.3. Describe characters in a story (e.g., their traits, motivations, or feelings) and explain how their actions contribute to the sequence of events.	RI.3.3. Describe the relationship between a series of historical events, scientific ideas, or concepts, or steps in technical procedures in a text, using language that pertains to time, sequence, and cause/effect.
Craft and Structure	
RL.3.4. Determine the meaning of words and phrases as they are used in a text, distinguishing literal from non-literal language.	RI.3.4. Determine the meaning of general academic and domain-specific words and phrases in a text relevant to a *grade 3 topic or subject area*.
RL.3.5. Refer to parts of stories, dramas, and poems when writing or speaking about a text, using terms such as chapter, scene, and stanza; describe how each successive part builds on earlier sections.	RI.3.5. Use text features and search tools (e.g., key words, sidebars, hyperlinks) to locate information relevant to a given topic efficiently.

(Continued)

TABLE 15.3 (Continued)

RL.3.6. Distinguish their own point of view from that of the narrator or those of the characters.	RI.3.6. Distinguish their own point of view from that of the author of the text.

Integration of Knowledge and Ideas

RL.3.7. Explain how specific aspects of a text's illustrations contribute to what is conveyed by the words in a story (e.g., create mood, emphasize aspects of a character or setting.	RI.3.7. Use information gained from illustrations (e.g., maps, photographs) and the words in a text to demonstrate understanding of the text (e.g., where, when, why, and how key events occur).
8. (Not applicable to literature)	RI.3.8. Describe the logical connection between particular sentences and paragraphs in a text (e.g., comparison, cause/effect, first/second/third in a sequence).
RL.3.9. Compare and contrast the themes, settings, and plots of stories written by the same author about the same or similar characters (e.g., in books from a series).	RI.3.9. Compare and contrast the most important points presented by two texts on the same topic.

Range of Reading and Level of Text Complexity

RL.3.10. By the end of the year, read and comprehend literature, including stories, drama and poetry, in the grades 2–3 text complexity band independently and proficiently.	RI.3.10. By the end of the year, read and comprehend literature, including history/social studies, sciences, and technical texts, in the grades 2–3 text complexity band independently and proficiently.

TABLE 15.4

Reading Standards: Foundational Skills
Print Concepts
1. (Only in kindergarten and grade 1)
Phonological Awareness
2. (Only in kindergarten and grade 1)
Phonics and Word Recognition

RF.3.3. Know and apply grade-level phonics and word analysis skills in decoding words.
   a. Identify and know the meaning of the most common prefixes and derivational suffixes.
   b. Decode words with common Latin suffixes.
   c. Decode multisyllable words.
   d. Read grade-appropriate irregularly spelled words.

Fluency

RF.3.4. Read with sufficient accuracy and fluency to support comprehension.
   a. Read on-level text with purpose and understanding.
   b. Read on-level text orally with accuracy, appropriate rate, and expression on successive readings.
   c. Use context to confirm or self-correct word recognition and understanding, rereading as necessary.

Grade 3 Writing Standards

TABLE 15.5

Text Types and Purposes

W.3.1. Write opinion pieces on topic or texts, supporting a point of view with reasons.
   a. Introduce the topic or text they are writing about, state an opinion, and create an organizational structure that lists reasons.
   b. Provide reasons that support the opinion.
   c. Use linking words and phrases (e.g., *because, therefore, since, for example*) to connect opinion and reasons.
   d. Provide a concluding statement or section.

(Continued)

TABLE 15.5 (Continued)

W.3.2. Write informative/explanatory texts to examine a topic and convey ideas and information clearly.

    a.   Introduce a topic and group related information together; include illustrations when useful to aiding comprehension.

    b.   Develop the topic with facts, definitions, and details,

    c.   Use linking words and phrases (e.g., *also, another, and, more, but*) to connect ideas within categories of information

    d.   Provide a concluding statement or section.

W.3.3. Write narratives to develop real or imagined experiences of events using effective technique, descriptive details, and clear event sequences.

    a.   Establish a situation and introduce a narrator and/or characters; organize and event sequence that unfolds naturally.

    b.   Use dialogue and descriptions of actions, thoughts, and feelings to develop experiences and events or show the responses of characters to situations.

    c.   Use temporal words and phrases to signal event order.

    d.   Provide a sense of closure.

Production and Distribution of Writing

W.3.4. With guidance and support from adults, produce writing in which the development and organization are appropriate to task and purpose.

W.3.5. With guidance and support from peers and adults, develop and strengthen writing as needed by planning, revising, and editing.

W.3.6. With guidance and support from adults, technology to produce and publish writing (using keyboarding skills) as well as to interact and collaborate with others.

Research to Build and Present Knowledge

W.3.7. Conduct short research projects that build knowledge about a topic.

W.3.8. Recall information from experiences or gather information from print and digital sources; take brief notes on sources and sort evidence into provided categories.

9. (Begins in grade 4)

Range of Writing

W.3.10. Write routinely over extended time frames (time for research, reflection, and revision) and shorter time frames (a single sitting or a day or two) for a range of discipline-specific tasks, purposes, and audiences.

Grade 3 Speaking and Listening Standards

TABLE 15.6

Comprehension and Collaboration

SL.3.1. Engage effectively in a range of collaborative discussions (one-on-one, in groups, and teacher-led) with diverse partners on *grade 3 topics and texts,* building on others' ideas and expressing their own clearly.

    a.   Come to discussions prepared, having read or studied the required material, explicitly draw on that preparation and other information known about the topic to explore ideas under discussion.

    b.   Follow agreed-upon rules for discussions (e.g., gaining the floor in respectful ways, listening to others with care, speaking one at a time about the topics and texts under discussion).

    c.   Ask questions to check understanding of information presented, stay on topic, and link their comments to the remarks of others.

    d.   Explain their own ideas and understanding in light of the discussion.

SL.3.2. Determine the main ideas and supporting details of a text read aloud or information presented in diverse media and formats, including visually, quantitatively, and orally.

SL.3.3. Ask and answer questions about information from a speaker, offering appropriate elaborations and detail.

Presentation of Knowledge and Ideas

SL.3.4. Report on a topic or text, tell a story, or recount an experience with appropriate facts and relevant descriptive details, speaking clearly at an understandable pace.

SL.3.5. Create engaging audio recordings of stories or poems that demonstrate fluid reading at an understandable pace, add visual displays when appropriate to emphasize or enhance certain facts or details.

SL.3.6. Speak in complete sentences when appropriate to task and situation in order to provide requested detail or clarification.

Grade 3 Language Standards

TABLE 15.7

Conventions of Standard English
L.3.1. Demonstrate command of the conventions of standard English grammar when writing or speaking.

    (a) Explain the function of nouns, pronouns, verbs, adjectives, and adverbs in general and their functions in particular sentences.

    (b) Form and use regular and irregular plural nouns.

    (c) Use abstract nouns (e.g., *childhood*).

    (d) Form and use regular and irregular verbs.

    (e) Form and use the simple (e.g., *I walked; I walk; I will walk*) verb tenses.

    (f) Ensure subject-verb agreement and pronoun-antecedent agreement.

    (g) Form and use comparative and superlative adjectives and adverbs, and choose between them depending on what is to be modified.

    (h) Use coordinating and subordinating conjunctions.

    (i) Produce simple, compound, and complex sentences.

L.3.2. Demonstrate command of the conventions of standard English capitalization, punctuation, and spelling when writing.

    (a) Capitalize appropriate words in titles.

    (b) Use commas in addresses.

    (c) Use commas and quotation marks in dialogue.

    (d) Form and use possessives.

    (e) Use conventional spelling for high-frequency and other studied words and for adding suffixes to base words (e.g., *sitting, smiled, cries, happiness*).

    (f) Use spelling patterns and generalizations (e.g., word families, position-based spellings, syllable patterns, ending rules, meaningful word parts) in writing words.

    (g) Consult reference materials, including beginning dictionaries, as needed to check and correct spellings.

Knowledge of Language
L.3.3. Use knowledge of language and its conventions when writing, speaking, reading, or listening.

    (a) Choose words and phrases for effect.

    (b) Recognize and observe the differences between the conventions of spoken and written standard English.

Vocabulary Acquisition and Use

L.3.4. Determine or clarify the meaning of unknown and multiple-meaning words and phrases based on *grade 3 reading and content*, choosing flexibly from an array of strategies.

   (a) Use sentence-level context as a clue to the meaning of a word or phrase.

   (b) Determine the meaning of the new word formed when a known affix is added to a known word (e.g., *agreeable/disagreeable. comfortable/uncomfortable; care/careless, heat/preheat*).

   (c) Use a known root word as a clue to the meaning of an unknown word with the same root (e.g., company, companion).

   (d) Use glossaries and beginning dictionaries, both print and digital, to determine or clarify the meaning of words and phrases.

L.3.5. Demonstrate understanding of word relationships and nuances in word meanings.

   (a) Distinguish the literal and non-literal meanings of words and phrases in contexts (e.g., *take steps*).

   (b) Identify real-life connections between words and their use (e.g., *describe people who are friendly or helpful*).

   (c) Distinguish shades of meaning among related words that describe states of mind or degrees of certainty (e.g., *knew, believed, suspected, heard, wondered*).

L.3.6. Acquire and use accurately grade-appropriate conversation, general academic, and domain-specific words and phrases, including those that signal spatial and temporal relationships (e.g., *After dinner that night we went looking for them*).

ANNOTATED

Grade 3 Reading Standards

TABLE 15.8

Reading Standards: Literature	Reading Standards: Informational Text
Key Ideas and Details	
RL.3.1. Ask and answer such questions to demonstrate understanding of a text, referring explicitly to the text as the basis for the answers.	RI.3.1. Ask and answer questions to demonstrate understanding of a text, referring explicitly to the text as the basis for the answers.

(Continued)

TABLE 15.8 (Continued)

RL.3.2. Recount stories, including fables and folktales from diverse cultures, determine their central message, lesson, or moral and explain how it is conveyed through key details in the text.	2 RI.3. Determine the main idea of a text; recount the key details and explain how they support the main idea.
RL.3.3. Describe characters in a story (e.g., their traits, motivations, or feelings) and explain how their actions contribute to the sequence of events.	RI.3.3. Describe the relationship between a series of historical events, scientific ideas, or concepts, or steps in technical procedures in a text, using language that pertains to time, sequence, and cause/effect.
ANNOTATION	ANNOTATION
THIRD GRADERS ARE EXPECTED TO ASK AND ANSWER QUESTIONS ABOUT THE CHARACTERS, SETTING, IMPORTANT EVENTS, AND LESSON OF THE STORY; DEMANDS FOR SPECIFICITY INCREASE SIGNIFICANTLY. THE STANDARDS' FOCUS IS ON THE CHARACTERS' INFLUENCE ON PLOT DEVELOPMENT, SO STUDENTS MUST EXPLAIN HOW CHARACTERS FEEL AND WHY THEY ACTED IN CERTAIN WAYS AND SUPPORT THEIR ASSERTIONS WITH TEXTUAL EVIDENCE.	STUDENTS ARE REQUIRED TO REFER TO THE TEXT TO SUPPORT THEIR ANSWERS WHEN IDENTIFYING THE MAIN IDEA AND FINDING THE MOST IMPORTANT DETAILS THAT STRENGTHEN THE MAIN IDEA. CONTENT-AREA TEXTS ARE ANALYZED TO FIND A SEQUENCE OF EVENTS OR A CAUSE/EFFECT RELATIONSHIP BETWEEN THE STEPS OR A PROCEDURE OR WITHIN A SERIES OF EVENTS.
Craft and Structure	
RL.3.4. Determine the meaning of words and phrases as they are used in a text, distinguishing literal from non-literal language.	RI.3.4. Determine the meaning of general academic and domain-specific words and phrases in a text relevant to a *grade 3 topic or subject area*.

RL.3.5. Refer to parts of stories, dramas, and poems when writing or speaking about a text, using terms such as chapter, scene, and stanza; describe how each successive part builds on earlier sections.	RI.3.5. Use text features and search tools (e.g., key words, sidebars, hyperlinks) to locate information relevant to a given topic efficiently.
RL.3.6. Distinguish their own point of view from that of the narrator or those of the characters.	RI.3.6. Distinguish their own point of view from that of the author of the text.
ANNOTATION	ANNOTATION
GAINING NEW VOCABULARY BECOMES A FOCUS: STUDENTS ARE EXPECTED TO DEFINE WORDS AND PHRASES IN TEXT, TO NOTE THE DIFFERENCES BETWEEN LITERAL AND NONLITERAL LANGUAGE AS WELL AS TO NAME THE PARTS OF A STORY/DRAMA/POEM AND DISCUSS THE DIFFERENT STORY STRUCTURES USED. STUDENTS ALSO NEED TO IDENTIFY THE POINTS OF VIEW OF THE NARRATOR, THE CHARACTERS, AND THEMSELVES.	STUDENTS LEARN NEW VOCABULARY & USE THE UNIQUE FEATURES AND ORGANIZATION OF INFORMATIONAL TEXT (TEXT FEATURES, SEARCH TOOLS) TO FIND AND MANAGE INFORMATION ABOUT A TOPIC. STUDENTS COMPARE THEIR POINT OF VIEW WITH THAT OF THE AUTHOR AND DISCUSS WHETHER THEY AGREE OR DISAGREE WITH THE AUTHOR'S PERSPECTIVE ON THE TOPIC.
Integration of Knowledge and Ideas	
RL.3.7. Explain how specific aspects of a text's illustrations contribute to what is conveyed by the words in a story (e.g., create mood, emphasize aspects of a character or setting.	RI.3.7. Use information gained from illustrations (e.g., maps, photographs) and the words in a text to demonstrate understanding of the text (e.g., where, when, why, and how key events occur).

(Continued)

TABLE 15.8 (Continued)

8. (Not applicable to literature)	RI.3.8. Describe the logical connection between particular sentences and paragraphs in a text (e.g., comparison, cause/effect, first/second/ third in a sequence).
RL.3.9. Compare and contrast the themes, settings, and plots of stories written by the same author about the same or similar characters (e.g., in books from a series).	RI.3.9. Compare and contrast the most important points presented by two texts on the same topic.
ANNOTATION	ANNOTATION
STUDENTS COMPARE THE MOOD OF A BOOK'S TEXT AND ITS PICTURES TO IDENTIFY THE DIFFERENT EFFECTS HAD BY EACH TYPE OF INFORMATION. THEY ALSO READ STORIES WRITTEN BY THE SAME AUTHOR TO DETERMINE WHAT IS THE SAME AND DIFFERENT: PROBLEMS, SOLUTIONS, SITUATIONS, AND SO ON. IF THOSE BOOKS ARE ILLUSTRATED BY DIFFERENT ARTISTS, THE CONVERSATION ABOUT THE DIFFERENT IMPACTS OF INFORMATION DELIVERED VISUALLY AND TEXTUALLY CAN BE CONTINUED FURTHER.	STUDENTS USE A VARIETY OF MEDIA FORMATS—MAPS, DIAGRAMS, TABLES, PHOTOS, AUDIO, CHARTS—TO BUILD A RICH UNDERSTANDING OF THE INFORMATION IN A TEXT. THEY EXAMINE THE WAY AUTHORS CONNECT SENTENCES AND LINK ONE PARAGRAPH TO THE NEXT AS THEY MAKE THEIR ARGUMENT ABOUT THE TOPIC—STRUCTURING AN ARGUMENT IS A CENTRAL FEATURE OF READING, WRITING, AND UNDERSTANDING INFORMATIONAL TEXT. THEY COMPARE AND CONTRAST TWO TEXTS ABOUT THE SAME TOPIC AND DISCUSS THE PURPOSES AND GOALS OF EACH AUTHOR.

Range of Reading and Level of Text Complexity

RL.3.10. By the end of the year, read and comprehend literature, including stories, drama and poetry, in the grades 2–3 text complexity band independently and proficiently.	RI.3.10. By the end of the year, read and comprehend literature, including history/ social studies, sciences, and technical texts, in the grades 2–3 text complexity band independently and proficiently.

ANNOTATION	ANNOTATION
THE CCSS USES "GRADE BAND" RATHER THAN GRADE LEVEL TO PROVIDE A BROADER FRAMEWORK IN WHICH TO POSITION READERS.	

TABLE 15.9

Reading Standards: Foundational Skills
Print Concepts
1. (Only in kindergarten and grade 1)
Phonological Awareness
2. (Only in kindergarten and grade 1)
Phonics and Word Recognition

RF.3.3. Know and apply grade-level phonics and word analysis skills in decoding words.
   a. Identify and know the meaning of the most common prefixes and derivational suffixes.
   b. Decode words with common Latin suffixes.
   c. Decode multisyllable words.
   d. Read grade-appropriate irregularly spelled words.

ANNOTATION
STUDENTS LEARN PREFIXES, SUFFIXES, AND LATIN SUFFIXES TO IMPROVE THEIR DECODING SKILLS AND TO BUILD THEIR SPELLING AND VOCABULARY SKILLS.
Fluency

RF.3.4. Read with sufficient accuracy and fluency to support comprehension.
   a. Read on-level text with purpose and understanding.
   b. Read on-level text orally with accuracy, appropriate rate, and expression on successive readings.
   c. Use context to confirm or self-correct word recognition and understanding, rereading as necessary.

ANNOTATION
FLUENT READERS ARE ABLE TO FOCUS ON THE MEANING OF THE TEXT, WHICH IMPROVES THEIR COMPREHENSION.

ANNOTATED

Grade 3 Writing Standards

TABLE 15.10

Text Types and Purposes
W.3.1. Write opinion pieces on topic or texts, supporting a point of view with reasons.
a. Introduce the topic or text they are writing about, state an opinion, and create an organizational structure that lists reasons.
b. Provide reasons that support the opinion.
c. Use linking words and phrases (e.g., *because, therefore, since, for example*) to connect opinion and reasons.
d. Provide a concluding statement or section.
W.3.2. Write informative/explanatory texts to examine a topic and convey ideas and information clearly.
a. Introduce a topic and group related information together; include illustrations when useful to aiding comprehension.
b. Develop the topic with facts, definitions, and details,
c. Use linking words and phrases (e.g., *also, another, and, more, but*) to connect ideas within categories of information
d. Provide a concluding statement or section.
W.3.3. Write narratives to develop real or imagined experiences of events using effective technique, descriptive details, and clear event sequences.
a. Establish a situation and introduce a narrator and/or characters; organize and event sequence that unfolds naturally.
b. Use dialogue and descriptions of actions, thoughts, and feelings to develop experiences and events or show the responses of characters to situations.
c. Use temporal words and phrases to signal event order.
d. Provide a sense of closure.
ANNOTATION
STUDENTS IN GRADE 3 WRITE OPINION PIECES THAT CLEARLY STATE THEIR POSITION AND SUPPLY THE REASONING FOR THEIR THINKING. THEY NEED TO UNDERSTAND HOW THEIR REASONING SUPPORTS THEIR OPINION AND MUST BE ABLE TO SHARE THEIR IDEAS ABOUT THIS. STUDENTS BEGIN TO LINK IDEAS TOGETHER TO BUILD AN ARGUMENT.

THIRD GRADERS WRITE INFORMATIVE/EXPLANATORY PIECES INDE-
PENDENTLY AND MUST HAVE AND USE STRATEGIES FOR GATHERING
DATA, TAKING NOTES, GROUPING SIMILAR IDEAS, AND DEVELOPING A
WAY TO PRESENT THE IDEAS FROM BEGINNING TO END. THIRD GRADE
IS THE FIRST YEAR IN WHICH STUDENTS ARE EXPECTED TO DO THIS
WITHOUT A GROUP OR A PARTNER; SOME STUDENTS WILL NEED SUP-
PLEMENTAL SUPPORT.

STUDENTS ALSO WRITE NARRATIVES ABOUT REAL OR IMAGINED
EXPERIENCES. THESE STORIES SHOULD BE DESCRIPTIVE AND USE DIA-
LOGUE TO SHOW THE CHARACTERS' THOUGHTS, FEELINGS, AND THE
DETAILS OF THE CHARACTERS' INTERACTIONS. STUDENTS WILL NEED
TO DEVELOP SKILLS AND STRATEGIES FOR INTRODUCING CHARACTERS
AND ENGAGING CHARACTERS IN CONVERSATION IN THEIR WRITING.

Production and Distribution of Writing

W.3.4. With guidance and support from adults, produce writing in which
the development and organization are appropriate to task and purpose.

W.3.5. With guidance and support from peers and adults, develop and
strengthen writing as needed by planning, revising, and editing.

W.3.6. With guidance and support from adults, technology to produce and
publish writing (using keyboarding skills) as well as to interact and
collaborate with others.

ANNOTATION

STUDENTS ARE EXPECTED TO PRODUCE WRITING THAT IS CLEAR
AND UNDERSTANDABLE TO A READER. TASK (THE TYPE OF WRIT-
ING ASSIGNMENT) AND PURPOSE (THE AUTHOR'S REASON FOR WRIT-
ING) SHOULD BE REFLECTED IN THE STUDENT'S ORGANIZATION AND
DEVELOPMENT OF THE ASSIGNMENT. THIS EXPECTATION IS TO BE
ACCOMPLISHED WITH ASSISTANCE. ALSO WITH ASSISTANCE, THIRD
GRADERS SHOULD DEVELOP REVISING AND EDITING SKILLS, INCLUD-
ING UNDERSTANDING HOW TO IMPROVE WORD CHOICES, LEARNING
STRATEGIES FOR CHANGING SENTENCE STRUCTURE, AND PROOFREAD-
ING TO CATCH AND CORRECT ERRORS IN SPELLING, PUNCTUATION,
AND GRAMMAR. TEACHER-DEVELOPED CHECKLISTS, PEER EDITING,
AND SMALL GROUP DISCUSSIONS ARE HELPFUL WAYS TO BUILD MAS-
TERY OF THESE SKILLS. DIGITAL PUBLICATION OF WRITING CONTINUES
TO BE A FOCUS, PARTICULARLY SINCE IT WIDENS THE AUDIENCE OF
POTENTIAL READERS.

(Continued)

TABLE 15.10 (Continued)

Research to Build and Present Knowledge
W.3.7. Conduct short research projects that build knowledge about a topic.
W.3.8. Recall information from experiences or gather information from print and digital sources; take brief notes on sources and sort evidence into provided categories.
9. (Begins in grade 4)
ANNOTATION
THIRD GRADERS ARE REQUIRED TO RESEARCH A TOPIC ON THEIR OWN AND WRITE UP A REPORT. STUDENTS LEARN HOW TO LOCATE INFORMATION FROM PRINT AND DIGITAL SOURCES AND USE THEIR OWN BACKGROUND KNOWLEDGE. THIRD GRADE STUDENTS HAVE VERY RUDIMENTARY RESEARCH SKILLS AND THIS PROJECT IS LIKELY TO BE EXTREMELY CHALLENGING. TEACHERS SHOULD CREATE STURDY SCAFFOLDS FOR EVERY STEP OF THE PROCESS: CREATE A SET FORMAT FOR THE REPORT THAT MUST BE USED BY EVERY STUDENT, ESTABLISH PREDETERMINED CATEGORIES INTO WHICH THE STUDENTS WILL ORGANIZE THEIR INFORMATION, AND SO ON. GRAPHIC ORGANIZERS, CHECK SHEETS, LISTS OF GOOD WEBSITES, RUBRICS TO EVALUATE TECHNICAL TOOLS WILL ALSO HELP THE STUDENTS. WHEN THE PROJECT IS COMPLETED, TEACHERS SHOULD HAVE A CONVERSATION WITH THEIR STUDENTS ABOUT WHAT THEY LEARNED—NOT ABOUT THEIR TOPIC, BUT ABOUT THE PROCESS OF DOING RESEARCH: THIS LEARNING (FROM MISTAKES AND FROM SUCCESSES) IS THE REAL GOAL OF THE PROJECT.
Range of Writing
W.3.10. Write routinely over extended time frames (time for research, reflection, and revision) and shorter time frames (a single sitting or a day or two) for a range of discipline-specific tasks, purposes, and audiences.
ANNOTATION
THE AMOUNT OF TIME SPENT WRITING WILL INCREASE AS STUDENTS WRITE FOR DIFFERENT REASONS AND PURPOSES, OVER DIFFERENT TIME FRAMES, ACROSS DIFFERENT DISCIPLINES, AND FOR DIFFERENT AUDIENCES. WRITING WILL BLEND INTO EVERY CONTENT AREA AND BE INTEGRATED ACROSS THE SCHOOL DAY.

ANNOTATED

Grade 3 Speaking and Listening Standards

TABLE 15.11

Comprehension and Collaboration

SL.3.1. Engage effectively in a range of collaborative discussions (one-on-one, in groups, and teacher-led) with diverse partners on *grade 3 topics and texts,* building on others' ideas and expressing their own clearly.
 	
   a. Come to discussions prepared, having read or studied the required material, explicitly draw on that preparation and other information known about the topic to explore ideas under discussion
 	
   b. Follow agreed-upon rules for discussions (e.g., gaining the floor in respectful ways, listening to others with care, speaking one at a time about the topics and texts under discussion).
 	
   c. Ask questions to check understanding of information presented, stay on topic, and link their comments to the remarks of others.
 	
   d. Explain their own ideas and understanding in light of the discussion.
 	
SL.3.2. Determine the main ideas and supporting details of a text read aloud or information presented in diverse media and formats, including visually, quantitatively, and orally.
 	
SL.3.3. Ask and answer questions about information from a speaker, offering appropriate elaborations and detail.

ANNOTATION
TEACHERS NEED TO HELP STUDENTS NOTICE WHEN THE CLASS OR GROUP IS HAVING A GOOD DISCUSSION AND ELICIT THEIR THOUGHTS ABOUT THE FEATURES OF A GOOD DISCUSSION. STUDENTS ENGAGE IN COLLABORATIVE CONVERSATIONS (BOOK GROUPS, BUDDY READING) AND DEVELOP SKILLS SUCH AS ACTIVE LISTENING, LOOKING AT THE SPEAKER, TAKING TURNS, LINKING IDEAS TO THE SPEAKER'S IDEAS, SHARING THE FLOOR, ETC. STUDENTS SHOULD BE ABLE TO LISTEN TO A SPEAKER AND ASK FOR CLARIFICATION IF NECESSARY. THEY NEED TO LEARN TO FORMULATE A QUESTION THAT IS ON TOPIC AND TO UNDERSTAND AND ANSWER QUESTIONS ASKED OF THEM.

(Continued)

TABLE 15.11 (Continued)

Presentation of Knowledge and Ideas
SL.3.4. Report on a topic or text, tell a story, or recount an experience with appropriate facts and relevant descriptive details, speaking clearly at an understandable pace.
SL.3.5. Create engaging audio recordings of stories or poems that demonstrate fluid reading at an understandable pace, add visual displays to when appropriate to emphasize or enhance certain facts or details.
SL.3.6. Speak in complete sentences when appropriate to task and situation in order to provide requested detail or clarification.
ANNOTATION
THIRD GRADERS USE AN AUDIBLE VOICE AND COHERENT, CONNECTED SENTENCES TO TELL STORIES OR DESCRIBE EXPERIENCES. THEY INCLUDE CAREFULLY CHOSEN WORDS, DESCRIPTIVE DETAILS, AND RELEVANT FACTS, AND ARE ABLE TO PROVIDE ADDITIONAL DETAIL OR CLARIFICATION AS NEEDED. THEY USE DIGITAL MEDIA TO CREATE AUDIO RECORDINGS OF STORIES OR POEMS AND CREATE VISUAL DISPLAYS THAT ENHANCE THE STORY/POEM BY CLARIFYING THE IDEAS, THOUGHTS, AND FEELINGS OF THE AUTHOR.

ANNOTATED

Grade 3 Language Standards

TABLE 15.12

Conventions of Standard English
L.3.1. Demonstrate command of the conventions of standard English grammar when writing or speaking.
(a) Explain the function of nouns, pronouns, verbs, adjectives, and adverbs in general and their functions in particular sentences.
(b) Form and use regular and irregular plural nouns.
(c) Use abstract nouns (e.g., childhood).
(d) Form and use regular and irregular verbs.
(e) Form and use the simple (e.g., *I walked; I walk; I will walk*) verb tenses.
(f) Ensure subject-verb agreement and pronoun-antecedent agreement.
(g) Form and use comparative and superlative adjectives and adverbs, and choose between them depending on what is to be modified.
(h) Use coordinating and subordinating conjunctions.
(i) Produce simple, compound, and complex sentences.

L.3.2. Demonstrate command of the conventions of standard English capitalization, punctuation, and spelling when writing.

(a) Capitalize appropriate words in titles.
(b) Use commas in addresses.
(c) Use commas and quotation marks in dialogue.
(d) Form and use possessives.
(e) Use conventional spelling for high-frequency and other studied words and for adding suffixes to base words (e.g., *sitting, smiled, cries, happiness*).
(f) Use spelling patterns and generalizations (e.g., word families, position-based spellings, syllable patterns, ending rules, meaningful word parts) in writing words.
(g) Consult reference materials, including beginning dictionaries, as needed to check and correct spellings.

ANNOTATION

YOUNG STUDENTS LOVE TO COMMUNICATE AND TO BE HEARD. SO, WHEN WORKING WITH SECOND GRADERS ON LANGUAGE CONVENTIONS, FOCUS ON THE WAYS IN WHICH ADHERING TO THESE CONVENTIONS MAKES IT EASIER FOR A READER OR LISTENER TO UNDERSTAND THE POINTS THEY ARE MAKING. TEACH STUDENTS HOW TO LOOK UP WORDS IN A PAPER OR ELECTRONIC DICTIONARY AND HOW TO USE A THESAURUS TO SHARPEN THE PRECISION OF THEIR WORD CHOICES.

Knowledge of Language

L.3.3. Use knowledge of language and its conventions when writing, speaking, reading, or listening.

(a) Choose words and phrases for effect.
(b) Recognize and observe the differences between the conventions of spoken and written standard English.

ANNOTATION

STUDENTS IN GRADE 3 CAN UNDERSTAND THAT FORMAL AND INFORMAL ENGLISH ARE THE SAME LANGUAGE, BUT EACH USES DIFFERENT RULES, VOCABULARY, SENTENCE STRUCTURE, AND GRAMMAR, AND EACH IS APPROPRIATE FOR USE IN DIFFERENT SETTINGS. BEING AWARE OF BOTH REGISTERS AND KNOWING WHEN TO USE EACH ONE HELPS SPEAKERS TO BE UNDERSTOOD BY OTHERS AND TO COMMUNICATE WITH MORE TYPES OF PEOPLE.

(Continued)

TABLE 15.12 (Continued)

Vocabulary Acquisition and Use

L.3.4. Determine or clarify the meaning of unknown and multiple-meaning words and phrases based on *grade 3 reading and content,* choosing flexibly from an array of strategies.

   (a) Use sentence-level context as a clue to the meaning of a word or phrase.

   (b) Determine the meaning of the new word formed when a known affix is added to a known word (e.g., *agreeable/disagreeable. comfortable/uncomfortable; care/careless, heat/preheat*).

   (c) Use a known root word as a clue to the meaning of an unknown word with the same root (e.g., *company, companion*).

   (d) Use glossaries and beginning dictionaries, both print and digital, to determine or clarify the meaning of words and phrases.

L.3.5. Demonstrate understanding of word relationships and nuances in word meanings.

   (a) Distinguish the literal and non-literal meanings of words and phrases in contexts (e.g., *take steps*).

   (b) Identify real-life connections between words and their use (e.g., describe people who are friendly or helpful).

   (c) Distinguish shades of meaning among related words that describe states of mind or degrees of certainty (e.g., *knew, believed, suspected, heard, wondered*).

L.3.6. Acquire and use accurately grade-appropriate conversation, general academic, and domain-specific words and phrases, including those that signal spatial and temporal relationships (e.g., *After dinner that night we went looking for them*).

ANNOTATION

THIRD GRADERS CONTINUE TO DEVELOP VOCABULARY SO THEY CAN MAKE PURPOSEFUL LANGUAGE CHOICES IN WRITING AND SPEAKING AND THUS COMMUNICATE EFFECTIVELY IN PRINT AND DIGITAL TEXTS. THEY USE REGISTERS APPROPRIATE TO THEIR AUDIENCE, CONTEXT, AND PURPOSE. STUDENTS IN GRADE 3 WILL READ ACROSS VARIOUS AUTHORS AND GENRES TO COMPARE WRITING STYLES AND THE EFFECTS OF LANGUAGE USAGE. THEY WILL DISTINGUISH SHADES OF MEANING AMONG RELATED WORDS AND USE WORDS ACQUIRED BY READING AND BEING READ TO, AT SCHOOL, IN CONVERSATIONS, AND IN SOCIAL SETTINGS.

Three Tips for Teachers of Third Grade Hipsters

1. Keep Your Students Closely Associated With the Primary Grades

Unsure of whether they're the oldest of the little kids (very cool) or the youngest of the older kids (not cool), third graders sometimes freeze up and lose track of who they are and what they should be doing. In today's culture, children are pushed to grow up quickly, even if the children themselves don't feel ready yet. However, third graders are certainly ready to be the leaders and role models of the primary grades. Maintaining your personal affiliation with the teachers in the primary grade cluster and helping to developing learning experiences that include all the primary grade students is an important way to support your students during a year of transition and growth.

2. Prepare Your Students Thoroughly for Their Standardized Testing Experience

As I indicated earlier, the standardized summative assessments of students' mastery of the CCSS-ELA and the CCSS-M are likely to be very challenging for all students. And I expect all Grade 3 teachers are already busy doing everything possible to prepare their students to meet and manage the academic demands of the assessments. However, it might be useful to discuss things above beyond the academic demands of the tests, such as

Big picture questions

Why do we have to take these tests?

Why do they begin in Grade 3?

Who sees our scores?

What do teachers do with the scores?

What do the scores mean for me?

Are these scores important?

Technical questions

What happens if my computer freezes up?

What if I lose my work halfway through?

Do I have to know how to keyboard to take the test?

Will there be people to help with the computers?

Can I have scratch paper for the math sections?

Will we know the people who are watching us test?

Nuts and bolts questions

When are we taking them?

Other questions

Do we have to take them? What if we're sick?

Where will we be taking them?	Will bad things happen to us if we don't do well?
How long will they take?	Will you get fired if we don't do well?
Can I go to the bathroom during the test?	Does the principal care about these tests?

There might be a lot of questions, but allaying students' fears and concerns is a great way for you to show support for their success. This will help them feel better prepared—mentally and emotionally—and relieve some of their anxiety.

3. Teach Your Students to Keyboard ASAP, Long Before the Tests Loom Large

Although most of our students are proficient technology users, my observations suggest young children are more familiar and comfortable with touchscreen technologies—like you'd see on an iPad or a classroom smartboard—than with using a QWERTY keyboard. If this is correct, our students' underdeveloped typing skills and their lack of familiarity with the operation and use of the types of applications typically found on laptop or desktop computers may become factors that impede their success on the standardized summative assessments.

The first mention of keyboarding skills in the CCSS-ELA comes in Grade 3 (Standard 3.W.6); this indicates third graders should master beginning keyboarding skills by the end of Grade 3. Ironically, third graders are required to use keyboarding skills to take the computer-based standardized summative assessments, which occur at least 8 weeks before the end of Grade 3. In other words, third graders are required to demonstrate keyboarding proficiency before they are actually expected to have mastered those skills.

I suggest primary grade teachers work together to ensure that all children are competent keyboarders before winter break begins in December of Grade 3. This plan will alleviate unnecessary stress in spring semester of third grade by allowing students and Grade 3 teachers to focus on academic content and test-taking skills rather than on typing practice.

References

Assessment 101. (2014). PARCC & SBAC. Retrieved from http://www.hmhco.com/educators/education-topics/by-topic/common-core/assessment-101-PARCC-and-SBAC

Keany, M. (2013). *Comparing the PARCC and the Smarter Balanced Assessments*. Retrieved from http://www.schoolleadership20.com/forum/topics/comparing-the-parcc-and-smarter-balanced-assessments

Partnership for Assessment of Readiness for College and Career (PARCC). (2013). Grade Three- The Field- Part A and Part B (Math). Retrieved from http://www.parcconline.org/sites/parcc/files/PARCC%20Math%20Sample%20Problems_GR3_The%20Field_PartAV2.pdf

Partnership for Assessment of Readiness for College and Career (PARCC). (2013). PARCC Grade Three Sample Items, pg. 10 (ELA). Retrieved from http://www.parcconline.org/sites/parcc/files/PARCCGrade3.pdf

National Governors Association Center for Best Practices, Council of Chief State School Officers. (2010). *Common Core State Standards in English language arts and literacy in history/social studies, science, and technical subjects.* Washington, DC: National Governors Association Center for Best Practices, Council of Chief State School Officers.

National Governors Association Center for Best Practices, Council of Chief State School Officers. (2010). *Common Core State Standards for mathematics.* Washington, DC: National Governors Association Center for Best Practices, Council of Chief State School Officers.

Smarter Balanced Assessment Consortium (SBAC). (2013a). Sample items-math. Retrieved from http://www.rcoe.us/educational-services/files/2013/11/asmt-sbac-math-gr3-sample-items1.pdf

Smarter Balanced Assessment Consortium (SBAC). (2013b). Sample items-ELA. Retrieved from http://www.rcoe.us/educational-services/files/2013/11/asmt-sbac-ela-gr3-sample-items.pdf

Smarter Balanced Assessment Consortium (SBAC). (n.d.). Gewertz, C. (2012, August 22). Consortia provide preview of common tests. *Education Week.* Retrieved from http://www.edweek.org/ew/articles/2012/08/14/01tests_ep.h32.html

White, J., & Dauksas, L. (2012). CCSSM: Getting started in K–grade 2. *Teaching Children Mathematics, 1* (7), 440–445.

INDEX

Note: Italicized numbers with the letter f or t represent figures and tables.